12/20/73

To
Lucy & Ben

I shall always cherish your friendship.

Love
Dr Bob

THEY CALL ME
THE SHOWBIZ PRIEST

THEY CALL ME THE SHOWBIZ PRIEST

by Rev. Robert Perrella ("Father Bob")

FRANCISCAN

TRIDENT PRESS   NEW YORK

Copyright © 1973 by Rev. Robert Perrella, O.F.M.
All rights reserved
including the right of reproduction
in whole or in part in any form
Published by Trident Press
A division of Simon & Schuster, Inc.
Rockefeller Center, 630 Fifth Avenue
New York, New York 10020

SBN 671-27112-1
Library of Congress Catalog Card Number: 73-82874
Designed by Jack Jaget
Manufactured in the United States of America
Printed by The Murray Printing Company, Forge Village, Mass.
Bound by The Plimpton Press, Norwood, Mass.

1   2   3   4   5   6   7   8   9   10

THE
CREDIT
SLOT

"Had you been a smart Jewish boy, you would have taken notes during these many years. But you happen to be a stupid *paesano* who disregarded notes and now find yourself in an awful mess endeavoring to recall the past thirty years of your life. You could have written a book four times the size with less work, sweat and aggravation." This demeaning accolade of prose was bestowed upon me by a friend and not a foe. And, ironically, every word is true and consistent. It was not my intention to write a book, although many friends had suggested it innumerable times. The seed to place my life between book covers fructified while reading Jim Bouton's *Ball Four*. If a ballplayer can narrate his experiences on the baseball diamond, the dugout and the locker room, why can't I chronicle my experiences among show people backstage, in the wings or the dressing room? The task appeared difficult and arduous and at times insurmountable. It demanded that I scratch my memory bag and practically empty it out to recall some events as far back as three decades. Hence the reader may possibly find some inconsistencies and discrepancies. Inadvertent, I assure you. Understandably, there were some occasions when certain characters had to remain unidentified.

The title of the book is purely my own creation, although Miss Penny Singleton suggested one possibly much more appropriate —"Shepherd Among the Stars." Other titles were offered, such as "Step Into My Life," "My 25 Years in Showbiz," "Backstage With Father" and "Years of Yesterdays." I would have preferred "Life With Father." However, such action would have necessitated a matriculation course at our neighborhood Manhattan House of Detention, popularly known in New York as the "Tombs."

My very special and sincere thanks to Mr. Sy Stewart and Mr. Leonard Forman, who helped to make the publication of this book a miraculous reality. The debonair man-about-town Mr. Earl Wilson, nationally syndicated columnist, graciously accepted my invitation to write the Foreword of the book. Since most of the characters relate to showbiz and Broadway, what greater authority could I seek than the "Dean of Showbiz and Broadway" and the author of *The Show Business Nobody Knows?* To Earl and Rosemary, my many thanks and love. A very gracious garland of gratitude to Miss Irene Sheehan of Rego Park, New York, for the many exhausting hours she sacrificed typing every single letter and word of the entire manuscript. Lastly, my "Impossible Dream" would never have been realized without the help and assistance of those people who embraced That Business . . . comparable to which . . . there is no other business.

To my beautiful mother and sister Jo, whose home is heaven

*To that trinity of gentle-men,
Perry Como, Joey Adams and Danny (Hideaway) Stradella,
who made* They Call Me the Showbiz Priest *possible*

*To my three deceased buddies,
the beloved Three Di's:*

*Father Mike Di Pietro
Father Chris Di Fiore
Father Ray Di Martini*

CONTENTS

FOREWORD BY EARL WILSON	11
THE SHOWBIZ PRIEST	13
HAVE COLLAR, WILL TRAVEL	33
NOT ALL MY FRIENDS ARE SAINTS	38
WHAT PRICE VEGAS?	61
THE HIDEAWAY, DANNY'S AND MINE	67
ANOTHER OPENING, ANOTHER SHOW	78
IT'S JUST IMPOSSIBLE	95
THE ACTORS YOUTH FUND	98
MR. CALABASH	105
THE MAN WITH THE GOLDEN VOICE	114
JEANNIE WEENIE	128

WE CALLED HIM "JOHN"	134
THE BEAUTIFUL BUFFOON	137
THE GUILD 146	
THE BROTHERS FIVE AND MARY	150
I WANT YOU ALL IN HEAVEN BECAUSE HEAVEN IS A SWINGING PLACE	154

FOREWORD

A priest by any standard is an eminent and distinguished figure in a society. The author, Father Bob Perrella, is not just a priest, a clergyman or a man of the cloth. His image in showbusiness far exceeds the periphery of a monkish-clad Franciscan Friar, reading his breviary or fingering his rosary, with a tableau of a California mission in the background. His parish is showbiz; his parishioners, those people who in any way are dependent on showbiz for a livelihood. This in multiple instances includes the Protestant and the Jew. Father Bob is as much at home with *Variety* as he is with the Holy Bible; as much at ease onstage as he is in a pulpit; as much conversant with the language of showbiz as he is with the theological language of the church; as cool and personable with showbiz characters as he is with his fellow clergymen. Many were the occasions when the good Padre and I crossed paths in the dressing room and backstage of theaters, in the colossal and renowned halls of New York hotels, at testimonials, opening nights, benefits and union meetings, in churches and synagogues, at weddings and funerals. Anywhere and everywhere he is "our priest."

By the very nature of his office, a clergyman's life is the embodiment of a psychologist, a consultant, an adviser and a confidant. During this past quarter century, Father Bob has rendered these priestly qualities and prerogatives to one and all regardless of race or creed. Without a shadow of doubt, he's been the recipient of more sensational and inside-showbiz stories muted and silenced, I'm sure, by the vow of the confessional. Had he revealed what he intimately knows and secretly harbors, this tome could triple in size.

In an era when ecumenism is thankfully so prevalent throughout the world, Father Bob promulgated and practiced this way of life long before it became so popular and acceptable. He knelt in synagogues before the mortal remains of Sophie Tucker, Al "Doubletalk" Kelly and many others. At the funeral home, he conducted the final prayer rituals of superagents Protestant Tom Rockwell and Jewish George Wood; he delivered the eulogy for music publisher Jewish Loring Buzzell, husband of LuAnn Simms. In a tiny Baptist church in Corona, New York, he prayed before the bier of Louis Armstrong. Father Bob Perrella is in deed and in truth "all things to all men" . . . verily, The Showbiz Priest.

EARL WILSON

THE SHOWBIZ PRIEST

They call me "The Showbiz Priest." Whether I am entitled to such an honored distinction is a question only the readers can decide. For twenty-six years, almost all of my priestly life, I have been in the midst of show people. Not only the greats but the unknowns, the stagehands, the technicians, writers, producers, directors, etc., became my unofficial flock. Shepherd among the stars. Not only the Catholic but the Jew and the Protestant. In showbiz the cursed barrier of race and religion does not exist, thank God. No one cares what your color is and cares even less what religion you profess. The one indispensable, unconditional prerequisite, the sine qua non, is Talent. This brings to mind the story of comic Alan Drake. He was about to be married and asked if I would perform the ceremony. "How can I, Alan, when she is a Protestant and you are Jewish?" "I thought," he replied, "they settled that matter when they held *that big meeting* in Rome a few years ago!" They should have!

Show people are a very unique people. They are a class unto their own. They are human, it's true. They bleed when cut, cry when sorrowful, laugh when happy. Yet they are emphatically different from the rest of humanity. They speak a language all their own; they act in a manner characteristic only to themselves. All troupers are members of that great, gigantic, ethereal family called showbusiness. Be their talents as diversified and polarized as the North and South Poles, they are, nonetheless, all children of the same family. There exist absolutely no hangups about the color of anybody's skin or if from the chain around your neck hangs a medal of Saint Christopher or the Star of David. And just as each individual family possesses its peculiar traits, traditions, culture, customs, idiosyncrasies, so too these identical qualities will be found in that titanic household called showbiz. No one crashes showbiz; they either accept you or they don't.

The entertainer is an exhibitionist, an extrovert, a show-off. Unfortunately, the actor is expected to be "on" twenty-four hours a day. The roles he portrays on screen and television are the very same we expect he would portray in real life. Wittingly or unwittingly, we stereotype these people into different categories: the lover boy; the sex symbol; suave, debonair, sophisticated; rough, unruly, gangster-type. The sex symbol must exude the Eros from the very moment she opens the windows of her soul. She's not permitted to cough in public or spit up something, even a particle of food lodged in her windpipe. Spitting and coughing are alien to sex. We contemplate the sex goddess with parted, painted lips, mouth wide open, as though she was suffering from a fatal case of asphyxiation or enjoying a delirious orgiastic experience. Her gait is that of a panther ready to stalk, seduce or rape every son of Adam. To see a Loretta Young wearing a diaphanous garment, a Perry Como shouting blasphemies, a Jimmy Durante insulting a citizen, a Mike Douglas telling "blue" stories, a tuxedoed Cary Grant wearing white sneakers would constitute a sacrilege far beyond redemption. However, statistics inform us their suicide rate is high; their divorce rate is incredibly higher. We begin to realize they are fallible and defective people like most of us. When the seeds fall off the gingerbread, the shine is gone! Generally speaking, showfolks are nice people. They give of themselves unstintingly if the cause is deserving. The annual Jerry Lewis telethon for muscular dystrophy is a monumental example. Bob Hope's annual Christmas excursions to faraway places to entertain our servicemen; the indomitable Martha Raye and hundreds like her risking their very lives to "let me entertain you"; Joey Adams and his Actors Youth Fund bringing joy and laughter to the inmates of joyless prisons and laughless hospitals. These are but samplings of the countless benefits performed by troupers throughout the world. Years ago Jimmy Durante was prohibited by his management from performing benefits. He had done so many that people refused to pay good money to see him in nightclubs. Why buy the cow when the milk is free?

Certainly you will find the cheat, the liar, the braggart, the inhuman among them just as you would discover the same in your own backyard. Their lives are so different from ours. We are commanded to avoid temptation; they live in temptation. On many occasions these people are the recipients of phone calls and written notes propositioning every type of sexual activity. I spent a few days with a well-known bachelor vocalist while he was appearing on a Chicago stage. Each night upon our return to the hotel his manager and entourage would look under the bed, in the closets, behind the couch to see that there were no female intruders hanging around. During that visit, I awoke one morning in the wee hours to find this young man on his knees reciting his rosary. In Detroit an actor returned to his hotel suite to discover a teen-aged girl lying on his bed, stark naked. She achieved this brilliant maneuver of infiltration by staking a bellhop. Showfolks do not have to go to the mountains; the mountains come to them.

Very often I posed this question to myself: How would I have lived my life if my name had been Sinatra, Dean Martin, Cary Grant? Would I succumb to the adulation of my fans? The fifty thousand dollars a week? The palatial homes with the giant-sized pools? The best of food and drink? The most expensive of clothing? The European sport cars? Would I have been faithful to one woman when hundreds of them were throwing themselves at my feet? Would I deny myself membership to the cult of Sybaris? Would my concept of reality be as real in this world of make-believe and tinsel? I would not even attempt to answer these questions—knowing what human nature is and, better still, knowing myself. Only the sinless can play the game of rock-throwing.

Showbusiness has always been characterized by two symbols, Comedy and Tragedy. Isn't this what life is all about? The fact remains if you're a Hollywood femme fatale or a Broadway favorite son, if you're a circus king or a rodeo queen, it doesn't transform the symbol of life one iota. It's still comedy and tragedy, laughter and tears, life and death. Unfortunately, too many of us fail to comprehend the vast realities of life; we look upon this earthly existence as a little girl would gaze on the pages of *Alice in Wonderland*. It is so comparable to the story of the little boy who desires to become a priest one week, a doctor on the second week and perhaps a fireman on the third. He is fascinated by the Roman collar, the doctor's hospital gown, the fireman's uniform. Fascination! Pure veneer! As a youngster I too always attached a certain quality of the unreal to the priesthood. Priests weren't human; they were superhuman—quasisupernatural. I could not imagine a priest awaking in the morning, bathing, cleaning his teeth, taking care of his personal needs. I couldn't imagine a priest being tempted and, God forbid, succumbing to the temptations. They were little gods doing Big God's work on earth.

The news media created the same aura of unreality in the vast expanse of entertainment. To read some of the tripe emanating from the press agents would have you believe there wasn't a toilet bowl in all of Hollywood. Just comedy without tragedy, laughter without tears, life without death. Hundreds of magazines depicting La Dolce Vita, the tuxedoed idol and his bejeweled mistress, the fabulous yachts, the supersized pools, the sumptuous homes of Lucullan splendor, the marble staircase, the imported cars. Not a word about the heartaches and pain to reach the top, not a word about the vocalist, the bands, the one-night stands, "on the road," away from home and family. The bedroom contract! Years of frustration and despair. "Don't call me, I'll call you." Endless hours of practice. Acting school. Vocal coaches. Childless lives! "I'll make you a star—if I can make you first!" Christmas, holidays spent in fleabag hotels in Hopscotch, U.S.A. Not a word about the underpaid, overworked ballerina who could only open the show but never close it. Not a word about the thousands walking the streets, hungry and anguished, looking for work or standing in line to collect unemployment. It is as though the actor were imperishable—insensitive to pain, incapable of contracting diseases, incapable of tears, incapable of dying.

I have seen much fear and much death among the fearless and deathless. I have seen the awful apprehension in the eyes of the Sinatras when Frank, Jr., was kidnapped. And the sigh of relief and godly gratitude when Mrs. Nancy Sinatra penned a note thanking me for my prayers. I have seen the tears of a mother when Mama Dorsey stood beside the biers of her two sons, Tommy and Jimmy. I have seen the tears of a frightened girl, LuAnn Simms, as she stood beside the lifeless body of her husband lying in bed. I have seen the tears of Mamie Farinola and her son, Vic Damone, as we viewed the remains of Pop Farinola. I have seen the tears of a Perry Como as we laid Lucia, his mother, to her eternal rest. I heard the quivering voice of Mrs. O'Keefe telling us that Dennis had passed on. The wife of the beloved Al "Doubletalk" Kelly confiding to me that I had lost a pal. And I have heard the plaintive strains of "Some of These Days" as I watched Sophie carried off to keep her last and final engagement. I have seen the tears of a funnyman, Jack E. Leonard, standing beside a hospital bed holding the remains of his beloved wife, Kay, and telling me, "My Cissie is gone." I have seen the tears of a Jerry Vale as we prayed at the bier of his mother. I have seen the tears of the Sinatras as Frank and Junior assisted Natalie at the graveside and I bade Marty, his dad, a prayerful farewell. I have gazed at the sorrow-filled face of Ed Sullivan as he said farewell to Sylvia, his wife of forty-three years.

Certainly entertainers are a part of the human family. They are not insulated against the vicissitudes of life nor immune to the devastating viruses of everyday living. They have their moments of joy and sorrow, moments of pleasure and pain; they laugh and they cry just as you and I. As Perry Como once stated in an interview: "The things I've always wanted are the things I've always possessed, long before fame and fortune—things like a family, love and loyalty." The loveliest of songbirds, Judy Garland, once asked me to escort her up a long flight of stairs at the Waldorf Astoria, fearing she might fall because of the length of her gown. As we reached the final step, she observed: "It's the story of your life, Father. Always helping people upward and forward." I replied, "Judy, all I want out of life is to reach that *Somewhere* over the rainbow you're always singing about." Maybe that's what it's all about!

To help people reach that *Somewhere* over the rainbow is my job and the job of every clergyman who ever walked the earth. Many were the times when I've been asked what business would a priest have with showpeople. First let me ask: Who and what is a priest? He is a mediator between God and man when with hands consecrated with the holy oils he celebrates the supreme sacrifice of the holy Mass. His work is apostolic, his earthly mission the salvation of all men. He is a soldier in the vast army of Christ pledging to uphold virtue and declaring a lifelong struggle against sin and all of sin's ramifications. He is a laborer in the vineyard of God. He counsels the doubtful, gives aid to troubled souls; he administers to the poor, the sick and dying; he comforts the afflicted. He is our father on earth doing the labor of his Father in heaven. What business does any priest have with his people? He marries them, baptizes their children, absolves them of any transgressions, brings them communion, ministers to their sick and dying and buries their dead. He admonishes and counsels, he gives aid and comfort, he seeks to be a fair arbitrator in marital problems and prays for their solution; he seeks employment for the unemployed; he helps in the adoption of children, especially for those bereft of youngsters. He must have kind, gentle, understanding words for those who are troubled in soul and in body. He must be available at all times, for all occasions. Available when his people unfurl the glittering tinsel of Comedy. Even more available when they unfurl the black crepe of Tragedy.

My vocation to work among people in the entertainment world was not planned or blueprinted. It just happened. The Church of Saint Anthony of Padua is my home parish, located in the southern district of New York's famed Greenwich Village. It is a towering, massive stone edifice, and within its stained-glass-windowed walls I served as an altar boy. It was here also I celebrated my first Mass as a newly ordained priest. And here I was stationed as a young curate. Each year Saint Anthony's would sponsor a dance and reunion of parishioners at Manhattan Center Hall. The object of this annual festivity was to reunite not only the actual parishioners but those who moved to the trees and manicured-lawn areas of the suburbs. My superior asked me to try to obtain some entertainment for the occasion. Suddenly I remembered that only a few weeks before I had seen a young vocalist at the Strand Theater on Broadway. His name was Perry Como. ("Perry" is obviously a strange name for anyone of Italian extraction. I learned later his baptismal nomenclature was spelled Pierino.) Then I learned that a young teen-ager from the parish belonged to his embryonic fan club. She provided me with the necessary information. I telephoned the Lexington Hotel, where Perry, Roselle and their child, Ronald, were living in a one-room apartment. Roselle answered the call and informed me I could contact her husband at the *Chesterfield Supper Club* show in the RCA Building of Rockefeller Center. This five-a-week radio show had just begun, with Martin Block, a nationally known disk jockey, as master of ceremonies. It was rumored in the trade that Block was earning more money than the Star.

Worried and fearful of being denied the favor, I prayed my way to the NBC headquarters. And there for the first time I met the youthful Mr. Perry Como with a pipe stuck between his lips. The picture puzzled me. Here's a man, I thought to myself, who works for a cigarette company and smokes a pipe.

We sat in the studio and I explained to him the purpose of my visit. He grinned understandingly, puffed a bit on his pipe, placed his arm around my shoulder and whispered into my ear, "I think we can make it. But," he continued—and my heart practically exploded—"on one condition. I want you to come here frequently. I want you and me to be friends."

In my earlier priestly years I was befriended by Jimmy Durante and the team of Joey Adams, Tony Canzoneri and Mark Plant. They had graciously performed benefits for the church to which I was assigned. Actually, Mr. Adams was my first contact with showbiz. Thus, I became involved with the entertainment field because of my passionate love for prizefighting. My boyhood idol was Tony Canzoneri. I first met him through a mutual friend and stablemate of his, Lenny Del Genio. Whenever he fought, I would glue my ears to the radio and pray Tony home. Whenever he fought in New York, I would be in the gallery, the cheapest seats in the house, shouting words of encouragement in between Hail Marys. Then one day as I passed the Loew's State my eyes caught sight of the glittering marquee:

JOEY ADAMS   TONY CANZONERI   MARK PLANT

I decided to visit with Tony backstage, and there I met America's goodwill ambassador, Mr. Joey Adams. And ironically enough, because of this first meeting with Joey another chapter of my life was written. I had become involved with the theatrical end of the union business, since Joey in later years was elected president of the American Guild of Variety Artists. And now here I sat, in a studio glorified as the Chesterfield Supper Club, speaking to a stranger who was to become a friend, a pauper who was to become a multimillionaire. Mr. Lucky! Perry was the second choice for the show; Andy Russell had declined the offer. Never in my wildest dream could I imagine that this first meeting with P. C. would be my first faltering step in the Land of Make-Believe.

I've spent many delightful hours in the company of Mr. Nice Guy and his family. I traveled to many parts of the country with him. We became inseparable buddies. We would invariably share the same hotel room. In fact, in Boston he kidded me about my nightly orchestrations and the way I would hold my thumb and index finger against my nose. Nick Kenny, a columnist for the now defunct New York *Daily Mirror*, once observed that Como enjoyed a thick, juicy steak every Wednesday and Friday of the week at Danny's Hideaway or Joe & Rose. Angered by the lie, I picked up the phone to inform Mr. Kenny that I've sat with Como on many Fridays and never was he guilty of that transgression. Nick printed this fact in his next-day column—and this explains the birth of my first sobriquet, "Perry's Priest."

It was a tradition in those days for Mr. C. to entertain the song pluggers one night a week. On one particular evening a group of them, Perry and myself went to a restaurant named Headquarters —so named because the proprietors, John Schwarz and Charles Fodor, were General Eisenhower's chefs during World War II. It was my first encounter with waiters and booze. In my seminary days, Manhattan was the place of my birth and Martini was a good Italian name. As we sat for dinner, the waiter came to me first and asked if I would like a cocktail before dinner. My face flushed with embarrassment. I didn't know one drink from the other. Politely, I asked him to serve the other guests and come to me last. At this point I kept my eyes and ears on Como. Whatever he orders, be it even poison, I'll order. "I'll have," crooned the Crooner, "a double extra-dry martini." As though I was rattling off my rosary, I kept repeating these words to myself over and over. Finally, the waiter reappears. With the poise of a country gentleman and the enunciative ability of a speech major, I declared my order. "I'll have a double extra-dry martini." He placed a huge champagne glass before me. My eyes and ears were no longer pivoted on Perry. I drank the stuff in two or three gulps. And Headquarters almost became my "Lost Head" Quarters.

The caption THE DAY A CROONER KISSED A NUN may sound terribly sacrilegious, but I can assure you it did occur. And the scene of this romantic interlude was the Holy Cross College Athletic Field, with a sellout audience. Monsignor Sullivan, director of the Catholic Charities of the diocese of Worcester, Massachusetts, convinced Como to make a personal appearance in behalf of the poor and needy. Perry decided to bring along the entire show: Mitch Ayres and his orchestra, Ray Charles and the Ray Charles Singers. We arrived at the airport, a battalion of cars—all convertibles—awaiting us. When we reached our destination, they drove us around the field a couple of times. Perry spotted a group of nuns and asked the chauffeur to stop. "Which of you sisters is the Mother Superior?" the crooner asked. They pointed to an elderly woman, who literally shook at the sight of the man she watched for so many years on TV. He gently sat on her lap and softly kissed her on each cheek. She giggled, blushed and seemed quite content. All I could think of at the time was the line of the Great One, "Oh, how sweet it is!"

At another dinner gathering, attended mostly by song pluggers, someone posed a question to me. He prefaced it by saying he was cognizant of the many, many years a priest must study. Hence, he felt I would be able to present him with a very wise and prudent answer. Is it true, he was saying, when two people—a husband and wife—a man and woman—are deeply in love, a love almost superhuman, their babies must of necessity be extraordinarily beautiful? The question astonished me. What the hell do I know about lovemaking? Finally, I had to admit my ignorance. Whereupon, song plugger Eddie Shore cast a hard gaze at song plugger Murry Weisel, not the handsomest of men, and yells out, "What a hell of a fight your parents must have had the night they conceived you."

Como's career was skyrocketing. His rating was very high; his records were selling in the millions; his personal appearances in theaters were sellouts. With the advent of television, the Canonsburg barber's profile became recognizable to most Americans. I recall the incident on our Boston-bound train, in the dining area, of a little girl pointing towards Perry and telling her mother, "Look Mommy, it's the Chesterfield man." In one of his earlier TV appearances, they dressed him in a striped prisoner's uniform and placed him behind bars as he crooned "Prisoner of Love." Hundreds of protesting letters were received by NBC, decrying the fact that Wardrobe had the unmitigated gall to dress their hero in such fashion. On another occasion, Don Rickles was performing as Como and retinue made their entrance into the club. Rickles is probably the greatest character assassin in the world. He spares no one, big or small; he devastates all. As Perry was walking in, Don placed his finger on his lips, asking the audience for absolute silence—sh, sh, sh. And with the softness of a snowflake touching ground, he whispered; "Here comes God."

The name Como became a symbol of some sort—beloved by the general public, admired and revered by the trade. His personal life remained untarnished. A family man with no scandal attached to his biography. He went to church on Sundays and wasn't ashamed to be seen on his knees. Everyone, in and out of the trade, looked up to him. While playing the New York Paramount, a young usher visited his dressing room and introduced himself. "I'm Vito Farinola. I'm also a singer and hope someday to be like you, Mr. Como." Vito Farinola yesterday is Vic Damone today. One day I met Vic at a recording studio and he told me he was seriously looking for a priest-companion. The statement baffled me. "How come, Vic?" I inquired. "If having a priest around Como can do so much for his career, I want a priest around me." Andy Williams vowed he would follow Perry up the path of success. From the format of his shows it is obvious he's keeping his promise. The stool is there in Andy's shows; the only thing missing is the single long-stemmed rose.

Richard Cardinal Cushing, the prelate who ordained me to the priesthood, sent an SOS. The archbishop of Boston was suffering financial upsets, needed money desperately to materialize the many charitable projects he had planned—one of them a youth center in a poorer section of the city. Danny Thomas and Frank Sinatra had helped the cause previously. Would I approach Como and intercede? Would I ask him to bring along an entire show to Boston? Perry was most cooperative; in fact, we journeyed to Boston not once but on three different occasions in behalf of the beloved Cardinal. And today in the North End district of Boston, called Little Italy, there is a room in the Christopher Columbus Youth Center dedicated to the millionaire ex-barber.

The Comos purchased a large, inviting home in the Gold Coast of Long Island in Sands Point. There was a sizable amount of land attached to the house—acreage of green sylvan beauty. A perfect setting for a religious theme. Hence, he wanted to surprise his wife with a marble statue of Saint Francis of Assisi, the patron saint of all animal life and nature itself. He informed me of his need and I promised to look around. I finally located a statue that perfectly fit his need and told him so. "Please pick it up and take it to my office." There were no cabs in sight, so the only alternative I enjoyed was the subway. Can you visualize a man of the cloth carrying a statue, about three feet high, of solid white Carrara marble and weighing, in my estimation, a ton? As good Saint Francis grew heavier and heavier, I began to regret my friendship with the Comos and denounced myself for not minding my business. You must understand Saint Francis is one of my favorite heaven-dwellers; he is the Founder of the Franciscan Order, of which I am a member. However, with both my arms practically torn from their sockets and my legs throbbing with pain, I began to suspect my destination was not the Como office but a Hill named Calvary and the object I held so securely was not a statue at all. It was the Cross of Calvary.

Como's career rose meteorically, yet it always seemed overshadowed by another vocalist. Perry could never shake the Avis Complex. Hertz happened to be a guy named Francis Albert Sinatra. On one occasion when Frank appeared at the New York Paramount stage, his dad became ill. Mr. Sinatra contacted the Paramount's manager, Bob Weitman, and he in turn asked Como to fill in. As we rode to the theater, Como nervously notified us, "If any of those Sinatra fans boo me, I'll throw the mikes at them." To the contrary, after some moans of disappointment, he was wildly accepted and cheered—so much so, he introduced his priest from the audience. In later years, Frank returned the favor when Perry's father passed on in Canonsburg, Pennsylvania.

Como's calm serenity characterized the man. Nothing in God's creation could shake or disturb Mr. Cool onstage. Nevertheless, he quietly harbored one covert idiosyncrasy: a fierce sense of competition with his fellow vocalists. At every rehearsal and dress, he remained unchanged, nonchalantly doing his thing. Calmly, dispassionately he performed his routine weekly shows. However, if anyone with the stature of a Crosby, a Dean Martin or a Tony Bennett appeared with him, Como would put his heart and soul into every note he sang. He refused to be Mr. Avis to anyone on stage—especially his stage. Jane Wyman, who gueststarred on his show several times, once wryly remarked, "At rehearsal Como looks like he's ready for the mortician; at show time he comes on like a bat out of hell."

Oftentimes the media can be indiscriminately cruel. It can paint a picture into whatever size, shape, form and proportion it desires. It can induce people to think in one manner while the media writes in another. A false allegation is as valid as a guilty verdict. I personally experienced an incident that left a very bad taste in my mouth where the media is concerned. Mr. Joseph McCarthy, a writer on the *Look* Magazine staff, was appointed to write a story on Como. There were many interviews, and on one particular Saturday night, after the weekly show, Perry turned to me and suggested I take the reporter to the Essex House, where Mr. C. had rented a luxurious apartment facing Central Park. "I'll be there in about a half hour," the singer promised. When we arrived at the suite, I asked Mr. McCarthy if he would be interested in a drink. The answer being affirmative, I called Room Service for some ice and a half-dozen splits of soda. The drink poured, I presented it to the writer. He must have enjoyed it, because he had a second. Later, Perry, Dee Belline and Mickey Glass arrived, and I poured a drink for Como while Mickey and Dee took care of themselves. We went to Joe & Rose's Restaurant for dinner, and the day ended. When the article appeared in *Look* Magazine, I was shocked beyond belief. Yes, Mr. Joe McCarthy wrote many nice things about me which are comme il faut on such an occasion. However, he destroyed the entire priestly image by describing me as the official bartender of the group. And with an Irish name like McCarthy, no less. Even my superior demanded an explanation. When I explained to my boss what actually had occurred, he succinctly and pungently qualified this indiscreet act of bad penman manners: "That guy had one hell of a nerve."

Have you ever witnessed a lifetime love affair among men? I'm not necessarily speaking of homosexuality or the erotic. Many are the times I witnessed a lifelong relationship between a manager and his client where a handshake and a bear hug are their seal and bond—where aside from the money involved, there exists an honest-to-God rapport between two people. Tom Rockwell and Perry Como, Harry Steinman and Tony Martin, Robert Coe and Ed McMahon, Tino Barzie and young Frank Sinatra, Jr., to mention some, are glittering examples of the quasi–father-and-son relationship between a manager and his protégé. Like the cliché notes, there are exceptions to the rule. Many moons ago when I was a young priest and Como well established in the trade, a young man, a former Bostonian, almost miraculously appeared in our midst. Until World War Two, this young man had worked with the Dorsey brothers as a road manager. His return from the service to civilian life found him broke and jobless. Honest to the core, he returned every cent he ever borrowed. However, he would ask me to intercede with our many friends in borrowing money for him. I was sort of the middle-man without the vig (interest). Through a bold stroke of luck or perhaps, in my parlance, divine intercession, this young man came upon a hot piece of property in the person of a male vocalist. The singer made himself a millionaire and made his manager a very rich man. Both moved to the Coast, where the singer does television shows, makes movies and personal appearances throughout the world, and where his manager enjoys a luxurious office suite on Wilshire Boulevard. Once, during my stay in Los Angeles, I visited my old friend and the nouveau riche at his Wilshire office. My reception was friendly and hospitable. However, I expected for old times' sake an invitation to his home and received none. I expected an invitation to dinner and received none. I expected perhaps an invitation to a drink in the edifice's barroom and received none. I expected maybe an invitation to a cup of coffee or tea in the office building's restaurant and received none. Finally the Big Spender asked where was I staying. The Beverly Hills Hotel, I informed him. Placing his arm around my shoulder, he walked me to a window and pointing to the corner, gave me instructions. "If you stand on that corner and take any bus, it will bring you right to the doors of the Beverly Hills Hotel." The singer's children call him "Uncle"—and believe me, he'll make you cry "Uncle" before he comes up with a dime from his fishhooks-lined pockets.

Many were the trips I made with the Como ensemble. Boston, Detroit, Buffalo, Chicago, Cleveland, to mention a few. One journey, however, impressed me as no other has. Durham, North Carolina. The Liggett and Myers Tobacco Company, of which Chesterfield Cigarettes is an affiliate and for whom Perry worked, requested their client to perform a benefit for their employees in Durham. A special train was rigged up with sleeping compartments, dining area, bar, etc. In my entire lifetime I never again enjoyed the privilege to ride a private train. Such a journey created an aura of prominence as though I were part of a Presidential convoy. The entire Como show became involved in the benefit: Mitch Ayres and his orchestra, Ray Charles and his choral group. When we arrived in Durham, we were met by another participant, comic Jay Lawrence, younger brother of funnyman Larry Storch.

During rehearsal I grasped the opportunity to visit Duke University campus and the city. My first glance of the cross-shaped edifices of the University led me to believe the institution shared some religious affiliation. Then I learned, much to my consternation, that the University had originally been named Trinity College. However, due to the fantastic contributions of the millionaire philanthropist Mr. Duke, Trinity became Duke University.

As a native New Yorker, I resented some of the southern traditions so foreign to my Northeastern upbringing. At restaurants, water fountains, toilets, the signs WHITES ONLY; BLACKS ONLY. The entertainment took place in the cavernous university auditorium. A lone horse stood conspicuously in front of the building. Once again, Whites Only occupied the main floor. Blacks Only occupied the balcony. Later, we were treated to a dinner of steak and grits. As Jay Lawrence attempted repeatedly and unsuccessfully to cut his steak, he thundered, "See if that horse is still outside the auditorium."

Why is this trip so somberly and vividly etched in my heart? Many are the times I dream of that sojourn. White Only, Blacks Only! I dream of another private train, riding those identical rails, each clack of the wheels a dirge of hate and violence, riding not to Durham but to Washington, D.C. A journey not as ours, filled with laughter and gaiety; rather, sad and mournful. The train I dream of carried the assassinated body of Bob Kennedy, a man I knew and loved. Whites Only! Blacks Only!

Undoubtedly, mine is a glamorous job. Not infrequently, the reverend Brother in charge of answering doorbells and telephones would list my personal calls on a piece of paper if I wasn't available. "Father Bob. Call from the Como office, Jack Entratter. Jane Wyman in town; call the Plaza. Julius La Rosa. Mrs. Natalie Sinatra. George Woods of the William Morris office. Mr. Phil Rizzuto"—ad infinitum. I realized sooner or later something had to give. My confreres are priests; priests are humans; humans are susceptible to the infirmities of human weaknesses, such as envy, jealousy and rancor. And sometimes hate. Soon the telephonic list became the object of scornful eyes and smiles of contempt. I was rechristened "Broadway Bob" and, *Variety* (paper) being the Showbiz Bible, "The *Variety* Priest" by a goodly number of my Franciscan confreres.

Through some "spiritual and prayerful" collusion, a transfer was conveniently negotiated whereby I spent three years in an Albany suburb. *Promoveatur ut moveatur.* Literal translation: Promote to a higher position and move. Figuratively translated: Promote the bastard and get him the hell out of New York and showbiz. These very words were offered as a toast in my behalf spoken by one of my Franciscan brothers and drunk to by a dozen of my Franciscan family in view of a crucifix hanging from a refectory wall. It seemed my friends were intent and determined to deglamorize me.

At that particular time, I held the title of New York Chaplain of the American Guild of Variety Artists. By the time my three-year tenure expired, away from the New York scene and showbiz, I was elected unanimously Permanent National Chaplain of AGVA. Many were the congratulatory caresses I received from my fellow priests. Yet the demons of envy, rancor, jealousy still persisted in many priestly hearts. They still resented my appearance on the television screen; they still resented the appearance of my name in print. Nevertheless, when neighboring priests from Old Saint Patrick's Cathedral on Mott Street refused to accept the role of the baptizing priest in *The Godfather* while horrible and cruel scenes of murder and violence were being perpetrated, my bosses immediately accepted the offer and money. Their very first shot at Hollywood and they grabbed. True, I've been the recipient of many shimmering bouquets, one of which I particularly relish. A fellow priest once remarked to me: "I could never be a showbiz priest and remain in the priesthood. It's too much of a challenge." Unlike Augustine, I don't intend to write an Apologia pro Vita Mea.

Two decades and six years is quite a span of time in any profession, more so in showbiz. During that interim you witness the strange transformation in the life of the theater and its people. Unknowns reaching stardom; yesterday's stars vanishing into the realm of anonymity. The superstars gliding along unaffected, untossed by the winds of the capriciousness of man or the whims of society. Watching artists emancipate themselves from the rank of the amateur to the level of the full-grown professional.

To review twenty-six years in retrospect without a single written note is a difficult task. A smattering of memorabilia might be the answer: Meeting the Clooney sisters in the New York Paramount Theater's elevator with Tony Pastor; Rosemary was eighteen, Betty barely sixteen. At Miss Page's pad a delicious home-cooked, Oklahoman dinner with Patti, her lovely mother and sisters. Frank Sinatra leaving the Tommy Dorsey band to make it on his own and Dick Haymes replacing him. Breakfast with Vinnie Carbone from the Glenn Miller ork and two other gentlemen, Dean Martin and Jerry Lewis, who only weeks before had formed a partnership at Skinny D'Amato's 500 Club in Atlantic City. The triumph of young Eddie Fisher at Ben Marden's Riviera substituting for ailing Fran Warren. Shaking hands with a baby-faced unknown, Pat Boone, wearing his ubiquitous white buck shoes. Anne Bancroft, Sandy Dennis, struggling thespians. Buddy Hackett, Jack Carter, Alan King, Jack E. Leonard working saloons in the Jewish Alps for pocket money. Little Connie Francis introducing herself and her dad, George, backstage after her first coast-to-coast TV appearance. Interceding with Sammy Kaye to let Don Cornell go on his own as a soloist. Comic Jackie Miles headlining the show at Arthur Jarwood's Rio Bamba; opening the show, a new vocalist, Dean Martin. Bringing blessed palms to Xavier Cugat working at Broadway's Capitol Theater. Temple Texas, Ethel Merman and I enjoying fettuccine Alfredo at Danny's. Eddie Fisher's "It's too bad you can't marry Debbie and me." Ditto Eydie and Steve Lawrence. On a cold wintry night, hat brim turned down, coat collar pushed up, Dagmar mistakes me for a "second-story man." Welcoming the McGuire Sisters to showbiz. Accidentally meeting Phil Silvers at the Toronto airport and during the flight listening to the funnyman's heartaches. Comic Gary Morton, who never really made it in showbiz but managed to marry the comedienne of the century, Lucille Ball. Jack Carter introduced them. A large age gap in the children of a well-known actress. She explains away the youngsters as "martini babies." Leon and Eddie's, the incubator of stars!

I made mention from the very beginning that my life in showbusiness had not been planned or blueprinted. Such plans would necessitate its own demise. They would constitute a practical impossibility. Imagine the reactions of fellow seminarians discussing their future apostolates. The foreign missions, parish work, education, home missions, prison, hospital and narcotic chaplains, preaching and lecturing. Suddenly I would declare my apostolate: to work among people in showbiz. This statement would sound so bizarre and absurd to their ears as to make them incredulous. The late, beloved Rabbi Bernard Bernstein of the Actors' Temple was of the same opinion. The Rabbi held the unique distinction of being one of the most powerful spiritual figures showbiz has ever embraced. His contacts were countless, his influence unlimited. Nevertheless, he too expressed the opinion on many occasions that the very chemistry of showbusiness demands acceptance and longevity. The fact one is a clergyman helps, but not to that extent. The number of reverends destroys the absolute of supply and demand. An artist is by nature suspicious. Especially one who made it big, is continuously in the limelight, is supposedly a multimillionaire. Like the hoodlum who hates cops because they are trying to separate him from his home and family, so too most entertainers believe clergymen are trying to separate them from their money. The same may be said of relatives and friends.

Frank Barone, onetime manager and counselor of Julius La Rosa, called me to his office. He had received a telephone call from a priest, recently arrived from Italy, and requested I act as interpreter. The Italian cited his case very briefly. In order to repair his church in his native town, he drew the names of thirty outstanding personalities in entertainment and athletics. If each of these would present him with a thousand or more dollars, his problem would be solved. On many other occasions similar incidents occurred. Mr. Jack Katz, Perry's lawyer, telephoned to inform me a fellow priest had requested a goodly sum of money, employing my friendship with his boss as the basis for almsgiving.

My introduction of a man of the cloth to a famous restaurateur and within a matter of weeks the good padre returns to the establishment. He reminds the restaurateur they had met through a mutual friend. And would he like to contribute to a very worthy cause. Later the clergyman admitted the cause was his own. Another time, Mr. Katz verbally castigated me because of the large amounts of the Como-show tickets the clergy was picking up in my name.

Tony Bennett believed me to be the most famous priest in the world. Nobody can have that many friends, he'd remind me. In New York, Boston, Pittsburgh, Toronto, Tony would receive backstage notes informing him the signee was a dear friend of mine and would he, Mr. Bennett, come to the table and meet the family. The most startling request of all came from the pen of a very naive Catholic sister. She believes in miracles and mistook me for St. Jude, the saint of the impossible. Was it possible for me to collect from my friends the sum of three hundred thousand dollars to pay the mortgage on their convent? In return, they would repay every dollar—time limit indefinite—and with no interest.

In dwelling on the number of people I've met in and out of showbusiness, I'm reminded of the cell-splitting process of the nuclear world. One cell splits into two, and two into four, the four into eight. This compares admirably with the story of my life. A visit to the Como rehearsal and I'm sharing a Coke with Steve Lawrence, Eydie Gormé and Jane Wyman; a lunch date with the late bandleader Tony Pastor and I'm face to face with Rosemary and Betty Clooney; an afternoon at Danny Stradella's summer home and I'm playing volleyball with Red Buttons, Robert Strauss and Esther Tobi; attending a National Advisory Committee meeting of the Actors Youth Fund and I'm cocking a glass with Joey Adams, Bert Bacharach, Virginia Graham, Horace McMahon, Robert Alda and the late Anita Louise. Dinner with Harry Guardino and a subsequent introduction to Anne Jackson. She wants to know if I'm the priest who supplied Harry with his Sunday spaghetti dinners during the New York filming of *Lovers and Other Strangers;* an appearance on the Mike Douglas Show and I am nervously twitching in my chair as Gig Young, Ann Blyth and the comedy team of Stiller and Meara are trying to calm me. Ethel Merman tells us there's no business like showbusiness. To which I can prayerfully reply, "You ain't just whistling 'Dixie,' Ethel."

HAVE
COLLAR,
WILL
TRAVEL

I dislike begging. It somehow conveys a feeling of degradation and pity. Certainly contributions must be sought for the upkeep of a church, a synagogue, a mosque. However, more money is always needed. To achieve this surplus I adhere strongly to the philosophy of giving people something for their money. Be it a card party, a dance, a social, bingo, a benefit . . . give something—just so the community will not feel they contributed and received nothing in return. Benefits have always been a tremendous source of revenue. Most of our parishes are located in the poorer, blighted areas of the eastern border. The greater majority of these parishioners have never attended a concert or reserved a table at a club. They couldn't afford it. Many of these same poor people have seen Sinatra, Martin and Lewis, Frankie Laine, Perry Como, Vic Damone, Jimmy Durante, the McGuire Sisters, Rosemary and Betty Clooney, Julius La Rosa, Patti Page, Eddie Fisher, Nat "King" Cole and many, many more. This bonanza of talent over the course of many years was available for the price of a one- or two-dollar ticket—and the selfless generosity of the artists. It's a little cheaper than the Copacabana or the Cocoanut Grove.

There is another area for healthy and profitable fund-raising. World premieres. Hence, when I learned Hollywood was about to put the Jimmy Durante story on film, I immediately hopped a plane and headed for Beverly Hills. Jimmy listened to my plan very patiently. When I finished, Jimmy merely shook his head sadly and gave me some perplexing news. "Yes, it's my life story, but I don't own the property anymore. Sinatra and Crosby bought the rights. I'm sure you won't have any trouble with them," Durante encouraged me. "If you get the premiere and need help, call Jules Podell at the Copa and ask him for a list of all his patrons" was his last fatherly recommendation.

Frank, Dean, Sammy Davis, Joey Bishop and Peter Lawford—the Clan—were doing their thing at Jack Entratter's Sands in Las Vegas. Once again I boarded a plane; this time Vegas was my destination. Frank greeted me warmly. At the same time, he was surprised to see me and realized I had some sort of a problem. "Frank," I hedged, a little embarrassed, "I understand you, Crosby and Dean are doing the Durante story in the roles of Clayton, Jackson and Durante. Is it true?" "Yes, we're contemplating it in the very near future, Padre." At this point I decided, Rather than beat around the bush let me give it to him straight. "May I have the New York premiere?" His answer sounded even more straightforward than my question. "You've got it! I've just one request to ask of you. I'll take a planeload of friends to New York for the premiere; make sure Como and the rest of your cronies also attend." Every fiber of my body shook with excitement. I visualized a mountain of money and so little effort. Some time elapsed and not a word about production on the Durante story. Then one day while scanning a Hollywood column in a local newspaper my eyes fell on a three-line news item. Frank Capra, director, and Frank Sinatra, actor, disagreed on several factors in the production of *The Jimmy Durante Story*. The deal has been canceled. Oh, my God! How could two good Sicilians, Capra and Sinatra, do this to me, a Neapolitan?

Mr. Sinatra invited me to spend a few days at The Sands as his guest. I accepted. An invitation was also extended for me to catch the dinner show that night. Again, I accepted. I sat at a table with Mr. and Mrs. Jack Entratter and their daughters and Mrs. Jeanie Martin. While the five were cavorting onstage, something happened that escaped me. It appeared that Dean was the butt of some sort of an inside joke. Not realizing the microphone was only a few feet from him, Dean turned to Joey Bishop and greeted him with a sonorous "You son of a bitch." Frank immediately signaled him with a "come-here" finger gesture. He whispered something into Dino's ear and Dean returned to the microphone. In a voice tinged with sorrow and amusement, he said, "Sorry, Father Bob, I didn't realize you were in the room." Everyone in the club was turning, laughing, looking for the Reverend Recipient of the apology. Dressed in sport clothes, I too turned, laughed and looked for the Clerical Scoundrel.

The following morning I arose rather early and made a beeline for the breakfast nook. Walking through the casino, I thought I saw a mirage. I couldn't believe my eyes. There was Dino, still dressed in his tuxedo from the night before, playing blackjack. Kiddingly I scolded him for staying up all night. Pleading guilty, he told me he had an early call on location for the movie *Ocean's Eleven*. We had a cup of coffee while he continued to play. Then came the now famous Martin drawl: "I'm taking one hell of a beating at this table. You better start praying for your old buddy." No sooner had these words left his mouth, the cards almost miraculously came his way. He couldn't lose a hand. A large crowd started gathering around the table. With each winning hand they would shout words of cheers and encouragement. Suddenly Dino turned to me and whispered: "Hey, Buddy, you better stop praying. This is getting embarrassing. I'll be late for work," he informed me, handing me a double fistful of chips. "Take these to the cashier and tell her to give me credit." When she informed me as to the exact amount of money I presented her, a vicious thought streaked across my mind. Why didn't I keep a couple of chips for myself? Why, even rabbis get paid for praying.

That evening the Clan was shooting a scene in front of the Thunderbird Hotel. It was a cold, biting, desert night. Dean wore his long johns underneath his silk tuxedo. He kept beating his hands against his legs and body to keep warm. "Would you believe this," he quivered, "I'm freezing, there's a bar only twenty feet from here and I can't get a drink." He's the only man I know who has a credit card for Alka-Seltzer.

Dean was working Las Vegas when I visited the gorgeous Martin household on Mountain Drive in Beverly Hills. On this occasion I was there at the invitation of Mrs. Jeanie Martin. We had spoken, coast to coast, by telephone and after I had described the nature of my forthcoming trip, she asked me to drop in. Sitting in the Martin study was quite a treat. It seemed that kids were coming out of the seams in the wall. One youngster walking through with a baseball glove and bat, a young lady pirouetting in a ballerina costume, two other kids sprinting by in bathing suits. It's no wonder Dean would never ask his Jeanie, "What's new?"

Mrs. Martin's invitation to "drop in" was in fulfillment of a pledge they had made. She presented me with a very generous check. The Martins decided to donate a stained-glass window to the Chapel of Saint Anthony's Seminary in Catskill, New York. The name MR. AND MRS. DEAN MARTIN has been seen in print and in lights. Now it can be seen amid the sylvan beauty of the Catskill mountains—in the House of God.

A new marriage between politics and the concert as a fund-raiser found its consummation recently in the campaign of Senator George McGovern in Inglewood, California. The funds for the Senator's campaign in California were swiftly dwindling and in dire need for replenishing. Warren Beatty, the actor, who had previously worked for McGovern, conceived the idea of a concert as a political money-raiser. It is common knowledge that Frank Sinatra, Sammy Davis and Dean Martin campaigned for John F. Kennedy; Paul Newman, Joanne Woodward and many more similarly worked in behalf of other Presidential candidates.

However, insisted Mr. Beatty and other involved entertainers, this exhibition would not be a political rally. To the contrary, politics would be kept to a minimum; it would be, pure and simple, a concert. With the aid of Barbra Streisand, Quincy Jones, rock singers James Taylor and Carole King, the McGovern coffers were replenished with three hundred thousand dollars. In less than twenty hours, the sixteen thousand seats of the Inglewood Forum were sold. As an extra attraction, such names as Oscar-winner Gene Hackman, Burt Lancaster, Mama Cass, Sally Kellerman, Julie Christie and Jack Nicholson volunteered their services to act as ushers and usherettes to the one-hundred-dollars-a-ticket patrons.

NOT
ALL
MY
FRIENDS
ARE
SAINTS

In showbiz there is a startling interweaving of people, personalities and just plain characters. You don't know with whom or to whom you are speaking most of the time. "You can't tell the players without a scorecard." Introductions are plentiful, but no one wears signs across their breast stating, I AM A BOOKIE, I'M A HOOKER, I'M A HOOD. You just don't know. You might meet a Ralph Bellamy at the barbershop or a Mr. Wise Guy at the shirtmaker. You could run into a Billy Wilder at the shoe store or be seated next to a madam at a restaurant. The problem is, you are one and people are legion; you wear a Roman collar and they are devoid of any career-indicators. Unless you know people personally or are gifted with a photographic memory, an introduction and a handshake could spell embarrassment and oftentimes trouble.

A vocal coach, a friend, invited me to hear one of his protégés. The invitation was accepted. As we rode over the Williamsburg Bridge, the young baritone politely asked if he could momentarily stop at his home to change his street clothes to a tuxedo. We stayed at the home for a short time, enjoyed a cup of coffee and proceeded to the club. The young man was a delight; he possessed a large, booming baritone voice very similar to Robert Goulet. Seated at the table with me were his in-laws. It wasn't until a week later that I learned I had been at the home of and sat at the table of Mr. Big of Brooklyn.

A friend and I walk into the Fontainebleau Restaurant to the strains of soft, romantic piped-in music. At one of the tables a celebration of some sort is taking place. Most of the party people knew my friend, so they insisted we join their company. As the introductions are spilling out like litanies, I hear the title "Countess." For a brief moment I become confused. Then I thought someone was putting me on. However, I was assured the lady was a real, live, genuine countess. We joined the party and enjoyed a lovely, refreshing time. Months later I became the victim of a literary time bomb. As I perused the local newspapers, my eyes pinpointed a large photograph of the Countess. She was indeed of royal heritage. She also operated the biggest brothel chain on the East Coast. The police apprehended her and deported her to Canada. Later, she made the headlines again. On this occasion she furtively returned to the States and once again she was regally escorted across Niagara's International Bridge.

A preaching assignment brings me to Chicago. I knew Durante was there working at the Chez Paree. Through some friendly channels I managed to learn the name of the hotel at which he was staying. One telephone call and I have a dinner date with the Schnozz. While we're dining Jimmy suddenly raised two fingers before my eyes as a young man approached our table. Deciding the two fingers indicated two drinks, I asked him not to order the drinks. I just did not feel like drinking. "Who's ordering drinks?" he commented. "I just want you to know that the guy who's coming over here is the number two guy in Chicago. So watch what you say."

I sat in a chair at Rudy's barbershop in the Warwick Hotel. Rudy is a celebrity in his own right. He belongs to that elite tonsorial dynasty frequented by many celebrities. As Rudy was studiously clipping the few locks I have left, a man entered the shop. "Sorry, Albert," Rudy apologized, "not today or tomorrow. My appointment book is filled." The man left. On the following day a man was murdered while seated in a barber's chair in the Park Sheraton Hotel. His name was Albert Anastasia.

"The FBI was looking for you," Brother Luke informed me. "They'll be back tomorrow." The FBI! Why would they want to see me? was my startled reaction. My only association with that group of infallible supersleuths is to occasionally watch them on TV's Sunday show. The following day they reappeared, placing before my squinting eyes an identification card reading THE FEDERAL BUREAU OF INVESTIGATION. They immediately assured me the matter at hand was not personal. All they sought was some information. Did I perform a certain marriage between so and so? Did I know the best man? His real name . . . his nickname. Could I tell them who attended the wedding? I tried to explain that during such services the large floodlights are directed toward the altar, practically blinding the minister, who faces them, and the church is of such large proportions it is almost impossible to see anyone except the first few rows. They weren't referring to the church but to the reception, they corrected me. I mentioned some attendants—really BIG stars, as Ed Sullivan would say. The groom was a well-known, high-priced theatrical agent; the bride, a Broadway showgal. Did you notice any unsavory characters at the reception? All the characters I recognized were quite savory, I assured them, including Jimmy Durante, Marlene Dietrich, Jane Powell, Hal March, among others. P.S.: It's the only wedding I've attended where tables were designated by cities.

"How about the fights Friday night, Padre?" inquired a friend who had just introduced me to three well-dressed gentlemen. We were in my friend's clothing establishment, where the trio made some purchases. Upon their departure, I asked about the professions of the elegantly dressed threesome and was informed they were legitimate hoodlums. A "legitimate hoodlum" is one who made his money dishonestly and now is involved in legitimate businesses. It is now Friday, fight night at the Madison Square Garden. I meet my haberdasher friend and he in turn introduces me to three Internal Revenue agents who were to be our companions as spectators. As the usher led us down the long aisle of the Garden, he suddenly stopped and pointed out our seats. I proceeded first and the others followed. Just as I was about to sit, a gruff voice greeted me: "Hi, Fa-der." It was the Unholy Three. This is my concept of a perfect dilemma: three hoods and three IRS men and I sit smack in the middle. I didn't look right or left, I didn't speak east or west. "Between the devil and the deep blue sea" makes sense to me now.

How many men of the cloth can make the notorious claim of being refused entry to a public restaurant? I can! As I entered the door of the Amalfi Restaurant one evening, Jimmy Toriello, the manager, stopped me and politely informed me I wasn't welcome that particular night. Embarrassed, confused, chagrined, I made my way home. Why in heaven's name would Jimmy do a thing like that? I tried to come up with an answer but could not. It was like one big crossword puzzle; the empty boxes were there but I couldn't fill them in. The following day I telephoned him. "What I did last night," he explained, "I did for your own good. Doesn't your buddy George Woods always invite you to sit and have a drink with him? Well, he was here last night and dined with Frank Costello."

A wise guy approached me to inquire if I would christen his child. I accepted the offer. On the afternoon of the baptism I noticed that the godfather was also a wise guy, perhaps of greater eminence in the organization. During the baptismal ritual, the minister asks the child several questions, which are answered by the godparents in the name of the baby. Do you renounce Satan? And all his works? And all his allurement, etc.? I do renounce them. Having asked questions and christened babies for twenty-eight years, I now naturally presumed that the sponsors would do their job. They didn't. The godfather thought it was the godmother's task to respond and not his. So he interrupts me and informs the young lady of her responsibility to answer all interrogations. At this point, the baby's father seriously advised me: "This is my kid. I want this thing done right." Then came the command "Repeat the questions, Father." An amusing observation crossed my mind. Here are two bastards who have been taking the Fifth all their lives. Now they've got me repeating questions.

Here are some classic nuggets garnered from the guys and dolls who cross paths on Broadway. "What does Shorty do for a living?" I asked a mutual friend. "He's a book publisher," I was told. "What's the name of the publishing house?" came the next question. "He has no name—he just makes book," I was enlightened.

Another compulsive horseplayer, who probably owes his life and blood to the shylocks, described his plight saying, "Pray for me, I'm in the hands of the Philistines."

A devout bookmaker—there are some—tells me, "Here's a fin; light five; the public is knocking me off." Translated into the vernacular this statement would read, Here's five dollars; light five candles; the bettors are murdering me.

"Requiem for a heavyweight!" Such a title is not inappropriate considering the stature of Joe Gallo in the hierarchy of the underworld. I met Joey several times during my willing but regretful visits to the Green Haven State Correctional Facility in Stormville, New York. On my very first trip I found myself nervously waiting for the Catholic chaplain in one of the cellblocks. A slight figure, blond hair, a mold caressing his face, beaming a toothy smile, stood before me. "Hi, Bob," he smiled, "I heard you were coming. Welcome to Green Haven." "Hell, Joey," I kiddingly snapped, "I haven't been here twenty minutes and already you robbed me of my title." "Sorry, Father Bob," came the apology; "welcome to Green Haven anyway." "Will you make the three-day retreat, Joey?" He grinned and slowly walked away. Released from prison, I hadn't seen or heard from Joe even once. But we almost did meet again. . . .

It is a traditional practice on the part of Danny Stradella to invite favorite friends to the Copacabana on opening nights. Especially when the entertainer/entertainers are special friends and steady customers at his restaurant. Such an invite was extended to me. It's been a long time—in fact, years—since I've attended an opening-night show. There's too much excitement and commotion plus the loss of sleep to make such an offer personally inviting. So I declined to catch Don Rickles' opening. My friends were there en masse. After the show Mr. Rickles, Danny Stradella, Robert Strauss, Morty Morton and many others sat at a large table. Two men appeared, Joey and his bodyguard, and began talking to Rickles, who in turn made the proper introductions. The mere sight of Bob Strauss' familiar cinematic face caused Joey Gallo to stir like an adolescent movie fan. "You're a big star in the Big House," he excitedly informed Strauss. "They all love you in the House—the niggers, the Portos, the whites [*sic*], everybody loves you. They can't wait for your pictures to be shown." This garland of esteem was further complemented by an invitation to dinner. "Why don't all you lovely people be my guests? I'm going to Mulberry Street for dinner." The familiar ring of Mulberry Street produced a glowing smile on the massive face of Mr. Strauss as he menacingly reminded Joey, "I thought Mulberry Street was Father Bob's territory." My name startled Joey. "Father Bob—you know him too?" "He's my friend; I've known him for years." Thank God, no one accepted Joey Gallo's generous invitation to dinner; it might well have been for many of my friends their Last Supper.

A diminutive gentleman, a big, black cigar protruding from the side of his mouth, the speech, clothes and mannerisms of a television mobster, approached me in the lobby of the Sands Hotel in Vegas. "Hey," he greeted me warmly, "the boys tell me you're a priest." I assured him that this earthshaking morsel of information was true. Encouraged with my confirmation, he continued to enlighten me with certain other facts. He's a devout Catholic, but only his wife and kids attend Mass on Sundays; he provides many contributions to the church. By this time he almost assumed a fatherly interest in me. He walked me to a quiet corner of the room and informed me his youngest son attends a seminary in a suburb of Detroit, where he and his family reside. When I inquired what kind of a priest, a secular or a religious, he beamed with his thesaurus of religious knowledge. "He's going to be a San Francisco priest!" Having been a son of Saint Francis of Assisi—a Franciscan—for the past thirty-seven years, I felt I enjoyed a perfect right to say, "I'm a San Francisco priest too!" We shook hands, content with the thought that his son and I might possibly work someday in the same union and perhaps the same local.

Life is a mélange of joy and sorrow, love and hate. There's much sorrow and little joy, much hate and little love in our penal institutions. We attempt to bring some element of the euphoria not only by providing entertainment but also to provide spiritual diversion. Preaching a three-day retreat at the Green Haven State Correctional Facility at Stormville, I received a letter from an inmate. A young man in his early twenties; narcotics was his crime—user and pusher. Though his identity will remain anonymous, I would like to reveal his note in toto:

Dear Father:

Today on March 23, 1970, I was present at your retreat. When you spoke of how people time after time hurt Jesus Christ by what they do, I looked at myself. In the past and present I hurt Jesus, I nailed him to the cross, I crucified him. I felt guilty even though I am trying and doing my best to go to heaven. Then when you spoke of praying and looking at Jesus, I kept it in my mind. Tonight I prayed to Jesus as I always do. This time I looked at him from one of the pictures I have in my room. I asked him for help and I told him I was hurt for hurting him in my past actions. Then I cried, because of what I did to him. Never in my life has this happened. Tonight it did, because when I looked at him I could really see how I hurt him and how wrong I was. After crying I felt good because I do love Jesus and I know he forgives me, as I forgive others who hurt me, and visa versa. I thanked Jesus and God for all they have given me, past and present. I thank them for giving me life, a soul, the light and the road to heaven. This is my goal. I will help others to go to heaven too. I will stand up for my Father, even if it's the cost of my death. Because I will live forever in heaven with him. Because I love him, and most of all because he has finally given me freedom.

Sincerely in love,

P.S. Thank you.

"Father, I'm pretty busy at the moment. Why don't you step into my private office. I'll see you in a few moments." The offer accepted, I stepped into his rather shabby, manly office. Inside the office stood a man elegantly dressed, his jacket resting flawlessly on the back of a chair. "Hi" came my greeting. His reply lay in the area between a grunt and a groin pain. This constituted the beginning and end of our conversation. Puffing hard and long on my cigarette, feeling terribly uncomfortable and unwanted, my primary thought was to get the hell out of there as soon as possible. In the meantime, those bulletlike eyes kept glancing at me. I returned to my friend with the stammering question "Who in hell is that character in your office?" "Oh, he's just a fag from Chicago." "A fag?" I chuckled. "He almost paralyzed me with a glance." Later I learned that "the fag from Chicago" was none other than Chicago's Salvatore "Momo" Giancona. Yet the man must have possessed some sophisticated charm and warmth to turn the head of a lady as lovely as Miss Phyllis McGuire.

The Drakes, Janice and Alan, always held a special place in my heart. Alan is a comic, big-time enough to be managed by Lloyd Greenfield, who is the American representative of Tom Jones and Engelbert (we call him "Engela") Humperdinck. Handsome and well tailored, Mr. Drake fits the mold of the American comedian perfectly. Flamboyant, fast-talking, exuberant, he comes up with quick hilarious lines which he claims are original. He is always "on," and the occasion could be a dinner date, a visit to a hospital, a ball game or a trip to the mortuary. An ex-Bostonian for many years, he still retains a tint of the broad A. Janice was something else. A product of the Jersey Shore, she won several beauty contests, including the most beautiful girl in the state. Quiet and shy, she was a delight. The Drakes had agreed to a mutual understanding. Whenever Alan was out of town and Janice desired a night "on the town," just call "Uncle Augie." With this adopted Uncle, no one would be on the make or in any way disturb the lovely young lady. As fate would have it, Alan was out of town when Janice called Uncle for a date at the Copacabana. At closing time, Augie called the doorman for his Cadillac. Here they were found, hours later, Janice and "Little Augie" Pisano, murdered. A victim of circumstance. She was at the right place at the wrong time.

It's all in a day's work! Attending the dying, visiting the sick and infirm, encouraging the imprisoned; it's all a part of the life of a priest. Included in this mélange of chores, on several occasions I also testified in court as a character witness. Tino Barzie, manager of Frank Sinatra, Jr., became the hoodwinked victim of a masterminded fraud. A travel agent with whom he had done business kept supplying him with tickets which unbeknown to him were stolen. The Feds claimed Tino was aware of the larceny. Jack E. Leonard and I were requested to testify as to the character of Tino. I informed the judge that I had known Mr. Barzie for many years—in fact, back to the Glenn Miller days; I was personally acquainted with his wife and children; I visited his home in Pittsfield, Massachusetts, and on occasions had dinner with them. Jack E. likewise testified to his close personal relationship with Tino and his lovely family. The case, thank God, was dismissed.

Again I find myself in a federal court in Newark, New Jersey. This time comic Phil Foster is the victim. A telephone call from manager Harry Steinman and within hours I'm traveling with Rabbi Mann and New York disk jockey "Long John" Nebel to testify in Phil's behalf. What was Phil's crime? He made plans to buy some furnishings and carpeting from an Englewood, New Jersey, neighbor, who intended to move elsewhere and more importantly was considered a "capo mafioso" by the Federal Government. Phil, the government claimed, quoted two prices. Ironically, when Rabbi Mann, "Long John" and I arrived at the

Newark Federal Court Building, the case had already been reviewed and thrown out of court. Phil played it smart. He and his family moved to Vegas. Guilt by association!

The sylvan beauty of Pennsylvania's rolling hills were small recompense for the long, arduous and monotonous bus ride to the Lewisburg Federal Penitentiary. The bus itself, of exceptionally old vintage, created more difficulties. We embraced every bump on the very bumpy country roads without the aid of an air conditioner. Four hours later the entourage arrived at the high, gray, forbidding walls. What is it like walking into a prison? *Hell!* The tower guards permitted a number of us to enter through the first gate; remained there for a few moments. We are now caged between the gleaming steel. The second gate does not open until the first is closed. To hear the excruciating clash of steel kissing steel is the God-awfulest sound I've ever heard. A short walk, about fifty feet, brings us to the prison itself. Again more gates—three huge barriers, to be exact, located at the north, east and west positions of the institution. And once again the agonizingly shrill cry of the steel. It's a surprisingly long walk to the auditorium; all of us helped carry band instruments, costumes, props, music sheets, attachés, etc. Upon arrival in the auditorium, an inmate removed my coat and kiddingly informed his confreres, "If any creep tries to rob Father Bob's coat, he'll answer to me."

While Enzo Stuarti, Mama Lou Parks and the Parkettes, Morty Storm, III, and Ada Cavallo were performing, I made my way around the auditorium. Blacks and whites greeted me. Amazing the amount of prisoners I knew; faces I recognized and did not really know. East Side . . . West Side . . . All around the town. Brooklyn . . . Bronx . . . Staten Island. Hello, Mike . . . Hi, Tony . . . Hello, Willie . . . Hi, Eddie . . . Hello, Sal . . . Instantly an ominous thought struck me: Let me get the hell backstage where I belong before I'm elected an honorary citizen by popular vote. After the entertainment, the warden cordially invited us to the officers' mess hall for sandwiches, coffee and cake. Nothing short of a miracle convinced the warden to permit two of my neighborhood inmates to escort me to the mess hall. Elated at this unexpected turn of event, one prisoner said to the other, "Jesus, did we 'score' tonight!" "Damn you"—my cool slightly ruffled—"don't use that word 'score' around here. That's why you're both here."

The rolling hills of Pennsylvania were no longer visible; it was pitch black. The ride home was long and tedious. No one had much to say. Smoke if you want; sleep if you can. The music ended, the songs sung, the jokes finished; all that remained for us—the entertainers and the priest—a revolting sense of depression, weariness, melancholy and the blues.

It was a pretty great show, even for the imprisoned souls of Lewisburg Federal Penitentiary. Tony Martin, Corbett Monica, Mama Lou Parks and the Parkettes and Israeli singer Esther Tobi. The most agonizing part of the day was the eight hours'—go and return—bus trip to the prison. However, it was worth the price when I witnessed the cheering, smiling faces of every member of the audience. The day was spring and sunny, so rather than use the prison auditorium, as we had done on previous occasions, the ball field became our amphitheater. The inmates built a two-foot-high stage and at show time the prisoners sat and stood around two-thirds of the stage. Mama Lou and the Parkettes, an all-black act of three girls and four boys, singers and dancers, were invited by popular request. On their first appearance in the prison with Enzo Stuarti, they virtually fractured the audience.

When the show ended, the entire cast reappeared on stage to take their final bow. At this point a very small number of the prisoners, closest to the stage, jumped to their feet, approached the three girls and grabbed. Hands flew all over the place as the girls shrieked and screamed and one of them cried uncontrollably. The whole scene lasted less than a minute. Weeks later I was informed that the other inmates did not approve this ungentlemanly action. The word was out to kill each and every offender. The culprits, realizing their sad mistake, spent more than a week in their cells, never leaving their *refugium peccatorum*, not even for food and church services. Unfortunately for the "good guys," will they suffer and be deprived of live shows for the sins of a few?

In the argot of the professional gambler, a "junket" signifies a free airline trip to and from the gambling locale, free rooms, food and drinks. In Vegas it is expressed as "comp" (complimentary). In return, the gambler is expected to play a certain amount of money. In the event you go broke, you may borrow some money —the amount depending on the credit the hotel allots you. This is negotiated by signing your signature on a "marker," a piece of paper denoting the amount of money loaned with your John Hancock.

The women's lib should be instructed that the junket is a male-chauvinist thing. About ninety percent of the passengers are male. Consequently, the hotels promoting junkets become the mecca of many filles de joie. Or to employ the vernacular—hookers. It was in one such hotel I spoke with a young Jewish boy from Brooklyn. As we parted, a girlish blonde stopped him and inquired, "Who's the creep you were just talking to?" "Creep? What creep?" Pointing in my direction, she croaked, "The guy with the blue shirt." "Why are you calling him a creep?" "Because"—her pride crushed—"I've been trying to make him for the last two hours and he wouldn't even move an eyelash." "Oh, my God . . . he's a clergyman—he's a Catholic priest," my friend moaned. She walked directly towards me. "Hello. I'm Bunny. I want to apologize; I didn't know who you were." Assuring her the mistake was perfectly natural, I began to think in terms of evangelizing. Why not? Any time and any place is as good a time and place to do the Lord's work. "Bunny," I hedged, "did you ever consider marriage, a husband, children and a home? Did you ever toy with the idea of going legit?" "I tried, Reverend, and it didn't work. Moreover, where else could I make three hundred dollars a day and pay no taxes?"

Joe Willie Namath is first and foremost a supergreat quarterback. Second and secondmost a supergreat Hungarian lover. During the magnificent September Festa of San Gennaro on Mulberry Street, I met Joe through a mutual friend. I accompanied him to our rectory courtyard, where a bazaar was being held. He no sooner set a foot on the sacred grounds when he was blitzed by six starry-eyed young ladies. "Girls, girls," I pleaded. "It's all right, Father, we won't hurt him," one of them reassured me. "We're student nurses from St. Vincent's Hospital." My second meeting with Joe Willie occurred as I sat with Fat Jack Leonard at Danny's. Jack was about to introduce me when Mr. Quarterback informed the Fat Man we had already met. "Christ," Joe prayed, "I thought *I* got around." Finally, I was introduced to a young lady who attends C. W. Post College in Nassau County on Long Island. Post is the practicing grounds for the Jets during the preseason period. Joe Willie asked her for a date; she accepted. "Are you a football fan?" she questioned me. "I'm not just a fan, I'm addicted." "What do you think of Joe Namath?" again she questioned me. "I think he's the greatest." "Yes," she agreed, "he's the greatest on the gridiron, but he's one son of a bitch inside an automobile. . . ."

At times to reminisce is a difficult task, especially when it involves twenty-five long years. My God, twenty-five years. There's a lot of yesterdays to look back upon and a lot of tomorrows to look forward to. It was the last day of my very first vacation in Vegas as a guest of Jimmy Durante. We stayed at the Desert Inn, where the Schnozz was performing with Eddie Jackson, Jack Roth and pianist Julie Buffano. I believe the Desert Inn had recently opened under the auspices of Mr. Wilbur Clark. During my stay at the DI, I met a most respectful young man from Chicago. His name was Ralph, but everyone in the establishment called him Ralphie. In his early twenties, he was unbelievably obliging and ingratiating. He would help anyone under any circumstance—driving to the city, the airport, or to church on Sunday—at the drop of a mere "Will you please." Hearing that Friday spelled finis to my vacation and I would TWA to New York the following morning, Ralphie asked if I would spend my last evening with him and his friend. The invitation was accepted. That delightful evening we enjoyed a sumptuous dinner and caught two shows, including Durante's. The morning of my departure I filed the names and addresses of the people to whom I wished to mail a "thank-you" note. "Jimmy," I inquired, "what's Ralphie's last name?" "Ralphie who?" "Ralphie from Chicago." "Capone." "Capone?" I stammered. "Yes, he's Al's kid brother."

There's nothing comical about murder and death. Yet in the most gruesome of cases, a word, an act or a detail could lead people into compulsive laughter. A clam house in our neighborhood was being readied for business—Umberto's. As the work was almost completed, I suspected the owners, unknown to me, would request to have the establishment blessed by a priest. One day as I passed the now "open-for-business" Umberto's, I noticed a priest sprinkling holy water over the premises. The priest is a very dear friend from the Village. Business was slow and rather discouraging. When Joey Gallo got hit and killed there by "shots heard around the world," Umberto's became the recipient of the most publicized murder in the universe. A Catholic nun stationed in Kenya, Africa, wrote to friends she had read about Gallo's murder. Friends from Sydney, Australia, notified relatives living in our neighborhood about Joey's demise. Suddenly Umberto's became a landmark. Tourist buses stop there for lunch. Tourists walking the local streets point a finger at the restaurant and talk in whispers. Business expanded incredibly. One day I remarked to Bobby, one of the owners, how well businesswise Umberto's was doing. "Yes, Father," Bobby observed; "that blessing Father John gave Umberto's really did the trick."

This story is not apocryphal or contrived. Were it necessary for me to take a solemn oath before God to prove its veracity, I would gladly do so. A would-be actress with no more talent for the stage than John Wayne's talent for the ballet fell prey to alcoholism and men. Twice married, twice divorced, she was the mother of a five-year-old daughter. Invariably she would sit at a bar until saturated with whiskey and return to her apartment with one of her retinue of boyfriends, each of whom was called "Uncle" by the five-year-old. One wintry morning when the little girl asked Mother if they had any visitors last night, she informed the child "Uncle Ralph" was here; in fact, he just left the apartment a few moments ago. With this parcel of information, the youngster made a mad dash for the elevator just as "Uncle Ralph" was entering the opened doors. There he stood in the midst of the early-morning riders, unshaven and wearing a day-old wrinkled shirt. Her greeting was a classic: "Uncle Ralph, thanks for sleeping with Mama last night and keeping her nice and warm."

She was no Betty Grable or Betty Hutton. Nevertheless, she remained on the perimeter of stardom long enough to star in a dozen or more cinematic musical comedies. As she made her entrance into a restaurant, the two gentlemen with whom I was seated began a litany of invectives. They were hesitant to reveal the story but finally decided to confess. It seems she was "very nice and condescending" to both of them in every appreciable way. After some time she informed the two individually—one did not know about the other—she was "that way." One thousand dollars for an abortion or a paternity suit for the prospective father. Her demand for money was acknowledged by the two Lotharios. Why the invectives? Seeking advice and comfort, one confided in the other. They soon learned she was never in a "delicate way." There were no pregnancy, no baby, no city, state or federal taxes. Smart girl!

A holdup and a robbery in the diamond-center area of Manhattan is no great news-maker. These crimes occur with the frequency of the sun setting in the west. One day, as was my custom, I visited a dear friend, a jeweler, in the diamond center. To my surprise, I found the inner door of the office bolted. Someone peered through a small glass window and assured my friend, "It's O.K. It's Father Bob." "When did you convert this joint into Fort Knox?" I wisecracked. "It's no joking matter," my friend whined. "Jesus, what an experience we had. Wow!" Now the jeweler began to expound. Three men marched into this place, each holding a terrifying revolver. The mere verbal reenactment of the frightening scene caused beads of sweat to spring out of his skull. "One man," he continued, "stood at the door; the other two grabbed me, my uncle and my helper and pushed us into the extra room. Then one of them handcuffed us to a water pipe while the other kept the Goddamn gun staring at our heads. Why is it," he questioned me, "crooks are just like cops? You'll always find a wise guy and a nice guy among them. One always ready to crack your skull and the other always so solicitous about your health." He resumed the story. "One guy went to the safe, the other to the showcase. As each piece of jewelry hit their attaché cases I could feel my heartbeat growing slower and slower. The final departing words were threats. 'Give us five minutes while we wait for the elevator. If you as much as gurgle during the five minutes, we'll return and kill you all.'" "What did you do when they left?" "Nothing—absolutely nothing," he replied, "I was too frightened even to whisper a prayer." There is a happy ending to the story, thank God. Most of the stolen jewelry was recovered. However, there's a surprisingly peculiar twist to this narrative. Most of the stolen jewelry was found in the apartment of one of the best-known, highest-priced, most successful female vocalists in the country. No names, please! Oh, how does one get minks? The way minks get minks!

"When are you leaving, Father?" "In a couple of days; we're staying just for the weekend," I informed the Vegas casino manager. "I wish I could say that," came a plea rather than a retort. "Why don't you?" I suggested. "Because we're prisoners on this Devil Island," came the retort rather than the plea. Las Vegas is unreal, ethereal, a make-believe world, a tinseled jungle. I often wondered what would happen were it possible to destroy the electric power of that citadel of sin. Would its gold be lost forever because its glitter has vanished? Would the nonworking one-armed bandits send the workingman back to his home? Would the hot, sunbaked Nevadan air deter the refrigerated-minded queues of tourists? How bad is Las Vegas?

Six churches and three parochial schools provide for the needs of the Catholic population. I attended Mass on a late Saturday afternoon in a church located behind the Desert Inn. Later the Actors' Mass takes place at 5:30 A.M., to be followed by three more Masses. There were many more Nevada-licensed automobiles in the parking area than those of out-of-towners. Like their casinos and supper clubs, the large-sized sacred edifice was packed to capacity—SRO. In his presermon announcements, the good padre reminded the congregation as long as they were vacationing in Las Vegas, where gambling is legal, the church would most cordially accept any hotel chips. Whether you win or lose at craps, blackjack or roulette, don't forget the Lord. In fact, praise the Lord and pass the ammunition. At communion time two more priests came to the assistance of the celebrant of the Mass. The three distributed the Eucharist for fifteen minutes while lines of natives and tourists returned reverently to their seats, having received the sacred species. To say I was mildly shocked is an understatement. I was pleasantly awakened. Incidentally, through the concentrated efforts of Mr. Jack Entratter, a synagogue reposes eloquently upon the property adjacent to Entratter's Sands Hotel. How bad is Vegas? You tell me!

Mr. and Mrs. Val Sorrento are friends. They, their two sons and daughters-in-law were about to embark on that once-in-a-lifetime vacation to Hawaii, San Francisco and lastly and smartly, Las Vegas. Mr. Val worked hard for thirty-nine years to achieve the renowned title as one of the finest pastry bakers in all New York. My business plans also included Vegas, so I decided to coincide my dates with theirs and surprise them. The surprise was indeed realized as I touched their shoulders when we were leaving church after Saturday-evening mass. One of our fun things included a show at Howard Hughes' Landmark Hotel. We wisely asked the waiter the price of a bottle of Dewar's White Label. He didn't know, because the occasions were far and in between when people ordered Scotch by the bottle. We asked him to inquire. He returned with the bottle, however, without any knowledge of the price of the bottle. He then promised to find out. By that time, Miss Bobby Gentry and others began the show. No waiters were in sight. Finally, we opened the bottle and enjoyed both the show and the golden firewater.

Now came the time of reckoning. Check in hand, his eyes bewildered, Mr. Sorrento looked at me astonished. Is it possible? he inquired, as he handed me the bill. Eighty-two dollars, it stated:

seventy dollars for the Dewar and twelve dollars for taxes. My sense of justice raged. No two-bit phony is going to make a jackass out of me and my friends, I cursed sotto voce.

I dismissed the waiter as he pleaded ignorance once more. I demanded to speak to the person in charge of the room. The manager, or whatever, suddenly appeared. A man in his early forties; very slight of build; a sneer powered his face as though a toothache had just set in. I've lived a lifetime with wise guys, so it's not too difficult for me to perceive what's genuine and who's stage-acting. He must have been a great fan of *Naked City* or such TV trash, because his efforts to assume a tough-guy portrait were overbalanced.

What's wrong here? he gruffly wanted to know. "We refuse to pay that ridiculous sum of money for a bottle of Scotch." The sneer now climaxed into a growl. "You had better know somebody in town or you'll stay here all night," he threatened us. I commenced by reminding him we weren't some farmers from Nebraska or Kansas; we were city slickers from New York and would not be duped or threatened. And, yes, we do know someone in town.

A telephone call to a friend; a return call to the Landmark Hotel for me. I resumed my conversation with the manager. "Your boss wants to talk with you, mister," I informed him. "My what?" he stammered. "Your boss," I replied. "Are you kidding me?" His voice quivered a bit at this point. "Do you work here?" I questioned him. "If you do, your boss wants to talk with you."

He went to the phone and returned shortly afterward. A transformation occurred incredible to the human eyes. He exuded meekness, understanding, compassion and a great deal of humility. Evidently the bottom fell out of his charade—and the hotel's check. "Just give me, if you want, forty dollars, and we'll call it even." We gladly paid the check. Our exit, quite satisfactory and victorious, gleamed with the Continental. He kissed the hands of our three ladies and shook the hands of the four men as he bade us adieu.

Hours later I found out, much to my hurt and chagrin, consternation and anger, the entire check had been cancelled through the intervention of my friend. While we were the recipients of a comp (complimentary) courtesy of the Landmark Hotel, the Bum took us for forty dollars.

To succeed in showbiz, you need a gimmick. It is a condition sine qua non, as my philosophy prof so beautifully used to phrase it. The great Jolson did it blackfaced with a knee touching the ground; Crosby's bo-bo-bo-bo; Sinatra's emaciated frame; Como's working in two speeds, slow and stop; Jerry Lewis' frenzied antics and Dino's glass-in-hand policy; Elvis gyrating his lower transmission, while Tom Jones gyrates the whole transmission. Harry Belafonte's wide-open shirt with his peekaboo navel. Johnny Ray wailed while Connie Francis cried her way through a song. The humorist Fred Allen and parsimonious Jack Benny started a feud which lasted a decade, from the days of radio to the days of television. The roaring success of the Harmonica Rascals sat precipitously on the absence of Johnny Puleo's stature. Fame came to George Raft not as an actor but as the King of the Roseland Dance Hall adagio gigolos. Durante's nose didn't hurt the cause, nor did Bob Hope's ski-jump make him any poorer. Now, what happens when you're a male sex symbol? What's the gimmick? How do you inspire women to perform such muliebrian rituals as to toss their panties, bras and house keys to their sex god? Ask Tom Jones.

For a week or so, it seemed Hollywood had been transported into our neighborhood. On Mott Street, Marlon Brando, James Caan, Al Pacino, Al Martino and the young dynamic director Francis Coppola were filming *The Godfather,* while on Mulberry Street, Red Buttons and Sylvia Miles performed their histrionics for *Who Killed Mary What's Her Name?* and the radiant Sophia Loren contributed her talents to *Mortadella.*

For a good number of years I enjoyed a very pleasant chore every Saturday night. Having heard confessions in my parish church, I would dress and rush to the Hotel New Yorker. Bernie Cummins, the hotel orchestra leader, and some of the musicians would line up in the corridor. Using the musicians' dressing room, I would hear their confessions, one by one. One night, while hearing confessions, I heard a loud, gruff voice informing the lined-up men that he was the new house detective. "What the hell is going on in there?" he growled. Not until I left my quarters and explained the situation was he pacified. Imagine—"The Night They Raided Father Bob!"

I was invited to the home of comic Archie and Rose Robbins. There I met a young, very attractive lady and her escort. And for one perplexing hour I kept watching the girl tugging down on her skirt. It wasn't that short, not by the standards of the modern mini. Was it my presence causing her such nervousness? Whatever the reason, I decided to leave the living room and spend a little time with the host and hostess in the kitchen. "Archie," I inquired, "who is that Sherry—and why is she forever tugging down at her skirt?" He grinned broadly. "She's probably the best-known stripper in the world—Sherry Britton."

I arrived at Columbus Circle about a half-hour after the near-fatal shooting of Joe Colombo. The scene was absolute pandemonium, the air suffused with shock, hate and anger. The enormous throng had gathered at the Circle to participate in a "unity" demonstration sponsored by the Italian-American Civil Rights League, as they had done the year before. On this occasion it developed into a bloodbath. I was ignorant of the murderous attempt until my arrival at the scene. Someone ran by and shouted, "Bob, follow me!" It was my friend Father Louis Gigante, chaplain of the League. I followed instructions, although I had no idea of my destination. Suddenly I realized we were headed for Roosevelt Hospital, where doctors were preparing to operate on the victim.

Father Louis ushered me into a private room on the same floor as the operating room. There the Colombo family sat speaking in hushed tones. Lucille, his wife, and children Anthony and Joseph, Jr., with their wives and young Vincent and some intimate friends had gathered there. I felt an air of dignity in that room. Moist eyes, wet cheeks; not one vituperative or vengeful word was spoken. Lucille portrayed a veritable fortress of strength, assuring her children their dad would be all right. I instinctively ignored the blood-spattered clothes and shoes the two elder sons and a few other men wore. I have witnessed such scenes many times in my life. On the second visit with Father Gigante, the hospital room seemed transformed into a chapel. Literally hundreds of get-well Mass cards, statuettes and medals were sent by anguished friends and concerned people from every part of the world. I've learned an unforgettable lesson from the Colombo family. Never in my entire life have I seen such unity, solidarity and harmony in any family I've known like the Colombos.

When Joey Adams conducts his annual Actors Youth Fund dinner in December, it is a certainty two personalities will be present: Sherri and Mickey Spillane. This seems to be the one and only time of the year I meet the Spillanes. Sherri is a professional singer-actress, while her husband, as the whole world knows, writes dirty and salacious books from which he makes a clean and modest (?) living. It sounds incredible, but the sale of his books throughout the world reached the astronomical figure of over fifty-five million. Mickey, to give a man his due, is peerless in his particular brand of literature. There's quite an age difference between the Spillanes. Mickey appears to be in his mid-fifties, while Sherri is in her mid-twenties. Theirs is a peculiar marital arrangement. When writing, Mickey lives alone on an estate in the wilderness of South Carolina. She lives in a penthouse in Manhattan's East Fifties. At that time, during Mickey's absence, she's free to do what she wants and go where she will, which invariably includes showpeople, swinging parties and nightclubs. When Mickey returns to his Manhattan pad, she must live his life: no showbiz, no clubs, no parties; early to bed and early to rise. Whenever we meet, Mickey kids me: "I presume you don't read my books, Father Bob." To which I retort: "And I presume you don't read mine—the Old and New Testament."

Jackie Robinson has entered the eternal dugout. Robby was a frequent visitor to Danny's Hideaway. I can still visualize him seated at the corner star-table of the Nook Room. Quiet and sedate yet friendly and affable, a gentleman under any circumstance, he was indeed a credit to his race. Jackie could not be described as a talkative man; rather, he was quite reticent. However, he always acknowledged my presence with a sincere "hi," a handshake and a toothy smile. As often as I felt the grip of his hand against my puny manipulator, I realized why he was so outstanding a baseball hitter. As I watched the film *The Jackie Robinson Story*, with Jackie and Ruby Dee, on my TV screen, I wondered where and how will history evaluate the status of this man as a black American. In breaking the color barrier in baseball, he devastated these barriers in every sport imaginable and for all times. Today because of Robby the black man dominates the professional gridiron, the baseball diamond, the boxing ring and certainly the basketball court. Today because of Robby every black man knows if he has the talent he'll be given the chance and opportunity to become another Jackie Robinson or another Sugar Ray. I shall always consider him the first black Moses. As a youngster, Jackie would always tell me Joe Di Maggio was his baseball hero. As a contemporary, Jackie was always mine. Whenever the memory of this fine human being comes to mind, I picture him at Danny's seated quietly on a bar stool or his huge frame resting comfortably at his favorite table, his salt-and-pepper hairdo neatly combed, a friendly, benign smile caressing his face. I'm sure he's made it Home right through the pearly gates.

Whenever I run into actress Terry Moore, we spontaneously recall the case of mistaken identity. An assistant director thought I was the actor to portray the role of the priest who would accompany Miss Moore down Death Row in the film *Why Must I Die?* The picture, a ten-day wonder to complete, made a lot of money.

In the "what's new?" department, I informed my vivacious friend I was in the throes of writing a book. At the mere sound of the word "writing," she jumped in delight. "I'm so thrilled for you, Padre. It's just great." Then she went on to add she too is about to have her poems published. Terry's taste in fashion leans more to the modern, outré style, giving her a much younger appearance. "Why don't you visit our church and parish house tomorrow?" I suggested. "Love to, but can't. I'm heading for Florida early tomorrow morning and then out to California. How about this evening after the theater?" she offered. "I'm on my way to see Melina Mercouri in *Lysistrata*." My mental adding machine went into immediate action. Show time seven-thirty; performance and intermission two hours thirty minutes—making it already ten P.M. Take into consideration at least a half-hour to an hour for a backstage gabfest with Miss Mercouri, and the transportation to my neighborhood will bring Miss Terry's arrival well over eleven P.M. At that hour it would be very indiscreet of me to be walking the streets of Little Italy and Chinatown with a gorgeous blond girl who just happens to be endowed with much Moore feminine attributes than most females. "No, Terry. Maybe some other time you can come and visit with me."

It's a lot cheaper making movies in Italy than in the United States, I learned during my stay in Rome. You can obtain triple the productivity for the same American dollar. This parcel of information was conveyed to me by an American producer who at the time was in the process of filming an English-speaking picture. Actor Harry Guardino introduced me to the gentleman, who in turn introduced me to the stars of his film, Michael Rennie and Elenora Brown. Miss Brown portrayed the little daughter of Sophia Loren in the magnificent war picture *Two Women*. Mr. Producer evidently did not catch the title that ordinarily precedes my name. Repeatedly, he called me "Bob." He delineated the showbiz phase of his life by informing me he operated a chain of theaters in and around New Orleans and Dallas. "I think I've got a hit movie, Bob." The statement was a hopeful plea rather than a conviction. "Do you know," he continued, "I've got everything going in this film. Fornication, sodomy, adultery, homosexuality, lesbianism, the whole works." "Do you know who I am?" I indignantly questioned him. "Sure—Harry told me your name is Bob." "You're only partly right, my poor man. Harry told you I'm Father Bob, a Catholic priest." There was a moment of silence, then embarrassment, then apology, all accompanied with a sunset blush. To make matters worse, I told him I was indirectly connected with the Legion of Decency office in the Archdiocese of New York. "Oi vey" were the last faltering words I heard stammer from his lips.

WHAT
PRICE
VEGAS?

There's no business like showbusiness. It's gospel! Nor does showbiz stand alone. An Ethel Merman extends an invitation—"Let me entertain you"—and a whole machinelike labyrinth of human endeavor goes into action. Once the final curtain falls, you return to your home without the slightest concept of how many lives were affected by the presentation you had just witnessed. The author, director, producer, set designer, lighting engineers, stagehands, wardrobe, costume tailors, house manager, stage manager, ticket takers, usherettes, ticket and souvenir-book printing, stage-door guards, ticket agencies, warehouses to store scenery and people and trucks to cart it, musicians, theatrical unions, literary critics, press agents, publicity department, personal management, etc., etc.—each department a small piece of colored glass placed together to create this singular theatrical mosaic.

This process repeats itself in every phase of entertainment—the cinema, the ice show, the rodeo, the circus, the supper club, the nightclub, theater in the round, the summer stock, the burlesque, etc. Things are no different in the newest of media, television. The vast empire of television staggers the complacent imagination. The gargantuan ad agencies from Madison Avenue to all parts of the globe, the countless thousands who either face the red-pimpled cameras or fabricate the box, the billions of dollars spent informing you which detergent will clean your filthy sink or which cigarette will soothe your dirty lungs at the fantastic prices ranging from forty to sixty thousand dollars a minute. Such is the power of television that even the President turns actor when he faces the camera. Impeccably dressed, every strand of hair in place, makeup applied, the script rehearsed and re-rehearsed, the proper gestures at the proper places, he faces America and the world with his State of the Union address.

Entertainment is the number two buy product of New York—the second-greatest industry. The city could not survive without showbiz. You needn't be a union card-carrying member to be affected by this industry. Like a monstrous squid, its tentacles all-embracing, it can affect you, the ticket buyer, and me, the moralist. The matinees and evening performances of Broadway and Off Broadway shows attract countless thousands of tourists. These people need transportation—hence the fast-talking, cigar-chewing hackie makes a buck; these people must eat—hence the hand-kissing maître d' palms a few; they might be thirsty—it's the bartender who will pour in that little extra touch of Scotch for that little extra tip. If the tourists remain in the city for any period of time, the hotels collect. If they intend to shop, it's the merchants who will add the seven-percent state and city sales tax to the bill. If they are on the town for the night, it's the nightclubs and supper clubs who will work up to the minimum or start from "the cover." If there are Sunday services, the church collects whatever remains. The story is repetitious. The rodeo, the ice show, the circus, live TV shows are the magnets that enhance the splendor of The Great White Way. Showbiz becomes the stable barometer of the financial world; when it's good at the box office, it's good everywhere.

WHAT PRICE VEGAS?

The elaborate emporiums of Las Vegas employ fourteen thousand souls—from the hatcheck girl to the No. 1 Star in the main room; from the cocktail girl to the No. 2 Star in the lounge. True, gambling is largely responsible for its success; however, gambling without entertainment would never succeed. In fact, in some sort of reverse psychology, Vegas hurts the business. In their quest for top-rate names—the superstars—the hotels are vying with each other, offering artists unbelievable, astronomical figures as much as one half million dollars for a month or two of work. A sum I would only pay to see the Last Supper with the original cast in Technicolor.

A very vivid example of the case in point is Perry Como's engagement in Las Vegas' International Hotel. Perry is prime material, a superstar, who hasn't worked a nightclub stage in almost three decades. His last club appearance was at the Copacabana in 1943, where Willie Howard starred and Como was the second banana. In those days, five hundred dollars per week, Perry's take-home, was a most welcomed and desirable salary. Throughout his career Como has been the prey of every nightclub operator in the country, especially Vegas. His popularity was unquestioned. He was the secret lover of every matron who ever held a broom in her hands, the ideal husband and exemplary father. Money would be the only catalyst to determine whether Perry would or would not succumb to the temptation. The International offered him for a six weeks' engagement the sum of a hundred and twenty-five thousand dollars per week—the total sum for six weeks' work of seven hundred and fifty thousand dollars. Plus the pretty extras as free board, food, drink, transportation, etc., for the entire Como ensemble, which normally would cost a small fortune. Como succumbed!

Nowadays artists vie with artists not personally but through their personal managers or representatives. Mr. Comedian No. 1 received x amount of dollars for his engagement. Mr. Comedian No. 2 comes along, he wants the same amount as Mr. Comedian No. 1. Then when Mr. Comedian No. 1 returns for a repeat engagement and learns that Mr. Comedian No. 2 was paid exactly the same salary as he received, he's demanding a raise. Perhaps Las Vegas can afford these monetary fluctuations; certainly not the small-time operator in Boston, San Francisco, and Tin Buck Two. If the stars and superstars will not work the little man's room, neither will the ballerina, the acrobat, the magician, the chorus girl, the vocalist, the musicians. Nobody works. Mr. Little Man just closes up.

Recently Jerry Lewis emceed the annual dinner of the Motion Picture Pioneers organization at the Americana in New York. I delivered the benediction. Jerry expressed an inspirational quotation, author unknown. Later that evening, Jack Valenti informed Jerry and me of the author's identity and the book in which the quote could be found. Jerry then reminded Mr. Valenti that at a social meeting with President Jack Kennedy he was shown the same quotation in a bowl-like plaque. The quote: "Only three things in life are real: God . . . Human Folly . . . and Laughter." The author, Aubrey Menen. The book, *The Ramayana*.

God and Human Folly are inexplicable; laughter, and/or entertainment, we have to live with. Perhaps this explains why God created angels before men. Cognizant of the human folly that would be perpetrated upon the earthly stage, He created an angelic entertainment corps with Michael and Gabriel as the heavenly supermoguls. Perhaps this explains even further why everyone loves showbiz. To employ a cliché: Everyone has two businesses: showbiz and his own! Everyone is an actor . . . a vocalist . . . a songwriter—a ham. It brings to mind the story of the bathroom attendant in one of New York's theaters. He complained to a friend about the long hours he worked, the short tips and shorter salary he received. "Why don't you quit?" his friend admonished him. "And give up showbusiness?" God forbid.

A great amount of the egocentric comes into play when the dollar is discussed. Certainly everyone wants the top dollar. However, there are some who are interested not only in top dollar but also want to achieve top primacy. For example, a Johnny Carson will demand ten thousand dollars more than anyone has ever been paid before by a hotel. If Jack Benny had been the top-money recipient of the Sahara Hotel with a weekly paycheck of a hundred thousand dollars, a Mr. Carson will seek a weekly paycheck of a hundred and ten thousand dollars. The extra ten thousand is a bona fide message of goodwill to instruct the show-biz world that Mr. Carson is the top banana. It also aids and abets in bolstering the ego. Maybe Russia is the answer: Listen to these fantastic prices paid for by the sucker American public. Believe me, I do not disparage against the entertainer. However, my sense of justice, my sense of values dictates against such exorbitant, astronomical prices. Cast your eyes upon these figures and consider the affluent hard working American who earns thirty to forty thousand dollars a year is living far above the means of the hardworking American masses. These figures may not be precise, but what's the difference? When you're dealing with twenty-five, fifty, seventy-five and one hundred thousand dollars, what if you add a few or subtract a few? Actually, the agents are at fault, if "fault" is the proper word. To increase the weekly total figure means to multiply that figure by ten percent for their own pockets. Hence, they'll haggle, fight, threaten the owners to remove their properties elsewhere unless they come up with their prices. Reportedly these are the figures of some of the top American stars in Las Vegas:

Barbra Streisand, two hundred thousand dollars. Tom Jones, one hundred thousand and up. Engelbert Humperdinck worked for a paltry twenty-four thousand dollars weekly; now he's up to the one-hundred-thousand mark. Steve Lawrence and Eydie Gormé (together), one hundred thousand dollars and up. Sammy Davis, one hundred thousand and up. Nancy Sinatra, fifty thousand dollars. Jerry Vale, fifty thousand and up.

The opening acts tend to be more realistic only because of the comparable staggering figures we've just quoted. The "openers" in Vegas are paid ten thousand dollars weekly, and in the event the artist rates better than the average opening act, such as Barbara McNair, the price is seventeen thousand five hundred dollars weekly. The dry, desert Las Vegas atmosphere is filled with foreboding anticipation. What happens now with the completion of the MGM Grand Hotel? The competition for talent will become doubly acute. Instead of a paltry one hundred thousand a week, they'll raise the ante to two a week. Others, caught in the bind of financial exigencies, will offer artists certain points (ownership in the hotel) in return for their services. Again I repeat, for that kind of money I want to see the entire cast of the Last Supper—live—in Panavision.

THE HIDEAWAY, DANNY'S AND MINE

Danny's Hideaway is my second home in New York City; Danny, my twin brother. Not really. You see, there is such a striking similarity in the lives of Danny and myself that I call him "Twinny." We were both born of immigrant parents. They both migrated to New York's West Side. His surname is Stradella; mine is Perrella. Fantastically incredible is the fact we were both Born on the Same Day of the Same Year (he's a few hours older but refuses to admit it). And lastly, we are in the same profession: he distributes material food and I, spiritual food. There is only one major difference: I don't get his prices.

I first met Danny and the Hideaway with Perry Como, who carried his four-year-old son, Ronnie, into the restaurant piggyback. This must be some twenty-five years ago. The Hideaway was then a one-room affair with a bar and six tables. Today it pridefully boasts of nine rooms with a seating capacity anywhere between five and six hundred, and employs one hundred and fifteen people. The atmosphere is very intimate and friendly. A nice place for nice people.

One of the nine rooms is called The Nook—a very exclusive area where Danny seats celebrities in every profession of life and his longtime customers. This procedure can also complicate matters. The Boss and his maître d's are required to remember the exact seating location of each customer. God forbid Steve Rossi should find himself seated next to Marty Allen; Dean Martin next to Jerry Lewis; Cindy Adams next to the late Dorothy Kilgallen or some ex-husbands next to ex-wives.

Photographs play a very important part in the decor of the restaurant. Here again diplomacy must prevail. Once a year, Mr. Stradella must remove certain pictures from one position to another or even be required to cut out certain personalities if possible. I personally heard a young actress telling Danny, "What's that bastard's picture doing next to mine?" It was her ex-husband.

Another "Thou Shalt Not": Never offer any information to anyone regarding the presence of any patron unless the customer leaves a notice to that effect. Not being infallible, occasionally Danny pulls a blooper. One night Robert Strauss walked in greeting the host with his famous Animal smile. "A friend of yours is in The Nook," the Animal was informed. "Who is it? "John England." "Who in the hell is John England?" came the puzzled question. Danny pointed his finger: "Go into The Nook and you'll find out." Mr. Strauss walked a dozen steps, stared around the room and finally rested his eyes on the person of an old friend, John Ireland.

Danny is a great host, second to none. He knows his business and he should. He was born into the restaurant world, since his parents, Charles and Rose, operated a restaurant on the same East Forty-fifth Street; his sister, Frances, and her husband, John Bruno, were the founders of the famous steak house, the Pen and Pencil. To possess such savoir-faire as a restaurateur doesn't come easily. Papa Stradella made his boy earn his Fettucine working as a busboy, bartender, pantryman, waiter and, finally, day manager. It was in this capacity he changed uniforms and headed for Europe as a soldier. The recipient of a Purple Heart medal, having been wounded in the Salerno beachhead invasion, he returned home, where he decided to open the hole-in-the-wall, six-tables-and-bar eatery. Now the nightmare of Salerno, Sicily, the Battle of the Bulge appeared to be a daydream in comparison with his new life as a restaurateur. He was blitzed by the labor unions. Threats of every variety; picket lines demonstrating in front of his establishment. Danny would have gladly subscribed to their demands, but couldn't afford their prices. Most of his help consisted of family, relatives and friends. The Little Gladiator finally broke the Dragon's back and won the battle.

At Danny's if you are the recipient of an unordered bottle of fine *vino italiano* or an excellent native brand, it automatically means at the end of dinner you will also be the recipient of a check. This tradition has a deep-rooted significance. Many were the times Danny picked up the checks of the struggling actor, and the down-and-out vocalist, the frustrated writer, the tired girl dancer who did not possess rent money, let alone the price of a delicious filet mignon. Sammy Davis in his autobiography, *Yes I Can,* speaks of his earlier days, when it wasn't the chic thing to do, how frequently Danny invited the young, unknown black artist to dinner and hardly ever presented him with a check. Incidentally, a copy of this book is inscribed by Sammy in these grateful words: "To Danny. Thanks for your friendship. You helped to make it possible." These same people—the Charlton Hestons, the David Jansens, the Robert Taylors, the Kim Novaks, the Janet Leighs and many others—have reached the pinnacle of success. Stars should shine, stars should pay. It's Danny's theory: "Yesterday you could not afford the bill, today you can." There are still people frequenting his restaurant—a struggling actor, a down-and-out vocalist, a frustrated writer, a tired girl dancer . . . to these he never sends an unordered bottle of wine.

Another extraordinary trait in the character of Mr. Stradella is his deep awareness of people's right to privacy. In this I believe he is absolutely unique. In the twenty-five years I have known him and the equal amount of time I have frequented his bistro, unlike the majority of New York restaurateurs, I cannot recall Danny mingling with his guests or sitting at their table. The one and only exception to this astonishing feat was the occasion when he and I sat with Hy Gardner. We were to discuss a forthcoming TV show, with Hy the interviewer and Danny and I the interviewed. The total elapsed time of Danny's sitting posture was three minutes. To this we add another unusual phenomenon to be found at the Hideaway. Its telephone booths are beautifully and artistically decorated with many phony and bouncy checks Danny received from some of his clientele. It makes interesting reading if you have the wherewithal to analyze man's inhumanity to man. A car, a TV set, furniture is always returnable. How do you return masticated food? With a phony check?

Such is Danny's predilection for cowboys and western movies, Sinatra tagged him "The Cowboy." On numberless occasions his knowledge of the Westerns amazed me. He can recall not only the names of cowboys thirty and forty years ago but the names of their horses. As a gag, director Hal Wallis called Danny to Hollywood and gave him a ten-second, one-line role in a movie. "That's no way to treat a lady" were his immortal words. To enhance the gag even further, when the movie opened at the Brooklyn Paramount the marquee read:

KIRK DOUGLAS   ANTHONY QUINN   DANNY STRADELLA
"LAST TRAIN FROM GUN HILL"

There's a bit of ham in all of us, including the humble waiters. Al Ruddy, producer of *The Godfather,* dined in Danny's Hideaway and spotted one of my favorite waiters. Pointing to Mr. Marco Mitelli, he told Danny, "I want that man in *The Godfather* as one of the waiters." The scene for Marco's initiation to moviedom is one of the most important and brutal of the entire film. It takes place in Luigi's Restaurant in the Bronx, where a corrupt police captain and a racketeer enjoyed a sumptuous Italian dinner. Marco, naturally, dispensed all the goodies. In moves Michael—Al Pacino—directly to the bathroom in search of the hidden gun. He then proceeds to murder both the bad cop and the mobster. Marco is a slightly built man, about five foot two inches, in his early fifties. Now, in addition to serving excellent food, he also distributes his autograph. What with all the publicity he has received during the past year, it's surprising he's still dispensing food. You can see his slight frame and partly bald head in the more recent published *Godfather* issues, equipped with many still shots. Recently, a national German magazine published a large centerfold photograph of the Luigi's Restaurant scene with Mr. Marco Mitelli's image as big as life. "How's the movie star—Marco?" I often ask the Italian Marlon Brando. "I should have asked for a percentage piece of the picture instead of accepting a lousy check," he mourns.

Danny's introduction to horseflesh and the world of racing enjoyed quite an auspicious beginning. The owner of a racehorse convinced Danny that his animal should be christened "Danny's Hideaway." For his trouble, Danny became part owner of the trotter. On the night of "Danny's Hideaway's" debut, the part owner left his restaurant and rushed to the Yonkers Raceway, arriving moments before the race was scheduled. He went directly to the owner and the trainer, who informed him the horse was in bad shape: his feet were hurting and terribly sore. "We'll send him out for an airing," they groaned. In the meantime, many of Danny's steady customers, everyone in the Hideaway establishment from the busboys to the hatcheck girls, placed a wager on their favorite stallion—everyone except Danny Stradella, the part owner. The horse came in first by a length and paid sixty-eight dollars for two. Later, Danny confessed to the sin of lying. Too embarrassed to admit not betting his horse, he spread a rumor that he bet two hundred to win on his horse. Sixty-eight dollars for two. Or sixty-eight hundred for two hundred. Or zero for zero.

One day a white-bearded gentleman walked off Forty-fifth Street into the restaurant. "I'm Mr. George 'Gabby' Hayes," he introduced himself. He and Danny became inseparable friends. Perhaps the word "friend" doesn't really convey the true inner feelings Danny possessed for this extraordinary man—or vice versa. Maybe a "father–son" relationship would be more properly descriptive. In fact, all of us called him "Pappy." Danny would watch over him like a mother hen. Each evening around nine, Pappy would be told to return home and get into bed. The weekends were spent at the Stradellas' summer home in Point Lookout, Long Island. That house became the treasure chest of so many wonderful memories. Rose Stradella, Danny's mother, and Gabby conversing—a scene so hilariously funny not even the great Billy Wilder could capture it on celluloid. A bottle of wine between them, Rose with her heavily accented Italianized English and Gabby with his drawling, Southern vernacular trying their darnedest to talk and drink. Truly a Babel; we would hide in other rooms, listen in and practically burst into convulsions of laughter.

Gabby loved kids. Every Sunday afternoon a procession of children would stand by the house waiting for the white-bearded cowboy to make an appearance. Kids with their parents, kids of every age and description, paper and pen in hand for autographs while Pappy patiently signed each one, to the very end. Kids from Point Lookout, Lido Beach, Long Beach and the entire environs. Where kids were concerned, ten Tom Joneses couldn't reach the stature of one Gabby Hayes.

Some years ago Danny decided to honor Gabby by staging a Wild West party in his honor. It was the first such event I had ever attended. Everyone with one exception was dressed in Western style. The exception wore a Roman collar and ankle-high boots. A large, white-saddled make-believe horse stood in front of the restaurant. Joe Gallart, the doorman, gloriously garbed as John Wayne's competitor, held it by the reins. Ethel Merman, Johnny Carson, Ed Sullivan, Red Buttons, Jack E. Leonard, David Jansen, Charlton Heston were some of the many celebrities who came to play Cowboys and Indians.

It was a gray, mournful Sunday afternoon when Danny phoned to tell me Gabby had passed away. We made immediate plans to fly to California, attend the funeral rites and return the same day. The night before our departure, a savage snowstorm struck New York, paralyzing the city and grounding all planes. We were denied the privilege to attend Gabby's Last Roundup.

Let's segue to the Hideaway! I recall the occasion Patti Page was playing the New York Paramount. She called Danny and asked if she could possibly have dinner in between shows. Danny assured her it could be done. Patti, Jack Rael, her manager, and I enjoyed a delightful dinner—compliments of the house. And outside the restaurant there stood a big, black limousine and a chauffeur ready to return us to the theater—compliments of Danny. Or the occasion of Anne DeMarco's, of the DeMarco Sisters, wedding. Several hundred people eating and drinking, dancing and laughing; Danny working as a bartender, a waiter, a busboy. After the festivities were over, I learned, much to my consternation, the whole affair was a wedding gift from Danny.

Speaking of the DeMarco girls, they referred to Danny and myself as the Ambassadors of Peace. Many were the emergencies to the Copa and other establishments to quell an argument, stop a fight, convince one or two of them to do the next show.

If Mr. Stradella is the Pontifex Maximus of the nine rooms comprising the Hideaway, there is another who reigns supreme within the scented walls of the kitchen. He is Guido, the chef. There is an inspirational quality about the life of this young, successful man. To him cooking is not a job; it is a dedication. Where an artist would find so much pleasure placing the last bold strokes of his brush upon the canvas, so, too, Guido delights with the last pinch of salt and pepper upon his palatable masterpieces.

Born in the northern part of Italy, Guido at the very early age of ten decided to learn the culinary arts. After World War Two, he became an apprentice working in the finest hotels in Italy, France and Switzerland. In his native land he received a monthly salary of six hundred lire, the equivalent of less than one dollar in American exchange.

There is in the life of every man a moment supreme. A moment when the unexpected, the unforeseen, the unanticipated arrives. Such a moment did arrive in the life of Guido only recently. President Nixon dispatched some agents to New York in search of an exceptional chef for the White House. The agents were to interview two chefs, both employees of two distinctive New York hotels. Both refused the job because of age and health. However, both chefs, strangers to each other, recommended Guido from Danny's Hideaway. Imagine the emotional struggle when Guido from Italy opened a letter marked THE WHITE HOUSE and signed by the President of the United States of America. He too refused the job—not because of age, health or any other reason, but because of loyalty to Danny. "After twenty years, how can I leave Danny now, even in exchange for a President boss?" he was heard to say.

Once a year the Hotel/Motel Expo at the New York Coliseum holds a contest inviting the outstanding chefs of the nation to participate with unusual creative recipes. Among his many achievements, Guido humbly revels in the fact he's won two awards. Imagine creating an American eagle out of fish! And with the help of chicken, he submitted this year a thirty-inch-tall Statue of Liberty.

Danny Stradella and Guido Marchitelli! This is the combination that makes the restaurant a gathering place for ballplayers, fighters, hard-boiled labor leaders, politicians, music men and a great sprinkling of entertainers. Barbara Stanwyck, Bob Mitchum, Henry Fonda, Glenn Ford, Jane Russell, Frank Sinatra, Charlton Heston, Tony Curtis, Janet Leigh never fail to make the Hideaway their first stop on arriving in town. It's become the funnymen's hangout. Red Buttons, Alan King, Milton Berle, Henny Youngman, Joey Adams, Corbett Monica, Soupy Sales, Jack E. Leonard are frequently there to swap jokes or steal them.

Ed and Sylvia Sullivan made their way to the Hideaway at least once a week. Milton Rackmil, ex-president of Universal Pictures and Decca Records, is a regular on Monday nights. Songwriter Mitch Parrish comes in three or four times a week; ditto Mr. and Mrs. Eugene Pleshette, parents of Suzanne*; Jack

---

* Also Gil and Sally Rosenburg, nephew of Ira Rosenburg.

E. Leonard, the Hideaway court jester, appears nightly. The special-events party rooms on the third and fourth floors of the restaurant have been the scene of some unbelievable gatherings. Sammy Davis, Jr.—*Mr. Wonderful* Opening; Gabby Hayes—Fiftieth Anniversary in Show Business; Dean Martin—Birthday; Martha Raye—Thirtieth Anniversary in Show Business; New York Yankees—End of Season Party; Robert Sterling and Anne Jeffreys, Tony Curtis and Janet Leigh—Wedding Receptions; U.N. Correspondents—Luncheons; Bert Parks—New Year's Eve Party; Roy Rogers—Birthday Party; Joan Crawford—Fan Club Party; Frank Sinatra—celebrating *From Here to Eternity;* Perry Como—Christmas Party; Red Buttons—Twentieth Anniversary in Show Business; Como's party in honor of Bing Crosby. This is but a sampling of the success the Little Bantamweight Champ from Hell's Kitchen enjoys.

The Hideaway has been the stage of many festive and elegant parties, weddings and testimonials. However, on one occasion it almost became the scene of near disaster. A steady customer, a vice-president of a Coca-Cola bottling company, and his wife dined one evening in the back room of the restaurant. Seated beside them were an oral surgeon and his wife. At the same time, a large group of medical doctors and surgeons occupied the third-floor dining room. The wife of the Coca-Cola executive suddenly began to slump to the floor, gasping for breath while her countenance turned a darkish hue. Evidently a portion of unmasticated food lodged in her throat. To call a doctor from the third floor would consume too much time, and at that moment, time was of the essence. The oral surgeon calmly ordered Charlie, the maître d', to hold the dying woman's head back and asked Peter, maître d' and brother-in-law of Danny, for a steak knife. In the presence of the other diners, while she lay on the restaurant floor, the surgeon deftly inserted the knife into her neck and removed the wayward particle of food. In the meantime an ambulance sped to the scene, and within minutes she arrived at a hospital. Her wound stitched, she returned home after a brief hospital stay. Danny reappeared in the dining room, his face ashen. He informed the diners, if they so wished, to finish their dinners. There would be no checks for anyone in the room. Others, if they wished to leave, might do so and be his guests the following evening. No checks for anyone. Then the Little Guy left the restaurant and vomited. He can't stand the sight of blood. P.S.: The Coca-Cola executive and his wife are still steady customers at Danny's Hideaway.

Danny is blessed and cursed with certain idiosyncrasies. It's almost impossible to convince him to visit in a hospital; almost equally unlikely he'd pay his respects at a wake unless I accompany him. When we perform this act of common courtesy, after extending our sympathy to the bereaved, he will invariably say, "Now let's go up to the box"—referring to the bier in the purest of Hell's Kitchenese. One evening as I entered his establishment, he was about to leave. "Where are you going at a quarter after seven?" "Where you just came from," he laughingly replied. "I just came from church" came my fast retort. "That's where I'm going." The church is Saint Agnes, on East Forty-fourth Street, just around the corner from the Hideaway. I never realized, nor did anyone else, the sneak fifteen-minute getaways from the Hideaway were allotted to the Almighty.

The Hideaway is my office. Here I sit and listen to news, good and bad, from the little guy on the street to the big star on the screen. Now if I can only convince Danny to build me a confessional box in one little corner of any of his nine rooms . . .

Tributes are hard to come by, especially when they're undeserved. I've attended more testimonials where I thought the guest of honor died and the lie-packed eulogies caused me to vomit up my dinner. Not so with Danny Stradella. Only recently I enjoyed the extreme pleasure to escort him on a weekend excursion to Las Vegas. It is indeed a soul-tingling experience to see the respect and esteem with which the Little Restaurateur is held by showpeople. Ironically, each tribute touched not upon his fame as one of America's outstanding restaurateurs, rather his generosity toward the poor, especially of showbiz. On three consecutive nights, with rooms filled with celebrities, Danny alone was singled out to take a bow. At the Riviera, Shecky Green's very touching tribute: Danny never sent a hungry actor away from his restaurant. At The Sands, dynamic Sammy Davis spoke from his heart and experience: "I was young and hungry and this man fed me. He picked up my tabs when I didn't have a dollar in my pockets." At the Frontier, funny Jack E. Leonard: "The reason I'm so fat is that Danny is so generous." At the Sahara, Bernie Allen and Steve Rossi: "God bless you, Danny Boy. Like the Good Book says, we were hungry and you fed us; we were thirsty and you give us to drink. And we were broke."

ANOTHER
OPENING,
ANOTHER
SHOW

To witness a dress rehearsal is a very fascinating experience. Such a rehearsal is the cumulative result of many individual efforts. Because in every TV show everyone is involved, from the stagehands to the director, for the success or failure of the show. A meeting is held each week prior to the presentation. Anyone who is of any importance must attend that meeting. You will find their names on the credit columns after every TV effort. Someone comes up with an idea. That idea is discussed . . . hashed and rehashed . . . until it becomes an integral segment of the show. Then the star works individually with the guest stars, reading and timing the script; later with the choral group and later still with the dancers. Finally, after many hours of sweat and work onstage and off, it is all put together at the dress rehearsal.

At the Como dress rehearsal I would sit inconspicuous as possible at the very rear of the Ziegfeld Theater. The late and beloved Harry Anger, who represented General Artists Corporation, who in turn represented Mr. Perry Como, was practically the factotum of the show. He was the bagman. If there were any misunderstandings or involvements of any sort, it was Harry's job to protect his client come hell or high water.

One of the most common sources of quarrel was the female guest stars. Invariably, they would saunter out of the dressing room onto the stage dressed in expensive gowns revealing too much décolletage. At this point Harry would steal a glance at me. If I shook my head negatively, it meant "No good. Speak to her manager or a representative and try to convince her to change or at least to alter the gown." If the nod was affirmative, it meant things weren't really that bad. Nor is this distaff acquiescence very easily achieved. Some will fight like wildcats for hours before they concede to make one minor change.

Such incidents spell out the true role of the personal representative. He's the buff—the wise guy—the mean one. He protects his property in every department. In the meantime, the star goes along his merry way cognizant his show will offend no one's taste or morals.

Such an incident occurred with the exotic actress Sheree North. When Mr. Anger caught the "no" sign from me, he rushed backstage as though he were about to impose the curse of excommunication upon the head of the young lady. Warned that that expanse of carnal exposure might prove offensive to a priest sitting in the theater—the companion and confessor of Mr. Como—she proved quite adamant against any changes whatsoever. Finally, Harry convinced her to cover the décolletage with an artificial flower and an extra piece of material. Upon returning to the West Coast, Miss North gave a press interview deploring the show, the time, the effort and money expended to travel round trip, coast to coast, and, lastly, the expensive gown which after surgery was hardly recognizable to her. And all because of a priest sitting in the theater.

In those days a group of very young entertainers had formed some sort of "let's stick together" club. They had not quite reached any degree of prominent success, and money did not abound among them. We would bowl once a week at the Port Authority Building on the West Side and frequent a pizza joint for pizza and beer on another evening on the East Side where most of them lived. Two girls, three boys—two queens, three kings: a full house. One girl came from Rochester, New York. It was her aunt, Miss Laura Ciminelli, an excellent restaurant cook, who first entertained the idea of calling her niece to New York. Her next move was to find a sponsor, and she accomplished this end by employing the services of a Bronx florist. The girl from Rochester came to New York as a contestant on the *Arthur Godfrey's Talent Scouts* show. When Godfrey announced LuAnn as the winner of the contest, telegrams and phone calls arrived by the hundreds from producers, directors, casting agents, agencies, bandleaders, requesting Miss Simms' signature. Instead, she became an official member of Arthur Godfrey's TV family.

Girl No. 2 was a Californian—blond, blue-eyed, beautiful. She sang with a group of boys, all her brothers. In that era, singer groups were having a field day. However, it seemed showbiz was saturated with them. Groups of sisters. Groups of brothers. Groups of relatives and friends. The only other resort for public recognition was to do it alone, as a soloist. Today she appears regularly on the three coast-to-coast networks, works Vegas frequently: the Blond Bombshell with the financier's name—Miss Jaye P. Morgan.

The first young man wasn't an entertainer; rather, his interest dwelt more in the technical department of the business: writing and directing. Quiet, reticent, almost Carthusian. Yet he was incredibly ambitious—willing to work and learn every facet of the trade. New York remained his habitat as long as there were things to do and learn in the world of television. Departing for Hollywood, he immersed himself in the art of movie-making. No chore was too small or insignificant. After many years, he accomplished very well what he set out to do, because today he is an up-and-coming director-producer: Al Rafkin.

The second youngster is unknown in America except in the

trade. He originated from Cliffside, New Jersey; remained in his native land for many years, each a barometer of failures and more failures. His career always seemed to hang hopefully on the perimeter of success. He needed that one big chance, that one big song, that one big record which never arrived. In Chicago he stirred a lot of theatrical noise, but New York wasn't listening. He decided to bounce around in the Land of the Kangaroo. Today, vocalist Tommy Leonetti is the biggest and most outstanding TV star in Australia. He returned to America not as a national hero but a helpless victim of the Big C, as cancer is predominantly known in showbiz. With God's help he conquered the dread disease and now initiated his comeback with a booking at the Copa and another at the Maisonette Room of the St. Regis Hotel.

The last man is the most inspiring success story of all. He hailed from a San Francisco suburb. Sang with Freddie Martin's band. One-nighters weren't easy. How often do you find a Frank Sinatra, a Dick Haymes, a Perry Como, a Jack Leonard, a Don Cornell? All ex-band singers. During his New York days he was quite a Lothario, dating every pretty girl in sight—models, stewardesses, actresses—until he met a little girl from Michigan way, the daughter of a judge. Once he met Julann, his case was terminated and the verdict forthcoming: marriage. When Merv Griffin talks about Julann, he's talking about his wife.

In his day, Arthur Godfrey undoubtedly was one of the giants of the television industry with the weekly presentation of his family of friends. I became very friendly with a good number of the cast because the Como and Godfrey studios were adjacent to each other. Frequently there were interstudio visits. Julie, Christine, Phyllis, Dorothy McGuire, Archie Bleyer, LuAnn Simms were among my closest and dearest friends.

It was while La Rosa was working for the Godfrey crew he promised to appear at an Albany, New York, benefit for our Franciscan seminaries. At about this time, he was unexpectedly fired from his job while the show was in progress. Many million viewers contemplated the reenactment of the bloody biblical scene of Salome, the dancer, Herodias, her mother, and poor St. John the Baptist. It was a crucial period in the young life of the ex-sailor turned vocalist: screaming two-inch headlines on the New York *Journal American* front pages describing every lethal blow thrown by Godfrey and himself. Prior to this catastrophe, La Rosa had committed himself to another benefit for the Red Cross in Washington, D.C., sponsored by Mrs. Mamie Eisenhower, wife of the President. More headlines, more publicity. Godfrey claimed it was the total loss of Julius' humility that caused the breach and precipitated the firing. The truth of the matter is Julius had contracted a personal manager, Mr. Frank Barone, a move Godfrey bitterly opposed, and was guilty of impugning the sterling character of the Godfrey family by openly escorting a married woman, Miss Dorothy McGuire. After the firing, La Rosa came to see me. We tried within ecclesiastical limits to weigh the possibility of a Catholic marriage between him and Dorothy. It was utterly impossible. Completely submissive and cooperative, he said, "Whatever you say Padre, I'll do."

Time is still the greatest panacea. Some years later, Julie was introduced to Como's secretary, a vivacious, beautiful, Ava Gardner look-alike, Miss Rosemary "Rory" Meyer. If Wisconsin is the state of dairy products, she has the complexion and skin to prove it. Julie began courting steadily. Many were the times I reminded him if I had not been a priest he would have a fight on his hands for the hand of Miss Meyer. When he would "hit the road" for out-of-town personal appearances ranging from one week to eight weeks, he would tell Rory: "If you get lonely and want to have dinner out, call Father Bob. Him I can trust."

Several times during his absence from New York he telephoned immediately after his dinner show and there would be no answer. Absence makes the heart grow fonder. So too with Julie. "Where in the hell were you, honey?" his voice would rasp through the telephonic wires. "Out on a date with the man who is going to marry me," Rory would answer demurely. The decision was made! Julie proposed, Rory accepted. All of his friends, especially his boyhood companions, were invited to the wedding.

So large was the number of wedding guests they rented out completely two motels. In fact, with the hope of a sudden conversion we placed in one room a priest friend of Julie's with a Jewish music publisher. It was the priest who greeted us the following morning with "Vell, vat's new?"

In the picturesque village church, Saint Anne's, in Francis Creek, a suburb of Manitowoc in northern Wisconsin, I joined Rory and Julie together in the holy sacrament of matrimony. And just as their best man and maid of honor became the baptismal sponsors of their firstborn, it was I who poured the waters of baptism upon the head of the adorable Maria Lucia La Rosa. Julie wisecracked, "It sounds like the brand name of a spaghetti company."

Next to hit the matrimonial canvas was LuAnn Simms. While still a member of the Arthur Godfrey family, she met a handsome young man, a music executive, Loring Buzzell. In fact, shortly after dating him a number of times she escorted him to the rectory to meet with my approval, which I gave her unhesitatingly. This statement about my approval might sound strange to the reader. It isn't. LuAnn's father, Mr. Al Simms of American-International Pictures, charged me with keeping an eye on his daughter during her New York stay. Such is our bond of friendship, after the death of his wife some years ago, he decided to remarry. Because time would not permit me to travel to California, he and his future new bride traveled from Los Angeles to New York for me to perform the marriage rites.

Little LuAnn asked to be married in the church in which I was stationed at the time—Saint Raphael, in the Hell's Kitchen section of New York. Godfrey unwittingly announced the date of the marriage and its locale on his coast-to-coast TV broadcast. On the morning of the wedding, which was scheduled for eleven o'clock, we were scheduled for a funeral mass at ten o'clock. About eight o'clock that morning the entire neighborhood was swamped with people—the church itself jammed with wall-to-wall people. Frank Parker and the McGuire Sisters also attended. We were forced to employ the New York police to remove some of the spectators to provide enough room for the bereaved family. As they carried the bier up the nave of Saint Raphael's, an amusing but irreverent thought came to me: If that poor dead man could wake for a fleeting moment and see this tremendous throng of people in and out of the church, he would probably say to himself, "What a way to go!"

Immediately after LuAnn's reception I hopped a plane to meet with Como in Chicago. For a change, he was really hard at work. Jack E. Leonard tells a classic about Mr. Relaxation. Perry borrowed a self-winding wristwatch from Mr. Leonard, returned it a few days later and it hasn't worked since. Bud Avery, son of the Democratic leader of Chicago, had booked a show with General Artists Corporation to play Detroit, Chicago and Cleveland. Included in the cast were Como, Nat "King" Cole, Patti Page, Jill Corey, the Four Lads, Ray Anthony and his band.

We traveled by train, and we had a dining room, a barroom, sleeping sections for the entertainers and their guests. In Chicago, at Soldier Field, Perry requested each spectator to strike a match. The effect of sixty thousand burning matches glowing in the darkness of that Chicago night was incredibly eerie. "Better to light a match than struggle in the darkness . . ." We arrived in Cleveland on a Sunday morning. I began knocking on the door of each sleeping compartment advising its occupants that it was Sunday—time for Sunday mass. When I knocked on the "King's" door and told him we were going to Sunday services at the Cathedral, he quipped, "I love you, Father, but I'm Baptist and nobody is going to change that." When we arrived at the church doors—Perry, Patti, Jill, the Lads—Patti remarked, "I must be crazy . . . I'm not even Catholic!" (Patti is a member of the Church of Christ.) Then another problem arose. The two young ladies reminded me they had no hats. At which point Como removed a kerchief from his breast pocket, ripped it into two pieces and presented the girls with their headwear.

It has been my pleasure to dine with many entertainers of the opposite sex. Some psychologists might describe such action on the part of a clergyman as remedial sublimation. Jane Wyman, Ethel Merman, Eydie Gormé, Patti Page, Rosie and Betty Clooney, Temple Texas and Connie Francis are some among the many others. One day I received a telephone call from Troy, New York. It was from a young vocalist, Mickey Milan, who requested I purchase a couple of theater tickets for a Broadway show. They were for Mickey's sister, a Catholic nun, and her companion. This mission accomplished, the plans now were that I meet them in front of the theater. I presented the two good sisters with the tickets and advised them I would take them to dinner immediately after the matinee. As I have just noted, I've walked into restaurants with all kinds of female entertainers, including perhaps even a few strippers. But this was my first dinner with nuns. In fact, I suddenly felt a little embarrassed. In such circumstances, our speech prof taught us, try to get off the hook by saying something funny. I began groping for a funny line. Danny Stradella from Danny's Hideaway stood solemnly at the captain's desk as I whispered into his ear, "I've got two extras from *The Sound of Music*; may we have a table for three?"

Again at Danny's and dining alone, I was invited by two lovely friends to join them for an after-dinner drink. One was Miss Sharon Richie, former Miss America and wife of Kyle Rote, and the other Miss Dorothy Mack, a former TV personality and wife of the well-known disk jockey William B. Williams. I became the target for some good-natured kidding on the part of my friends. One wisecracked, "Hey Padre, you're always seen with the most beautiful women in the world." I tried hard for a hilarious retort and suddenly remembered the line of Fulton Sheen: "Just because I'm on a perpetual diet it doesn't mean I can't read the menu once in a while."

Stanley Kaye, a theatrical manager, handles a good number of names including actor Paul Burke and singer Michele Lee. One day he telephoned to inform me he had a very serious problem on hand. One of his clients, a Catholic, desired to marry a young lady, also Catholic, and they were having trouble with the arrangements. It seemed the two youngsters had mistakenly made arrangements with Tavern-on-the-Green Restaurant in New York's Central Park before inquiring at the rectory on the hour schedule of weddings in church. The reception was set from twelve to five in the afternoon. Sunday weddings in the girl's church started at two—because the last Sunday mass was held at one in the afternoon. Could I help? "Certainly," I assured him. "Have the boy and girl give me a call." Shortly afterwards the young lady telephoned and we set an appointment at the rectory.

The time arrived for the kids to make their appearance. I waited for the ring of the rectory doorbell, and when it rang, I opened the rectory front door. I stood there startled, perplexed, speechless. Before me stood a white girl and a black boy. Never in my score and better years as a priest have I ever been confronted with a similar situation. The consternation must have reflected in my eyes, my face, my whole being. Finally, I invited them into the office. In conformity with diocesan regulations, I spoke to both of them individually and then together. Notwithstanding the many racial and social barriers they would be forced to face, they wanted to be married . . . they were deeply in love . . . not even the combined forces of heaven and hell could stop them. The arrangements were made to be married on a Sunday morning in between the ten and twelve o'clock masses. Patricia and Gregory Hines, of Hines, Hines and Dad, are now man and wife. In the wedding party was Miss Patty Duke, a schoolmate of Gregory and Maurice Hines.

There was some resentment on the part of some parishioners who witnessed the wedding ceremony. This resentment was directed toward me personally for having performed the miscegenational rites. When asked why, I had only one answer: "I don't marry colors; I marry people."

At the Royal Box of the Hotel Americana, Patti and Gregory enlightened me with this bit of family gossip: Within a very short time there'd be another Hines added to the list.

It was a warm spring morning as I stood on Mulberry Street of New York's Little Italy and the mailman handed me a package. As I studied the return address I realized the package was a record album. Maria Lanza Cocozza had sent me an album of her son, Mario. Moments later a man from the neighborhood, watching me cradling a package in my hands, remarked how lucky I was to receive such goodies through the mail. I in turn informed him it was a recording—a Mario Lanza album. Then came the sickening news. At first I reprimanded him for saying what he said. He politely left and returned with a newspaper, the obituary column. Yes, my dear friend Maria had died the day after she mailed me the album. She inscribed on the album cover: "To Father Bob, as my son would say: 'May I wish you the very best of everything in life always.' Love! Maria Lanza 1970." The name of the album? *I'll Walk With God*.

I first met John F. Kennedy in the home of Archbishop Richard Cushing in Brighton, Massachusetts. At that time he was an assemblyman and Cushing the archbishop of Boston. It was only months away from my ordination to the priesthood in the year 1942—ordained by the same Cushing. There were other occasions when I met Mr. Kennedy during his meteoric rise to the Presidency. Upon his election, Mr. Frank Allen of New York, a very intimate friend of Jack and the entire Kennedy family, invited me to the inaugural ceremonies in Washington. Because of personal reasons, I had to decline the invitation. However, I felt I should participate in this auspicious event—the election of our first Catholic President of the United States. Through Mr. Allen I expedited a white leather Bible to the First Family tastefully inscribed, "To the President and Mrs. John F. Kennedy."

Often have I wondered if this could have been the first Catholic Bible in the White House, aside from the family biblical heirloom. In return Mrs. Allen presented me in the name of the President a sterling silver pen and pencil set inscribed "John F. Kennedy, January 20, 1961." A letter from the White House dated March 28, 1961, followed and read as follows:

Dear Father:
  Frank Allen came to my office today and presented me with the beautiful Bible that you had made for me. I want

you to know that I appreciate this very much. You were extremely kind.

With every good wish

Sincerely,
John F. Kennedy

There have been many crises that have crossed my path as a priest in showbusiness, but one particularly flashes across my mind as the most unforgettable. It concerned an Arab king and a young American Jewish actress. They were deeply and madly in love. Whenever he visited New York, many times incognito, she would fly from the Coast to be near him. His aides would conceal her in a huge rug or a very large laundry bag, use the freight elevator and carry her up to the King's suite. She showed me autographed photos he sent her and many amorous letters he had written from his homeland.

Many were the times when she visited me at the rectory or I visited her at her apartment to discuss and attempt to resolve this enigma of human relationship. Certainly two people in love —free to marry—can and should be married. But this was a love story woven in bitter conflicting colors. He was a king, she a commoner. He an Arab, she a Jewess. The most remote possibility of such a marriage was shattered when I hypothetically posed the question to my Jewish and Arab friends. Their reactions were identical: Disdain for anyone who would sacrifice their birthrights. Because of such a union the king could be dethroned or even assassinated; she an outcast among her own people for the rest of her natural life. To further stretch the imagination, such a marriage might even trigger an international war.

I begged and pleaded with her to forsake this wild dream. Finally, she acquiesced. Like the dream, she forsook even me. She vanished into the darkness of memories, never to be seen or heard from again.

My superior called me to his office to inform me he was in desperate need of money because of reconstruction work at our Seminary in West Andover, Massachusetts. This desperation for the monetary is a sine qua non condition for human existence, especially in religious circles. "Can you help me?" he pleaded. "Can you come up with some ideas?" The suggestion of a variety show with some very strong names suited him fine. "Now you must present your plans before my cabinet of advisers."

As I sat before this astute body of six intelligent men, my initial remark emphasized the need for money to cover expenses, perhaps a first loan of ten thousand dollars. Suddenly the heavens caved in. They completely failed to realize the existence of certain hidden (?) expenses such as renting the Boston Garden Arena or Madison Square Garden (just the four walls) at a price tag of five thousand dollars; the decorations; five stagehands; ushers; ticket sellers, lighting men; ticket printing; publicity; musicians; transportation and hotels for about forty people; special police, etc., etc. "We're looking for money and you want to take it away from us" was one sagacious response. Another remarkably intelligent gem sounded like this: "If show people can do benefits for others without pay, why not for we Franciscans?" "Now, let's be honest," I suggested. "What would Eddie Fisher, a Jew; Nat 'King' Cole, a Baptist; Patti Page, a member of the Church of Christ; Mitchell Ayres, a Christian Scientist, know about the word 'Franciscan'? They probably think it's some can company out of San Francisco." The fact of the matter is, not one of these artists would receive a penny from me.

The problem that confronted me now was the exact locale for the variety show. New York or Boston? I sought the advice of Ed Sullivan and he strongly suggested New York City, pointing out the fabulous success of the annual Night of Stars, sponsored by a Jewish philanthropic organization. Still, I felt New York was too blasé for such a project; there were the Copa and the Latin Quarter, where top names could be seen and heard every day of the week, not to mention the Paramount, Capitol, Strand, Loew's State theaters. After much deliberation, I decided on Boston.

While in Boston, protocol demanded that I contact His Eminence, Cardinal Cushing, for permission to hold the show within the confines of his archdiocese. My first move was to rent the Boston Garden Arena for a night. It was Harry Anger of General

Artists Corporation who strongly suggested the show be held during the Thanksgiving Day season. He claimed it was the best time of the year to run a benefit. People are in a holiday spirit, yet not hamstrung with money problems or Christmas gifts.

Next, I sought the advice and aid of practically every disk jockey in and around Boston. We discussed primarily the prices of tickets. Because of the caliber of the show and the number of superstars, I was thinking in terms of five and ten dollars per ticket. Unfortunately, they convinced me to agree to a dollar fifty, two seventy-five and three fifty per ticket. As the infallible Monday-morning quarterback predicts, my price scale was the right one. The entire show completely sold out in ten days. Filene's, Jordan Marsh, the Boston Garden did not have a single ticket available. One gentleman offered us a one-hundred-dollar bill for four three fifty tickets. "Please," he begged, "don't disappoint my kids." One phone call almost proved disastrous. An uninformed friar, asked about the availability of tickets, told the caller they would be on sale at the box office on the night of the show. Unfortunately, the call came from a newspaper reporter and the misinformation found its way into the papers on the very afternoon of the presentation. On that night, six or seven thousand souls tried to purchase a ducat and not a single one was to be had. The Better Business Bureau of Boston in no uncertain terms excoriated me in a letter about such unethical practices.

Como was the first of the artists I approached. The project was explained to him, and he readily agreed to appear and take along with him the Fontaine Sisters, Ray Charles and his choral group and Mitchell Ayres, his musical conductor. Next I visited Nat "King" Cole. It would be a pleasure, he assured me because at the time of the show he was contracted to appear at the Boston Latin Quarter. I had taken care of the Italians and the blacks; now I was interested in a nice young Jewish boy. Eddie Fisher was very responsive and filled the bill perfectly.

Three big, potent, solid names—all males. Obviously, a petite and beautiful female was needed. Pretty Patti Page came to my rescue. No pleading, no begging. A straightforward request, a straightforward answer. "Can you make it, Patti?" "I'll be there, Padre." And of all people to unintentionally offend, Patti was the victim. In the midst of the afternoon rehearsal, I forgot to dispatch a limousine to pick her up at the airport. And to make matters worse, she inexplicably entertained the idea that the benefit was being held for an orphanage. "Patti," I kidded her, "the only orphanage I'm involved with is myself. I have no father. I have no mother." When the news of "The Festival of Stars" began circulating in showbiz, many offered and volunteered their talents including Betty Clooney, LuAnn Simms, comic Leo DeLyon, dance team Hoctor & Byrd, music conductor Archie Bleyer, dancer Bobby Brandt, master of ceremonies Gary Morton and guest of honor, Rocky Marciano.

With such a lineup of names and talent, a very delicate and perplexing problem arises. Billing! There are times when an entertainer might compromise a little where money is concerned or sign with three fiddles instead of seven in the string section of the orchestra or humiliate themselves to occupy a small, filthy dressing room. But where billing is involved, even the good Lord would have to take a second spot.

Let me attempt to explain the simple billing system in the world of showbusiness. Given a case of a number of stars of equal caliber, the easiest method is to list the names alphabetically, in the same, identical size print. If two or three artists are of equal caliber, their names are placed on the same line, and the print is of the same size. However, if one actor is slightly more esteemed or presently more popular, his name is placed first in line on the extreme left side of the advertisement. This is because in reading from left to right, the reader's eyes fall first on the name at the extreme left. On the other hand, if a name is one to be reckoned with yet not on a par with the artist co-appearing, it will be categorized as ALSO STARRING and/or SPECIAL GUEST, EXTRA SPECIAL GUEST. The question arises, how to deal with husband-and-wife teams? Rest assured if the husband's name is at the extreme left side of the column, the wife will exert her feminine prerogatives by sleeping on the twin bed on the left side of the room.

As for the billing of the Boston "Festival of Stars," I naturally wanted Como's name heading the list. This plan could have been realized alphabetically with Fisher and Page. But we had to also contend with Cole. Moreover, at this particular time Fisher's vocal pipes were as hot as Satan's steam pipes, selling records by the millions; and to enhance the glamour, Eddie was about to marry the internationally popular Miss Debbie Reynolds. "King" Cole's position in the rank of superb vocalists remained unshakable; he was verily the musical Rock of Gibraltar. Perry's popularity remained uncontested, but he wasn't selling records as well as the younger Fisher.

Suddenly there came the inspiration. Cole was appearing only through the graciousness of the Boston Latin Quarter, for whom he was working at that time. The solution was perfect: we would list the others alphabetically and give credit where credit was due—to the Boston Latin Quarter. The program read: PERRY COMO, EDDIE FISHER, PATTI PAGE. COURTESY OF THE LATIN QUARTER, NAT KING COLE. When the King noticed the billboards, he looked at me with those black smiling eyes and grinned: "Padre, anytime you're ready to remove your collar and wear a tie, you've got me as a client."

Still, my troubles weren't over. In dealing with entertainers special precautions must be exerted not to offend an inflated ego in any shape, form or manner. This explains the presence of the ten-percenters: managers and agents. What will be the order of their appearance onstage? The man who presented this question to me was Milton Blackstone, Fisher's manager. Cole was no problem because he had to return to the Latin Quarter, necessitating an early appearance on our stage. In answer to Mr. Blackstone's query, I made my pontifical pronouncement: "Eddie will close the show." Had I at that very moment converted to Judaism, Milton could not have been more shocked. He stared at me in disbelief. "We're closing the show?" his voice crescendoing to an Irish-tenor pitch. "Well, not really," I hedged; "Eddie closes the first half before intermission. Como closes the second half." Fisher too proclaimed the requiem of my priesthood: "Father Bob, King Cole just made you a proposition. If you accept and wear a tie, I'll join your stable too."

Needless to say, the show was a tremendous success in every aspect. Fourteen thousand tickets sold in ten days—a stupendous sellout. Many Bostonians told me the show was the most talent-packed exhibition ever to be seen in Boston at any time and superbly directed—a tribute to Messrs. Harry Anger and Irving Chezar of General Artists Corporation. My return home to New York was triumphant. I could hardly wait to present that big, fat check to my superior as though he would knight me into the Knights of Malta. The expenses, totaling fifteen thousand dollars, were completely paid. Check in hand to the tune of forty-two thousand dollars, my superior thanked me, suggested I take a vacation to anywhere my heart desired and terminated our conversation with a bit of fatherly admonition: "Don't ask for any money. I'm broke!"

Only on one occasion do I recall being refused a benefit. The denial came as a shock to me. I was very friendly with the entertainer and much more friendly with one of his managers. Jack Spina, a Bostonian, came to New York and after a short while became a part and parcel of the Como ensemble. Those were not the caviar days of Jack's life, and I was instrumental a good number of times in obtaining help for him. One day he introduced me to a young man with a boyish, smiling face, a brilliant set of sparkling teeth, wearing white buck shoes. Randy Woods of Dot Records and Spina were set to guide the career of Mr. Pat Boone. In 1955 Pat performed his first coast-to-coast TV Como show. It was during this interim of time that I received the refusal. A deeply religious man, Boone's religious tenets forbade him to work for any cigarette or beer companies, kiss any girl in public or perform for any other religious affiliations. I found it hard to believe. On countless occasions I've seen the Jew entertain the Catholic and Protestants, the Catholic entertain the Jew. At the annual Actors' Temple Benefit in New York, you'll find five Christians to one Jewish entertainer. Pat and Shirley, Red Foley's daughter, and the four girls were friends. Thus, the hurt grew deeper when I learned he did a benefit for a Catholic church in Brooklyn at the request of Mrs. Roselle Como.

IT'S
JUST
IMPOSSIBLE

All stories should have a happy ending. Life, however, is not so benevolent or acquiescent. Some of the greatest love stories blessed at the foot of God's altar are terminated at the foot of a judge's bench. Mine is a very unhappy ending. Ironically, the pitiful finale lay completely outside my jurisdiction. I followed the rules de rigueur to shore up the broken dike of friendship, but my efforts were unaccepted, vain and worthless. I had been guilty of an unpardonable crime and the offended would not forgive.

In the summer of 1963 my superiors transferred me to the Church of Mount Carmel in Watervliet, New York. This Dutch-named city lies on the northern portion of the Hudson River opposite the shirt-manufacturing citadel of Troy. My departure from New York was negotiated without a single farewell to any of my friends. Truthfully, I was humiliated and too embarrassed. The transfer was triggered by sacerdotal jealousy and priestly venom. Ironically, during my stay in Watervliet I was elevated from the New York State Chaplain of the American Guild of Variety Artists to its national chaplaincy.

About a week after my arrival I received a long-distance call from Dee Belline, Mrs. Como's brother. In the friendliest of terms, he reprimanded me for leaving the New York scene without even so much as a word about my transfer. He further informed me to call Roselle and Perry; they were very anxious to hear from me. Thus began the telephonic romance of friends from Watervliet to Sands Point and from Sands Point to Watervliet. As often as Perry and I spoke on the phone, one conversation was a carbon copy of the previous one. I dislike phones to a greater extent than he. He would say: "How are you?" "How do you feel?" "Do you need anything?" "Why don't you come down to the city for a day or two?"

Thanksgiving was about a week away when I decided to call the Comos. Since each of his offers received a negative reply from me, I convinced myself to ask a millionaire friend for something for the rectory. "Perry," I said, "you keep asking me if I need anything: booze, radio—anything. Our rectory can certainly use a little color TV set. We have none—color or black-and-white. In fact, Thanksgiving is here, Christmas around the corner. Kill two birds with one stone; make it your Christmas gift to me."

The moment I heard the excruciating pause and then the tone of his voice, I knew I had made a catastrophic mistake. His "You'll get it! You'll get it!" fell upon my ears with the same cadence of "Heeeere's your TV set! Heeeeere's your TV set."

My many efforts to contact him failed; he was never around. How often was I a witness to this very same event when he wasn't interested in seeing someone. Once, when only he and the maid were at home and she answered the phone, he did speak to me. Steel could not be any more frigid. When I suggested seeing him at his home, as I had done literally hundreds of times, I was politely told to contact Mrs. Como for an appointment. I pleaded with her to enlighten me in regard to this rupture of our friendship of twenty years. Had I said something to antagonize her husband? Maybe some stupid rumor; perhaps the work of some jealous idiot (clergy not exempted). Was it perhaps the request for the color TV set?

To this question she did not commit herself. She did, however, suggest, "It could be the reason." Once I took it upon myself to visit him at his Roncom office. He hadn't arrived as yet. Suddenly I find myself in a Rockefeller Center bar staring at Dee Belline and realizing I've been maneuvered into this spot to keep me out of Someone's presence. That was my last attempt to contact him.

I've seen many heads roll down the bloody *salle d'armes* corridors of the *Chesterfield Supper Club* and the *Kraft Music Hall*. Stupidly, my pride convinced me I could not possibly fall victim as so many others had in the past. Not when a Sydney, Australia, newspaper described the friends of Frank Sinatra as unsavory characters, Dean Martin's constant companion as "Killer" Gray and Perry Como and his ever-present priest-companion. Not when a question submitted by an E. L. of Jamaica, New York . . . Question: I understand Perry Como is accompanied by a Franciscan priest wherever he goes. Can you identify the priest? Answer: Father Bob Perella (my surname misspelled). Not when in a *Look* Magazine interview of many years ago on Como and Company, I was alluded to as a drink dispenser and an integral part of the Como syndrome. If pride caused this calamitous experience in my life, it is with pride I contemplate my friendship of twenty years with Mr. Como and my participation, insignificant as it might be, in helping to create the image of Mr. Nice Guy. Perry and his Priest! Como, the singer, who wore the solid-gold crucifix ring on the pinky of his left hand and Father Bob, the priest, who presented the ring to him some twenty-five years ago.

In retrospect, this sad, unreal, frightful experience seems to be in Perry's own words: "Just Impossible."

THE ACTORS YOUTH FUND

I am very proud to claim membership in the Actors Youth Fund and equally proud to be a member of its elite advisory committee. Mr. Joey Adams is the nonsalaried president of this theatrical organization, whose only purpose for existence is charity. The particular brand of charity is war: showbusiness war on juvenile delinquency. Oftentimes the avenues of communication are barred to the priest, minister and rabbi. These "holy jobs" represent the very thing the hoodlum despises. Who then will be the contact man? Who makes the connection between the juvenile delinquent and society? The idol of the blackboard jungle's toughies, be he or she an athlete, a vocalist, a comedian, an actor. Call a neighborhood meeting promising the presence of a Secretary of Transportation, Claude S. Brinegar, and the name would have absolutely no magnetic quality; call the same meeting and promise them a song or a handshake from Mickey Mantle, Bill Cosby, Ray Charles, Pearl Bailey or Muhammad Ali and the success of that gathering would be unquestioned. All kids are starry-eyed. To see a celebrity in the flesh, one he might occasionally see on the TV screen but never in a theater because the kids haven't the price of a ticket, is an unforgettable experience and thrill. I shook hands with Jack Dempsey at the age of nine and never forgot the occasion. An old Chinese proverb tells us: "The hook without bait catches no fish." The actor, the athlete, the singer, the comedian, the celebrity is the bait. They are the cup of hot soup the missions offer the Bowery derelicts; the outcasts will remain for divine services. In every war there is a basic and fundamental need for soldiers and ammunition. Mr. Adams has wisely employed the members of his profession and of the sports world as greasepaint soldiers and laughter-filled cartridges.

Headliners like Eddie Fisher, Louis Armstrong, Sammy Davis, Rocky Marciano, Rocky Graziano, Lionel Hampton, Barney Ross accompanied by prez Joey Adams invade neighborhoods where the words "tough and rough" are hardly descriptive. These are the areas referred to by comedians as "where they steal police cars with the cops in them" . . . or "steal hubcaps while the car is running" . . . "where station houses have peepholes in their doors for the policemen to look through." Each entertainer does his thing. In most of their professional endeavors, the artist will abide by a time schedule: he works fifty minutes at a supper club during the dinner show and perhaps twenty minutes more at the second show. When he appears before the kids, there is no timetable: just saturate the youngsters with talent and love. After the performance, the headliners and sports figures remain with the children. They mingle among the kids, shake hands, answer questions, sign autographs.

The second phase of this altruistically motivated program is teaching; hence the need for teachers, classes and classrooms and subject matter. The children are taught the varied and diversified crafts of showbusiness. They are instructed in every conceivable art that requires a spectator, from boxing to ballet, acrobats and magic to juggling and ventriloquism, from puppetry and mind-reading to costume design and the art of makeup.

Where entertainers freely give the only commodity they have to offer, their talent, the instructors of these children must of necessity be given salaries. You cannot keep body and soul together on Hail Marys. Once again we perceive the wisdom and knowledge of the architects of the Youth Fund. A majority of showpeople are unemployed most of the year. Why not, then, have recourse to the pragmatic principle of Demand and Supply? Create jobs! This is precisely what this project accomplishes: It creates jobs for the unemployed artists. It transforms him from an entertaining juggler, magician and acrobat to a teaching juggler, magician and acrobat.

The children are naturally suspicious of the do-gooders. The environment alone would trigger such emotions. Why would a galaxy of stars appear in this starless, brightless, blighted neighborhood? Pragmatically, they ask, "What's in it for them?" Hence, any promise solemnly made must be solemnly kept. As Mr. Adams told me, if you promise Jackie Robinson it would be in the best interest of your health, mental and physical, to have Jackie Robinson there. No substitutes. Willie Mays, Muhammad Ali, Richard Burton, Elizabeth Taylor will never do. It must be Jackie or it could be the start of World War III. Operating on such a dangerous premise, there were times when artists like Lionel Hampton, Mahalia Jackson, Phil Foster, Frankie Avalon have forfeited paid engagements to appear when their names were advertised. In fact, Sammy Davis felt obligated to push back a Boston nightclub engagement when he realized he committed himself by a longtime promise to appear before the kids.

Suspicion logically breeds distrust. "Entertainers, like everyone else, work for money; no one is coming here to work for beans," philosophized one youngster. In this era of materialism where the dollar bill has been practically elevated to divinity, it isn't difficult to assume a child's distrustfulness of any altruistic causes. "Nobody does something for nothing" is the slogan of today's merchants of greed. Joey recounted another of his soul-searching experiences. Only Louis Armstrong's name had been advertised to appear at a local auditorium of an Upper West

Side neighborhood. Hardly anyone was there; perhaps the first three rows of the arena were occupied. Widespread incredulity enveloped the neighborhood. "Why would Louis Armstrong come to this dump, man, just to entertain us?" were the sentiments of one Doubting Thomas. When Louis appeared, breaking away from a birthday party in his honor, the news circulated with the speed of a typhoon. The auditorium was jammed with smiling, delighted, delirious wall-to-wall children and adults, even before the beloved Satchmo could apply his famous handkerchief to his smiling face.

The program proliferated to far more extensive horizons. If it is our scope to prevent juvenile delinquency, how about the adult delinquent? The one already incarcerated and forgotten. Why not provide a measure of the hilarious among prisoners? The pleasure to preach a three days' retreat to the Catholic inmates of Green Haven Penitentiary in Stormville, New York, was mine in the not-distant past. Their schedule is practically bereft of any type of entertainment. While in cellblocks the convicts hear the sounds of TV but do not see the screen. Several sets are available in "the yard" for the prisoners' convenience. But when you realize there is a population of twenty-five hundred and only several sets, there isn't much of a choice in programming. The last live show they enjoyed took place several years ago.

Father Ed Donovan and Father Victor Cesario, the prison's Catholic chaplains, approached me with an idea. Why not try to provide these men with a live show during the Christmas festivities? Upon my return to the city, I spoke with Joey Adams; now we hope to instill a little joy and happiness within the drab and merciless walls of Green Haven. Thus, today the greasepaint troupe will travel from a penitentiary to a local jail, from reformatories to state institutions, bringing laughter and a few brief hours of contentment to people whose only heirloom is time.

It is interesting if not miraculous how Mr. Adams manages to accrue the voluminous amounts of money necessary to operate such an organization. Once a year he calls a meeting of the committeemen and women, usually held at a restaurant where hors d'oeuvres and drinks are served. Complimentary! The date of the annual Actors Youth Fund dinner is announced; forms for the souvenir book are distributed; the identity of the person to be honored the evening of the dinner is revealed. A glimpse of the caliber of men—not necessarily in showbiz, however; each a tycoon in his field of endeavor—so honored are the following names: Harold J. Gibbons of the Teamsters Union; Jerry Lewis; Lionel Hampton; Louis Armstrong; Danny Stradella of Danny's Hideaway Restaurant; Lawrence Tisch, president of the Americana Hotel and its chain and Joseph Kipness, Broadway producer and restaurateur. As the national chaplain of the American Guild of Variety Artists, invitations to many gatherings and testimonials of a showbusiness nature are part and parcel of my portfolio. However, most of them, if not all, vanish into oblivion when compared to the Youth Fund annual dinner. A double- and sometimes triple-terraced dais holds a glittering array of names from every segment of the world of government, theater, variety, finance, labor, literature and diplomacy. It is a fun-feast where annually the beloved octogenarian Harry Hershfield reminds us his doctor advised against remarriage because he was not heir-conditioned.

Aside from the two salaries allocated for the young women who are employed by the Youth Fund office, not a single penny is removed from the treasury. Be it foresight, shrewdness or divine guidance, Mr. Joey Adams accomplished the impossible. This achievement against insurmountable barriers native to a charitable organization was motivated by a deep-rooted, God-inspired belief in the cause for which he works so unstintingly. He convinced the powers that be of the urgency, need and necessity of the Actors Youth Fund to the extent the City of New York, the State of New York, the Federal Government, the Anti-Poverty agency contribute a "matching" dollar for dollar. Hence, whatever proceeds are realized with the annual dinner and souvenir book, these figures are quadrupled. What was originally one hundred thousand dollars is now a half a million dollars!!!

What measure of success has the Actors Youth Fund program

enjoyed? Considering today's increase in crime and violence, the demoralization of youth everywhere, the pornographic filth at their command, the devastating usage of drugs and narcotics among our children in every city, town and hamlet of America, the project achieved miracles, great and little. Dozens of the kids are now paying members of the American Guild of Variety Artists; dozens more are enrolled in the musicians' union; some are affiliated with the theater and Equity, others with television and radio and AFTRA—American Federation of Television and Radio Artists. A dance team reached such professional heights as to work Radio City Music Hall. Some signed recording contracts. Many troupes are traveling professionally. The greatest miracle of all is to see some of the alumni return to the Blackboard Jungle to teach the kids the things they have learned.

To fulfill our intense desire to avoid a repetition of the atrocities of Attica in our lifetime, to employ entertainment as part-time therapeutics, Mr. Adams at my suggestion wrote to Governor Nelson Rockefeller. To our dismay and disgust, the Governor refused our request. Like the great majority of "promises, promises" politicians, Governor Rockefeller relied on the old political cliché as a way out. The State has no money. However, they did find the money to heal the Attica wounds and bury the Attica dead. I live only a few short blocks from the Tombs. Much against my wishes, I witnessed the 1970 riot. I offered to speak to the riot leaders and was politely reminded only a lunatic would make such a proposal. Could the havoc of Attica and the Tombs have been avoided with "the sound of music"?

I asked many of the convicts in Green Haven and Lewisburg prisons how did live entertainment with strong-named personalities affect the population? The reactions, I'm told, were hilarious and pathetic. They learn the identities of the artists who will appear on the bill and the artist's particular talent, such as sing, dance, joke, ventriloquize or whatever. Now they assume the role of frustrated producers. They'll stage the entire show. A hardened, convicted criminal is supposedly emotionless. Don't believe it. The anticipation, the anxiety, the breathless impatience before the arrival of a show is as emotion-packed as a Saturday-afternoon football game in any American hamlet. After the show, the "boys" gather in the yards and the frustrated producers will discuss the myriad mistakes we committed. They should have made the ventriloquist open the show rather than the comedian, or the dance team should have been in the second spot rather than the third. Wonderful! Wonderful! Anything to sublimate the distorted, criminal mind. Anything. . . .

Defeat is not our name. We will not accept a gubernatorial denial. We'll strike at the moon hoping someday to hit the stars. We could not convince the State; we'll try the City—New York, naturally. Mr. Adams contacted the City Prisons Administrator and other officials. We hope someday to provide city prisons and other reform institutions with live variety shows and, God willing, stage plays. If the whip did not succeed, maybe entertainment will.

MR. CALABASH

My first visit to Hollywood was as a guest of Jimmy Durante. Until then it was the longest trip I had ever experienced. As a youngster geography had always been my favorite subject. The wild anticipation of flying over the Mississippi River, the Rockies, Pike's Peak, the Continental Divide, the Grand Canyon, to cast my eyes on the blue Pacific, caused such an emotional impact within me as to create an undesirable trauma. Born in Greenwich Village where the only real, live trees to be seen were in Washington Square Park, the thought of standing beneath a palm tree shook me with sheer excitement.

Jimmy had sent me a check for a round-trip airline ticket and an extra-generous amount of pocket money. When the stewardess announced we were about to land in Los Angeles, my heart began to pound with the staccato of a pneumatic drill. As the huge wheels of the American Airliner kissed the California earth, the miracle occurred. I was in California—the land my spiritual forefathers, Padre Junipero Serra and his companions, Christianized many years ago.

After what seemed to be an interminable wait, the plane door swung open. I walked toward the terminal. Suddenly and unbelievedly I heard my name being paged. Me—the kid from Thompson Street in the Village—being paged in Movieland!!! I immediately knew the page was Durante-inspired. It wasn't "Father Robert," or "Father Bob" but "Father Roberts," just as Sir James always addresses me. Jimmy's chauffeur introduced himself and off we drove, first for a Class A sight-seeing tour of Hollywood and then to the white brick house on North Beverly Drive.

What a reception committee! Lou Clayton and his Aida, Eddie Jackson and his Jean, Jimmy and his dog. That evening we all had dinner at Dave Chasen's, where I encountered my first big culinary surprise. Until that moment I thought the whole world was Italian. I wasn't too well acquainted with restaurants. Having spent thirteen years of my life in seminaries, from ages thirteen to twenty-six, my options in the selections of food were quite restricted. To add to the dilemma, everything sounded so Frenchy. I ordered the only recognizable item on the menu, Veal Parmesan. Much to my consternation, the waiter presented me with a dish of veal covered with Parmesan cheese. My mother, in fact most New York restaurants, served that dish with mozzarella cheese. I was quite perplexed and informed Durante about my problem. Gently but firmly he reminded me there was no forgery in California. You get what you order. You ordered Veal Parmesan and you got it!

My second surprise was the Durante household. There was a swimming pool he never used; a barbecue pit that never barbecued; a refrigerator that contained only milk and corn flakes and not a drop of whiskey in the house. In those days Jimmy was a confirmed bachelor. Friends would drop in any hour of the morning, noon and night. Jimmy would sit at the piano and entertain anyone willing to listen to a new piece of material. We dined out every night at different restaurants, where Jimmy would be sincerely welcomed by owners, staff and practically every patron. The mere sight of the little man with the big nose standing at the threshold of the restaurant caused immediate pandemonium. It seemed he loved everyone and everyone loved him.

About this time Lou Clayton was a very sick man. Jimmy and all of us knew it was only a question of time before Lou would play his last performance. Jimmy and I visited him every day. "We got to keep him happy. We got to make him laugh," Jimmy would remind the gang. It amazed me to see the transformation that occurred in the Durante character. He was a very sad man; the thought of losing his dearest friend was torturous and painful. Yet the moment we arrived at the Clayton apartment, there was a new Durante. He laughed, joked, told stories, mimicked until poor Lou would collapse from laughter. Shortly after, Clayton received his final curtain call from the Divine Director. And Jimmy has never forgotten Lou's widow, Aida.

One of the most unforgettable stories that Jimmy tells concerns his dog. His wife, Jeannie, had exacted from him a solemn promise that if and when the dog should pass on, Jimmy would provide a proper funeral for the animal. This entailed a funeral director, a coffin, a hearse, a limousine and a grave site. Eventually the dog died. And Jimmy entertained every intention to fulfill his promise. However, try as he might, he could not visualize himself in the role of a weeping mourner. After much coercion he convinced Julie Bufano, his pianist, to play the role. There was poor Julie, dressed completely in black, including hat and gloves, eyes downcast, hands crossed almost prayerfully, following the bier that contained the remains of the Durante Dog.

Each evening after supper Jimmy and I would return to his home while the rest of the gang returned to their own pads. He would religiously remove his jacket and shirt, put on a bathrobe, wrap a towel around his head turbanlike, light up a good Cuban cigar and place his weary body into a hammock. All I could see through the soft California moonlight were Jimmy's beautiful nose and Durante's expensive cigar rocking back and forth. I thought the sight was hilarious. He thought I'd make a good subject for a psycho ward.

On the second week of my vacation Durante was booked into

Wilbur Clark's Desert Inn in Las Vegas. This created a very bothersome problem. He had a tremendous decision to make: should he or should he not take this young Levite to the land of the devil's playground? At first he decided against it, suggesting I remain in Beverly Hills with his old and lovely black maid, Maggie. At this point everyone intervened in my behalf. Eddie Jackson, Julie Bufano, Jack Roth, Lou Cohan, Jackie Barnett kept pulverizing him with every sort of argument, legal and ecclesiastical, until he finally recanted and I was on my way to the fabulous city of Las Vegas, Nevada.

In Vegas the Durante entourage was enhanced with the presence of Jack Dempsey, his two lovely daughters, Ted Lewis and his Ada and writer Gene Fowler, who at the time was writing the Durante biography, *Schnozzola*. Among the guests at the Desert Inn were four lovely young ladies from Los Angeles. One of them, Ronnie Rondoni, approached me at poolside and said: "We have been trying to figure out what you do for a living. We see you having breakfast with Dempsey and his daughters, lunch with Ted Lewis and his Mrs. and dinner with Durante. You must be some sort of a big shot."

"What," I asked, "did you decide I do for a living?" "Well," she responded, "one girl thinks you're a performer, another guessed a gag writer for Durante, the third thought you were a theatrical agent and I—perhaps it's better left unsaid." At this point I encouraged her. "Please tell me! I really want to know." "I," she almost whispered, "thought you were a racketeer." "What in the name of God ever made you think that?" She proceeded to inform me I had NEW YORK written all over me and that ever-so-slight touch of Brooklynese accent. We made a pact. I would inform her of my profession on the afternoon before my departure for New York.

It was Friday afternoon and pretty Ronnie was ready to spear me with a barrage of questions. "Will you tell me now?" she pleaded. At the time I was sitting poolside in a beach chair. I suggested she do likewise, because when she hears who and what I am she will probably fall on her pretty derriere. When I enlightened her on my priestly profession, she could only exclaim, "Oh, my God—*no*! To which I amen-ed: "Oh, my God—yes."

If Jimmy suffers a human frailty, it is his generosity. He gives to every worthwhile cause and some not so worthwhile. He has been taken on more than one occasion. Whenever I browse through a local-church or a local-organization souvenir book, invariably the middle page carries the message YOUR FRIEND— JIMMY DURANTE. He was never known to refuse the extended hands of Broadway panhandlers waiting hours at the doors of the Astor Hotel for Sir James to make his entry or exit. During my Hollywood visits, I've watched some broken-down, washed-up, derelict actors queued at the doorway of the Brown Derby or Chasen's Restaurant to await the arrival of the Durante automobile. He had sent me a well-padded check to pay for my California excursion, enough for a round-trip airline ticket and then some. When it came time to leave, he presented me with a similar check, which I strongly refused. As I relaxed in the den of his home, Jimmy sat at a small desk paging through an ordinary scrapbook. He showed it to me—and I honestly believe I'm one of the very few to lay eyes on that ledger. It contained the names of many people, mostly from the Fourth Ward district of New York City, in the shadow of the Brooklyn Bridge, where Durante was born and raised. These were some of the people, Durante's people, he supported for so many years. Like Celeste Holm's Ado Annie of *Oklahoma!*, he "Can't Say No."

The question has often been asked, What makes a good comic? Most performers will tell you a comic is as good as his writers. There are some who are completely helpless without their scribes. This undoubtedly is true, but not in the case of Mr. James Durante. There exists a certain element of humility, spontaneity and naturalness in the Durante humor seldom found anywhere else. Jimmy's material doesn't necessarily have to be funny. It's the way he says it.

A few Durantistic gems are the following stories, funny and true to life. He was working the Copacabana in New York and living at his favorite haunt, the Astor Hotel, when he decided to phone me to ask me to hear his confession. In the Catholic Church it is obligatory for its members to confess and receive Communion during the Easter season. I arrived at the Astor and went directly to his suite. While Jimmy was phoning someone in California, Fatso Marco, the second banana to Milton Berle during his fantastic TV tenure, invited me to a drink. "Get me a tall Scotch and water and only one cube of ice."

Jimmy and I were alone in the living room. He finished his call and now the both of us went into his bedroom to assure ourselves the proper privacy. I am seated, with a purple stole around my neck, slightly bent forward with my head cupped in my hands. Jimmy kneels beside me, his eyeglasses on his face, a prayer book in his hands. He reverently begins: "Bless me, Father, for I have sinned." Suddenly there's a hard knock on the door. The same door is burst open and in walks Fatso holding a small tray with the Scotch, water and ice. Durante is aghast! "What kind of a nut are you, Fatso? Can't you see I'm going to confession?" Fatso looks Jimmy straight in the eye and said, "Durante, because you got problems the priest has to go dry!"

It was a Palm Sunday when I accompanied Jimmy to Calvary Cemetery, Queens, New York, where both his parents are buried. At my request some Catholic sisters wove a wreath of palms to place upon the sacred grounds. It was rather late, and we feared we would not be permitted entrance, because the cemetery gates are closed at four-thirty. We spotted a guard, and Jimmy delegated me to the envoy. "You're a priest and he can't say no to you" was his classic reminder. The guard consented, but reminded us we must leave in a very short time. Jimmy got out of the automobile and the guard spotted him for the very first time. Durante took out a ten-dollar bill and gave it to him. Stunned by his generosity, the guard enthused, "Jimmy, you can stay in there as long as you want." To which came the immortal reply: "The hell with you! I want to get out of That Place like everybody else."

On our return to the city, the Beloved Clown questioned me: "Whatdaya think about disturbing the dead?" "Disturb the dead?" A bewildered expression covered my face, and Jimmy immediately sensed this. "Let me explain," he added. "When I was a young man I tried very hard to be good to my parents. Now in older years I feel perhaps I didn't do enough. I would like to build them a . . ." Jimmy stopped. I knew he was searching for the word "mausoleum"—which, incidentally, is a four-syllable word. Any word with that amount of syllables must of necessity prove to be an insurmountable barrier to the Great Schnozz. The second attempt was made: "I want to build them a mussolini."

On another occasion in New York, a casual walk brought me in front of the Astor Hotel. Jimmy is in town, why not pay him a visit? In the lobby of the Astor, I picked up a house phone. Eddie Jackson answered and at my request gave the phone to Mr. Durante. "This is Father Bob." "Who????" Jimmy demanded. "Sorry; this is Father Roberts." "Where are you?" he wanted to know. "In the lobby of the Astor," I answered. "Come on up," came the invitation. In the suite were Jackson, Jack Roth and a man, a stranger. "Hello and sit down," Jimmy greeted me in his inimitable way. "I'll be busy for a while." The stranger, Jackson informed me, is an accountant. He's helping the Schnozz to fill his income-tax returns. At one point, during the question-and-answer session, Jimmy removed the glasses from his face, squinted at me and opined: "I'd rather rob a church than try to cheat the tax people—what do you call them . . . oh, yes, the Internal Revue [*sic*] Department. God is more forgiving."

At the Actors' Chapel in Saint Malachy's Church in New York, I assisted at the wedding of Miss Margie Little and Mr. James Durante. A priest friend of Margie's performed the ceremony. Immediately before the wedding, Jimmy and I were alone in one of the rectory offices. He was quite nervous and tense, pacing the floor. Suddenly there was a knock on the door and the good Monsignor called out, "Mr. Durante, the bride is here." Jimmy gave me one last, desperate look and in all seriousness said, "I hope I don't forget myself and take a bow when it's all over."

The phone rings. It's Father Sal Anastasia, one of the finest of priests and most gentle of men, calling for help. He requested the services of the Schnozz for the annual reunion and dance of his parish in the Bronx. Would I intercede? Jimmy had to deny the request because there wasn't enough time in between shows at the Copa. Finally I advised Jimmy that Father Sal was not only a priest and a dear friend but happened to be the brother of Albert Anastasia. "I've just changed my mind. I'll go!"

Who is "Mrs. Calabash"? That question has been directed at me at least a thousand times. Many years ago Jimmy revealed to me the identity of Mrs. Calabash with a promise I would never divulge it to anyone, not even my closest kin. Not until a year ago—when Jimmy, as a guest on the *Mike Douglas Show*, told the nationwide audience that Mrs. Calabash was his deceased wife, Jeannie. It seems as often as Mr. and Mrs. Durante boarded the *Super Chief* out of Chicago, they would pass a little town named Calabash. Jeannie fell in love with that particular locale. It represented the typical all-American town. The tree-lined streets, the manicured lawns, the big white church—everything Americana. Dynamic Jim would promise Jean, "Someday I'm going to buy you Calabash! All of Calabash!" While doing a show, the Schnozz searched for an appropriate closing line, and his efforts were hopeless. Suddenly he thought of Jeannie and Calabash. "Good night, Mrs. Calabash, wherever you are." Thousands of letters poured into Hollywood. Who is Mrs. Calabash? Jimmy realized he was now the proud possessor of a priceless gimmick. The world waited twenty years to learn what we already knew then.

In his column, "Little Old New York," Mr. Ed Sullivan speaks of the Broadway in the nineteen-twenties when Clayton, Jackson and Durante were jamming New York's Club Durante. He recalls how the late great John Barrymore said, "Jimmy, you ought to play Hamlet." And the classic response: "John, to hell with those small towns like Hamlet. Broadway's good enough for me."

Mr. Sullivan's recollections included a very touching, sensitive, compassionate vignette. He and Durante ferried across New York Bay to entertain the wounded servicemen at Halloran General Hospital on Staten Island. When Ed introduced Jimmy, he forewarned the audience that Durante had a radio show that evening and he must return to the city no later than eight o'clock. Hence, Jimmy must catch the seven o'clock ferry and could only sing one number. Much to Sullivan's consternation, Jimmy stayed onstage for an hour. When Ed reminded him he missed the ferry and consequently the radio show, Jimmy's reply were words that could fall only from the lips of a saint: "Ed, when I saw two wounded kids in the front row applauding—one with his left hand and the other with his right hand because each of them had lost an arm—I decided it wasn't so tragic to miss my radio show."

Some time ago I appeared on the *Mike Douglas Show*. During the interview Mike asked a rather sticky question, putting me on the proverbial spot: "Of all your friends in showbusiness, whom would you classify as the greatest performer?" I refused to answer directly. However, I did say if I had to pick one person who is loved and revered by all, has been around showbiz longer than most people have been on earth, has never used a smutty word or a blue joke, has performed more benefits than anyone in the business, then I must say it is Jimmy Durante. Jerry Lewis agreed with me. Frank Sinatra caught the show with Pat Henry in his Palm Springs home, and Pat said, "Frank thought the choice was perfect."

The Schnozz is a man small in stature, but in my books he stands twenty feet tall and glows in the dark. Good night, Mr. Calabash, wherever you are!

THE
MAN
WITH
THE
GOLDEN
VOICE

The name is magic; the voice . . . magical; the man . . . a magician. The name, the voice, the man belong to Francis Albert Sinatra. He is not svelte of hands, but certainly svelte of voice. The vocal tricks he has forgotten most vocalists do not possess in their repertoire. Many are the sobriquets attached to his name; the one I find most appropriate is The Voice. His is undoubtedly the most famous, the most publicized, the most talked-about name in the business. Others come and go, but although he has now retired from singing, he is a landmark in showbiz. He has been for better than a quarter of a century. In his young days, the scene of his many conquests was the Paramount Theater in New York; later it was Las Vegas. Many of my friends, not necessarily in the trade, would board a plane to Vegas for a weekend to hear the golden tones of the singer's Singer. He is recognized anywhere in the world. His films are still seen in every part of the globe. His recordings sell in astronomical figures. Each of his television appearances was considered a Special. More than an entertainer, he is today a wealthy financier—travels in his own planes with his own cast of pilots. The old Hoboken Ferry is a thing of the past. He is indeed "Chairman of the Board."

I was introduced to Mr. Sinatra as he was spiraling to success. I met him where most people have met him: backstage at the Paramount. When I was referred to as Perry Como's priest, he wisecracked: "Does Como need the clergy in his corner? I've got Saint Christopher!"

When young Frankie decided to leave the Tommy Dorsey band to sail alone the uncharted seas of success, he surrounded himself with a trio of showbiz-wise characters. Manager: Hank Sanicola; booker: Tom Rockwell; public relations: George Evans —each of whom in their own particular medium was responsible for Frank's unprecedented and meteoric career. Mr. Rockwell later developed into a gargantuan figure in the domain of personal management: the founder and president of the General Artists Corporation agency and the guiding hand in the careers of the Mills Brothers, Bing Crosby and Perry Como. Through some legalistic maneuvers, the Music Corporation of America paid an unknown sum of money to Dorsey's manager, thereby nullifying their ownership of Frank's contract and representing the star singer. At the same time, General Artists Corporation released Frank from his contractual obligations, still binding for several more years, and both agencies, MCA and GAC, became the recipients of five percent each of the Sinatra income. Many years later, another agent, representing the William Morris office, played a major role in the vocalist's miraculous comeback. At the time when the soaring popularity of the Singer had waned to almost a whisper, George Woods presented his client with a script and in so doing presented him with an Oscar and a new career. *From Here to Eternity.* The rest is history.

It was my extreme pleasure to have performed the wedding rites of George Woods and Lois O'Brien, a musical-comedy actress and one of the most beautiful women I have ever seen. It was likewise my pleasure to baptize their two lovely daughters.

Sinatra is a very controversial figure. It is not my desire to condone or condemn the things he has said and done. However, I would like to point out that Frank is a target, a victim of the mass media. The many good deeds he performs are hardly ever seen in the printed word; the many charities he maintains go unnoticed. But let him make one drunken, foolhardy mistake and it will be exploded into unimaginable size and shape, exaggerated beyond belief. There exists a very thin line of propriety among writers, newscasters and their ilk. If you are accepted, if you are considered a "nice guy" among the word-setters and are in reality a woman-chasing husband or a chronic female drunk, your evil deeds will never blemish the lily-white purity of the Fourth Estate. If, to the contrary, you're not accepted, if you are a "bad guy" in the eyes of the scribes, then prepare yourself for journalistic homicide.

Having performed a benefit in London, Mr. Sinatra planned a stopover in New York to participate in another such function for the Italian-American Civil Rights League at the Felt Forum in Madison Square Garden. A television commentator requested an interview with Sinatra and was denied. Can you imagine anything more sacrilegious than denying a news commentator or a reporter his request? The next evening on the TV news he and three fellow commentators ridiculed, belittled, disparaged Sinatra. They kept repeating Sinatra was too big a star to be interviewed by an unknown commentator.

I see herein several breaches of common courtesy and etiquette. Does the instant-omniscient presence of a news commentator demand that a person stop doing what he's doing to lay bare his soul to some idiotic questions? Isn't a man entitled to his rights of privacy? Doesn't a man have the right to decide whether he wants to be interviewed or not? It just so happened I was in the dressing room with Frank; it just so happened he was extremely busy planning the show and talking with friends; it just so happened he knew the nature of some of the questions the commentator would ask and he refused to be ridiculed, belittled and disparaged. Ironically, I've met some of these newly created

TV gods—the broadcasters—and the truth of the matter is, some do act as though their names were Sinatra.

This story came from the lips of Rosemary Clooney many years ago. It is no different today; the same story could have been written yesterday or tomorrow. Her younger sister, Betty, expressed a desire to meet Frank Sinatra. Rosemary called Frank and informed him of Betty's wish. Frank took Betty to dinner at the Starlight Room at the Waldorf and via a chauffeured limousine returned her to the Clooney residence. The following day the newspapers provided an idyllic description of the new romance in the life of Lover Boy Sinatra. They painted a veritable portrait of love: how rapturously they gazed into each other's eyes; how tenderly they held hands; how closely they danced together; how attentive and polite he had been toward his new love. Ironically, there wasn't a newspaperman in sight. The information was provided by one of the maître d's—a friend of the writer.

Recently, Frank got himself involved in another Las Vegas fracas. A gentleman running for the office of sheriff denounced the Singer in one of his campaign speeches. Every syndicated paper in the country picked up the newsworthy (?) item. The candidate was quoted as saying if he were elected, Mr. Sinatra won't set foot in Vegas—and if he did he would be forced to behave himself, to stop bothering waitresses, to stop pushing his weight around town. He failed, however, to mention the many millions of dollars the magical name Sinatra brought into Vegas; that the esteem and preeminence Las Vegas enjoys today as the entertainment center of the world is due vastly to the Sinatra hierarchy; that the name Las Vegas and the name Sinatra are synonymous.

Sinatra is a gentle-man. He loves his children and they love him. Recently I was in the company of the Sinatras. And I could see Nancy, Jr., and Tina holding, caressing, touching, fondling, kissing Daddy almost continuously. I shall never forget how proudly his chest expanded when I informed him that if I could have a son, I would want him to be the replica of his Junior. During the funeral rites of his dad, I noticed the Singer fumbling for something in his pocket. Then whatever it was he sought was palmed in his left hand. Moments later I saw the crucifix of his rosary shining in the sunlight.

Sinatra is a generous man. Many are the tales of his generosity, the majority of them unpublicized. The Hollywood chorus girl about to be fired because she was always late on the set. She couldn't afford a car, so she had to ride the buses. If this posed a big problem for the young thespian, it had an easy solution for Frank. "Here are my car keys. Take my car and keep it."

Death came to the proprietor of one of Hollywood's most famous nightclubs. The man's wife tried to operate the club and failed miserably, only to claim bankruptcy. When Sinatra heard of her plight, he had her reopen the club, hired a battery of musicians at his own expense and worked there for ten nights—and all "on the arm," to use that beautiful all-American cliché.

The Vegas waitress who presented him with several Jack Daniels and became the recipient of a one-hundred-dollar tip.

This is not the exception, it is practically the rule. Merely because I participated in the burial rites of his father, he instructed young Frank to pick out a very expensive wristwatch, have it engraved and sent it to me. A little Catholic nun, an intimate friend of Mom Sinatra, stayed at Natalie's side, inseparable for the three days of the wake. Today her convent sports a station wagon.

Friendship knows no boundaries in the philosophy and character of this man. If you're his friend, he will tear mountains apart with his bare hands to help. If you're an enemy, even mouth-to-mouth resuscitation would be considered an imposition. When tragedy struck the lives of the Judy Garlands, the Ethel Barrymores, the George Rafts, the Lee J. Cobbs, it was Sinatra who placed his John Hancock on blank checks. And in many more instances, these unlucky ones never knew the identity of the man who paid their rents and bought their food.

Mr. Sinatra is most modest about his charitable contributions. He has one motivating force when it comes to charity: he *must* believe in the cause. Once he does, he devotes the same drive, energy and personal involvement to it that he does to his professional undertakings.

Cognizant of the futility and frustrations I would experience asking Frank to enumerate the list of his charitable endeavors, I wrote to Mr. Jim Mahoney, his public relations man. Sinatra never speaks of his philanthropic works. Jim's reply was comparable to the Book of Revelation. The long, incredible list sounded like a long, endless litany of mercy. The four corners of the earth became the recipients of this man's love for suffering humanity, especially children.

A few years back he made a world tour for children's charities. He personally paid for all expenses and insisted that all moneys raised stay in the country in which he appeared and be donated to specific children's charities. The results of that tour are a monument to a man dedicated to raising money to ease the suffering of people in need.

In Japan his appearances resulted in the erection of buildings and supplying facilities for five orphanages, including six million yen for construction of the two-story concrete Sinatra Educational Hall at Shoja Yojien orphanage.

In Hong Kong the funds were used to continue the work of a children's orthopedic hospital, aid the children of fishing villages and to build a blind children's foundation.

In Israel, under sponsorship of the Israeli Labor Organization, Histadrut, a Frank Sinatra Youth Center in Nazareth was created, and Sinatra annually has endowed scholarships for children of the youth center.

In Athens the money provided operating funds for a nursery at the Saint Sophia Children's Hospital.

In Paris the money went toward a home for crippled children.

Many organizations benefited from his concert appearances in Great Britain, including the Invalid Children's Aid Society; Variety Group Fund; The Sunshine Home for Blind Children; SOS, an organization for spastic children, and a fund for mentally retarded children.

In Italy it was the Boys' Towns of Italy that reaped the major benefits from the appearances—and has been receiving aid ever since.

In the past year he realized one of his lifetime goals: dedication of the Martin Anthony Sinatra Medical Education Center in Palm Springs, named in honor of his late father. He also endowed the Christina Sinatra Teen Center for high school youths in Palm Desert.

The Martin Luther King College in Georgia; Reiss-Davis Clinic for Children in Los Angeles; Neighbors of Watts; Friars Club Charities; Eisenhower Medical Center; American Civil Liberties Union; Italian-American Civil Rights League; The Thalians, Share—the list of organizations to which he has given his time, energy and talents is endless.

In one three-year period, through appearances for which he personally absorbed all expenses, he raised more than one million dollars for a dozen charities in St. Louis.

He read of the plight of U.S. diplomat Don Mitrione, brutally kidnapped and slain in South America, and hastily arranged and appeared in concert in Richmond, Indiana—raising more than one hundred thousand dollars for the widow and family.

But these are the obvious, the publicized facets of Mr. Sinatra's generosity.

He is known in show business as the world's softest touch.

What a ten-year-old San Antonio girl doesn't know until now is that her series of vital operations were paid for by anonymous contributions made by Mr. Sinatra; schoolchildren in remote areas of San Francisco ride to school daily in buses supplied, again anonymously, by Mr. Sinatra. The list goes on and on.

A fatherless family in New York's Harlem: a mother and three sons. The boys decide to write to Mr. Sinatra. Youngsters though they be, they wrote a very touching and impassioned letter. Please, they pleaded, if it's possible, send us a bed. We have never slept in a bed; the floor has been our mattress since we were born. A fast transcountry call to Mr. Henri Gene, the Chairman's New York representative and grandfather of two beautiful babies. Since Frank is the recipient of thousands of such requests, he tells Henri to make the customary investigation: "Check it out." The check-out proved true. The apartment, unbelievable to the eyes of Gene in this day and age, possessed a few sticks of furniture: a kitchen table and a couple of chairs plus a stove. Notified of this inhumane tragedy, Frank tells his Man Friday to furnish the apartment. The next compassionate scene is soul-gratifying: Henri behind the wheel of a station wagon. Stocked to capacity, the station wagon carried a couch, chairs, lamps, linen, blankets, bed sheets, pillowcases, "God bless Santa Claus" mattresses, a bed for mother and a couple of double-bunkers for the boys. The Man can't be all bad.

Sinatra loves children, especially those deprived by nature or accident of some human faculty. During his London pilgrimage for children, he visited an institution for blind children. When he arrived the children were at play—a game called "Net." Comparable to a net thrown over the side of a ship, a net is thrown over the side of a strong structure and the children climb it. When he emerged from the automobile, someone politely and softly announced, "Mr. Sinatra is here." He and Mr. Henri Gene were escorted through every building on the grounds; they were shown the children's playroom and playthings. The children even entertained: the blind boys and girls sang for the Singer. The anticipation *to see him,* they informed Frank, was torturous. The wind blew hard. Photographers and TV cameramen clicked away when a young girl about eight years of age approached him. In a strong Cockney accent she addressed him. "Mr. Sinatra," her sightless eyes questioned him, "what color is the wind?" For a few moments, an excruciating silence. Henri looked on helplessly. His eyes pleaded with his boss: "Come on, big boy, you've got all the answers. Come up with one *now!*" Frank's words came out hesitantly: "You see, sweetheart, the wind blows so fast you can't see the color."

The mayor of Cathedral City, California, a suburb of Palm Springs, received a letter. His Honor, Francis Albert Sinatra is the mayor of Cathedral City. The epistle, written by a little Indian girl living high in the sun-bronzed mountains skirting the Springs, bore a request: would his honor, the Mayor, bring a little toy to her baby brother? She had no daddy—he ran off; just Mother and her baby brother. Frank decided to visit the young lady personally. Disguising himself with a few days' growth of beard, wearing a ragged jacket, sloppy pants and a broken-down fedora, he jumped into his station wagon and literally headed for the mountains. Again, "Check it out." When he saw the shack in which human lives are asked to vegetate, he remained in shocked disbelief. Furniture, food and sanitation were strangers to the shack. He thought to himself, Even animals are much too noble creatures to live in this cesspool. The disguise worked wonderfully. He palmed himself off as a local representative investigating the land. He returned to his "seat of power," Cathedral City. The following day a huge truck groaned its tortuous way up the meandering mountain roads jammed with toys, canned foods and clothing. Within forty-eight hours the shack was completely furnished and equipped with every piece of furniture and paraphernalia necessary to convert a Shack into a Home. To this day the Indian mother and her two Indian children don't know who the mayor of Cathedral City or the government representative is. The Guy can't be all bad.

There's a story told to me many years ago by my dad about World War I. Amid the havoc and horrors of that war, on each Christmas Eve and Christmas Day peace returned to the world. As the strains of "Silent Night," "Noël" and "O Little Town of Bethlehem" perfumed the gunpowdered air, the absence of a single gunshot or cannonade seemed almost miraculous. The devasted terrain in France, the immolated milieu of Germany suddenly became immersed with the divine presence of the Prince of Peace. Aside from the religious implications—the comparison is hardly fitting—such a story has been repeated: When Mr. Sinatra visited Israel recently, he sought governmental permission to stage a concert on the battlefields of that country. Having already performed a benefit for the children of Sion at Tel Aviv, he now wanted to entertain its brave and "come if you dare" fighting corps. In order to divert all the combatants, the arena was set, practically speaking, on the boundary lines of Egypt and Israel, within earshot of the enemy soldiers. Throughout the entertainment, as Sinatra vocalized song after song, some even in Yiddish, there wasn't a shot to be heard or a cannon fired. Minutes after the concert, all hell broke loose. "What fools we mortals be."

The whole spectrum of Mr. Sinatra's humanitarian activities can perhaps best be summarized by the fact that although of Italian-American descent, there hardly is a single ethnic, religious, racial or other charitable group that has not benefited from his continuing charitable efforts.

In his own words, Jim Mahoney graphically describes the man. "I personally would like to stress one point: He does not just give money. Many rich men can give varying amounts of money somewhat easily. But he goes a step further. He gives of himself. His time and his talents. He works for charity—with his voice, not just with his checkbook."

Mom Sinatra (she was christened Natale, is called "Dolly" by her friends and "Mom" by her son's friends) winged her way to Rome and was thrilled to participate in a semiprivate audience with Pope Paul. When she appeared before his Holiness and was introduced merely as Mrs. Martin Sinatra, the Pontiff whispered into her ears: "I know all about the charities your son has performed throughout the world. God bless him."

Recently I was invited to young Nancy's opening at Caesar's Palace in Las Vegas, where Frank had rented a couple of hundred rooms for his friends. When he spotted me that evening, he walked over, put his left arm around my neck (the right arm was in a sling) and kissed me on each cheek—Italian style. I overheard someone saying, "Those Sinatra lips have kissed many a face, but I'll bet it's the first time they've kissed the face of a priest."

At the Italian-American Civil Rights League's benefit show, where better than a half-million dollars was realized, Frank and his friends, Jilly Rizzo, Sammy Davis, Vic Damone, Connie Francis, Trini Lopez, Jerry Vale, Frankie Valli and the Four Seasons, Pat Henry, Don Costa, Ed McMahon, Rocky Graziano,

Ross Martin and others, were in his dressing room. To see some of the stars hedgingly asking the Superstar to pose for a picture with them reminded me of an amusingly comparable scene in Rome: some monsignors hedgingly requesting of the Pontiff the privilege to be photographed with him; they wanted a picture to take home. It was there in the dressing room when I presented Frank with a solid-gold crucifix ring. It did not cost more than twenty dollars; you would have thought I gave him a twenty-carat diamond. He displayed it to anyone interested enough to look, meaning everyone. "Now, Frank," I advised him, "you officially belong to Father Bob's stable."

Poverty was a household word and reigned supreme in the Dallas home of singer Trini Lopez. His familial fate was typical of most Mexican-Americans residing in the Lone Star State. His people have been victimized by filthy politics, capitalism and labor since they first crossed the Rio Grande. For years they toiled the harvest of the rich for no harvest of their own; they received nothing comparable to a decent wage, let alone a substantial day's pay. With such a poverty-stricken background, how did Trini make it so big? To whom does he owe his success as one of today's most sought-after and highest-priced vocalists? Trini told Ed Sullivan in an interview: "Frank Sinatra first heard me nine years ago at PJ's in Hollywood, signed me for his Reprise Record company and I've been with him ever since. The fact that Frank's been in my corner has made it much easier for me, and he's done it for many other young performers without ever taking a bow." Today when Mr. Lopez plays the plush Waldorf's Empire Room or Chicago's Ambassador or Los Angeles' Cocoanut Grove, I wonder if he ever recalls the dark, bleak days of Dallas or his migrant, oppressed and aggrieved people? I wonder, how must it feel to flounder in the quagmire of absolute destitution and then bask in the sun of plenty?

Were I to evaluate the social status of the New York cab driver, I would say he's comparable to any member of the ministry. He's everybody's "father confessor." Only the bartender runs a close second. His supposed knowledge of the Vietnam War or any other topical subject including busing, segregation, drugs, pollution, abortion and whatever is encyclopedic. The overwhelming majority of our cabbies are hardworking, honest, nice guys. However, you'll always find a rotten apple in every barrel of good ones. One such varmint appeared from beneath his bed of rock recently. An English tourist, a seventy-one-year-old Mrs. Margaret Morgan, took a cab from Kennedy airfield to suburban Woodbridge, New Jersey, a thirty-mile trek from the metropolis. What ordinarily would have been a thirty-five-dollar tab, the frightened woman ("the cab driver was a very big man") was charged two hundred thirty-seven dollars and seventy cents. She was forced to borrow a hundred and fifty dollars from her Jerseyite relatives. The *New York Post* carried this outrageous story. Mr. Sinatra immediately sent a two-hundred-and-fifty-dollar check to the victimized Britisher, explaining, "In England I have always been treated royally"; apologized for the varmint and his ilk and sincerely hoped the rest of her trip would be a delightful one.

Mr. Sinatra arrived at his favorite New York bistro, Jilly's, owned by his buddy and constant companion Jilly Rizzo. The time was not unusual for Mr. S.; it was four-fifteen A.M. The kitchen closed, the Chinese cook home in a warm, comfortable bed and the Crooner craving for chicken chow mein. Jilly decided to send the chauffeured limousine to Pike Street, on the Lower East Side of Manhattan, hoping the Cook would return to the restaurant. Twenty minutes later, the restaurant phone rang bearing the momentous message analogous to MacArthur's "I shall return." The chauffeur's declaration, "The cook and I are returning to the restaurant," was equally important. For his inconveniences and services rendered, Frank presented the cook with a three-hundred-dollar tip. "Any time, Mis-ta Sinatra, anytime," his little almond eyes gleamed.

Get yourself a name in showbiz and you'll probably get yourself a subpoena to appear before some racket committee in Washington. Ask Sammy. Ask Frank. Mr. Sinatra had been ordered to appear—he refused to have himself subpoenaed—before the Select

Committee on Crime. I watched his appearance on television and read about it in newspapers and magazines, and from what I saw and read, Frank came up smelling like roses. He challenged every Congressional committeeman, answered every question respectfully yet defiantly, firmly stood his ground, until the investigators soon appeared to be the investigated. When Mr. Sinatra left the Cannon Office Building in Washington that morning, in my eyes and those of all my friends his stature had grown twelve feet tall.

On July 24, 1972, a letter was published in *The New York Times* authored by the singer-actor. It read in part, "At one minute after 11 on the morning of July 18, I walked into a large hearing room in the Cannon Office Building in Washington to testify before a group called the Select Committee on Crime."

He alluded to the accusations and allegations of his friendship "with certain characters alleged to be in the crime business." The author asked, "Where is the rights of a private citizen in this country when faced with the huge machine of the central Government?" Later he spoke of "the ugly era of Joe McCarthy, in which 'facts' are confused with rumor, gossip and innuendo, and where reputations and character can be demolished in front of the largest possible audiences.

"In my case," he continued, "a convicted murderer was allowed to throw my name around with abandon, while the TV cameras rolled on. His vicious little fantasy was sent into millions of American homes, including my own. Sure, I was given a chance to refute it, but as we have all come to know, the accusation often remains longer in the public mind than the defense. In any case, an American citizen, no matter how famous or how obscure, should not be placed in the position of defending himself before baseless charges and no Congressional committee should become a forum for gutter hearsay that would not be admissible in a court of law."

Now he touches upon the real reason for governmental harassment, his ancestry. "Over the years I have acquired a certain fame and celebrity, and that is one reason why so much gossip and speculation goes on about me. It happens to a lot of stars. But it is complicated in my case because my name ends in a vowel. There is a form of bigotry abroad in this land which allows otherwise decent people, including many liberals, to believe the most scurrilous tales if they are connected to an Italian-American name. They seem to need the lurid fantasy; they want to believe that if an entertainer is introduced to someone in a nightclub, they become intimate friends forever. But it is one thing to watch a fantasy for a couple of hours on a movie screen and then go home. It is quite another thing when the fantasies are projected on real, live human beings, because it doesn't say 'the end' when they are finished. Those human beings have to go on living with their friends, family and business associates in the real world.

"We might call this the politics of fantasy. Sitting at that table the other day, I wondered whether it was any accident that I had been called down to Washington during an election year, a year in which Congressmen have difficulty getting their names into the newspapers because of the tremendous concentration on the race for the Presidency. It certainly seemed that way.

"And I wondered if the people out there in America knew how dangerous the whole proceeding was. My privacy had been robbed from me, I had lost hours of my life, I was being forced to defend myself in a place that was not even a court of law. It wasn't just a question of them getting off my back; it was a question of them getting off everyone's back. If this sort of thing could happen to me, it could happen to anyone, including those who cannot defend themselves properly. I would hope that a lot of Americans would begin to ask their representatives, in the Government and in the media, to start separating fantasy from reality, and to bring this sort of nonsense to an end once and for all."

JEANNIE
WEENIE

Miss Sarah Jane Fulks of St. Joseph, Missouri, is Miss Jane Wyman of Beverly Hills, California. We met, Jane and I, in a Sixth Avenue loft, dignified with the sobriquet "rehearsal hall." My true intention in visiting the hall was to "accidentally" run into Rosemary Clooney, also booked on the Como show. Rose and I hadn't spoken, written or met personally for a number of years—in fact, since her marriage to the divorced José Ferrer. I wanted to renew our friendship.

Meeting Jane was fun! She is a very gregarious person. She'll greet and "hello" anyone and everyone in sight. Jane talks with the staccato of a pneumatic drill. There's a New York bartender who still recalls how Miss Wyman pistol-whipped him with an order of nine different drinks within a span of thirty seconds. Dewar's—J&B—Jack Daniels—martini—Presbyterian—Bloody Mary —screwdriver—daiquiri—straight up—straight down—on the rocks —no ice! With such a cascade of words and names, the confused bartender suggested she come behind the bar and give him a hand. She did.

Her outlook on life—her *savoir-vivre*—startles me. It always culminates in five short words: "Play it by ear, honey." There isn't an ounce of phoniness in her entire makeup. She is at home in the dining room of a tenement apartment as she would be in the fashionable salon of the gilt-edged Plaza. One day she suggested dinner at the Edwardian Room of the Plaza. Having finished our predinner drink, she requested the check, paid it and spurted out, "Let's get out of here and eat where there are some real live people."

Notoriously candid, she will tell you precisely what's on her mind in friendly or unfriendly language. On my first visit to her Beverly Hills home, Jane assured me I was most welcome, anytime. With this ingratiating warranty, she asked if I would like a drink. When I responded affirmatively, she politely invited me to get off my behind and pour myself some booze. "Around here we do things ourselves, regardless of my star status or your Roman collar." Charlton Heston, a struggling unknown in Hollywood, played opposite Jane and became a first-rate star—but only after he listened to her advice to "lose that fat rear you're carrying around." Likewise Rock Hudson in *Magnificent Obsession*. While filming a segment of her TV series, she and an actor enacted a tender love scene. When he placed his lips upon hers, she realized he attempted to soul-kiss her. She gave no reaction, spoke no words. The segment completed, she fired him. And she thundered —sturdy, straight and strong: "The son of a bitch hasn't gotten a job since!"

What does it feel like to be a star? What emotions does one experience to walk Fifth Avenue and have people gawk at you, surprised and amazed? How does one react sitting in a plush restaurant, attempting to eat a meal, and have autograph hounds disturbing every forkful of food you try to thrust into your mouth? What impressions does one conjure when the star sees the facial expressions of surprise, incredulity and disbelief as he or she heads for the washroom? My God! A star is going to the bathroom. High is the price of stardom. And yet it is not always so. Miss Jane Wyman came to New York to audition for a lead role in a Broadway show. Certainly "Johnny Belinda" is, has been and always will be a superstar.

She described to me the cold savagery of the big-time Broadway theater. The stage doorman recognized her immediately and welcomed her most cordially. Once inside the theater, the stage manager greeted her with an impersonal "Hi." She's escorted onstage and told to sing. The theater is engulfed in total darkness and empty except for the producer, the director, the musical conductor and perhaps a couple of backers, or angels. It's a moment of complete helpless and hopeless loneliness. That's when you wish you were being gawked at, hounded by autograph pests and surprising people as you walked to the ladies room. Just to see a smiling, familiar face.

She didn't get the part. The whole scene terminated with a frigid and laconic "Thank you. Next . . ."

Miss Wyman's knowledge of film-making is all-encompassing. She enjoys that rarely achieved "factotum" reputation. The well-known veteran actor Gene Raymond, husband of the late Jeanette MacDonald, once eulogized Jane in this fashion: "There are some women who excel in their particular field of endeavor. The actress, lawyer, doctor, psychiatrist, painter, etc. But Miss Wyman is exceptional in every facet of the business. She is an astute producer, a gifted director and an intelligent, inspired star-actress. I'm not resentful toward any female excelling in some particular subject. But to excel in the three facets of film-making, disclaiming the title of a male chauvinist pig, is too much for any man."

Miss Wyman never speaks about her ex-husbands, especially the Governor of California, Ronald Reagan. Occasionally I would kid her about the prestigious positions she forfeited by divorce: the First Lady of California and possibly the First Lady of the Land. She merely grins. She admits being an absolute vacuum in political science: "I know nothing about politics." However, she also admits it was exasperating to awake in the middle of the night, prepare for work and have someone at the breakfast table, newspaper in hand, expounding on the far right, far left, the conservative right, the conservative left, the middle-of-the-roader. She harbors no ill feeling towards him. The photograph of the Governor, his present wife and Jane at the reception line of the lawn wedding of their daughter, Maureen, seems to prove this.

Whenever Jane writes or phones me, there transpires an immediate transformation of nomenclature. It is no longer Jane Wyman; rather, it's Jeannie Weenie. On one of her long-distance calls, I was absent from the rectory, so she left a message: "Tell Father Bob that Jeannie Weenie called." The priest who had taken the call was a foreigner, born in the sunny land of Sicily and spent twenty-five years in the foreign missions of China and Central America. When I returned home, he looked at me almost pathetically, conveyed the message, shook his head and said, "Crazy friends with crazy names."

Miss Wyman has two genuine traits in her lovely makeup. When she arrives in town she will unfailingly phone to arrange a dinner date, and she will attend my daily Mass and receive the Holy Eucharist. One morning, having attended Mass and received Communion, I invited her to breakfast. Antoinette, a buxom lady from good Neapolitan stock, was the cook at Saint Raphael's rectory. The formal introductions between Miss Wyman and Antoinette were completed with no mention of Jane's professional status. The following morning there was no breakfast prepared for me. The mere sight of yours truly caused a barrage, a cascade of harsh-sounding Italian words and broad Neapolitan gestures. "You'll be the death of me yet," she harangued. "Last night I almost died from palpitations of the heart when I watched my TV set and saw *that lady*." "What lady?" I feigned ignorance. "The one that was here yesterday morning—the one you introduced me to—the one with the funny name for a girl, Johnny."

During one of my California visits to Jane's home in Newport Beach, she asked me to escort her to the houseboat of one of her dearest friends, Claire Trevor and her husband, Milton Bren. Miss Trevor, incidentally, is an exceptionally talented painter. Someone suggested we play some poker. While the game was in progress, a guest arrived whom I recognized to be Rock Hudson. A thought kept recurring: Wyman, Trevor, Hudson. I wonder what the wealth of these three superstars could possibly be. The poker game ended. Five players. Four winners. One loser. Guess who? Me!

Mr. Hudson set out to regale our small party with a typical introduction to a funny story. "Did you hear the one about the queer baseball pitcher?" When we assured him that we had not, the actor turned comedian and began. "A queer baseball pitcher had just walked a man to first base. As he faced the next batter, the homosexual slinger returned to his pitching form. He extended his arms forward and back to his chest and then cocked his head toward first base to assure himself the base runner wasn't taking too much of a lead. He repeated this action five or six times and suddenly walked off the mound, made a complete turn toward first base, placed his hands on his hips and squishily mouthed these tender words to the base runner: 'I love you.' "

Jane is a gracious hostess, ever solicitous for each and every one of her guests. She'll wine and dine you at every opportunity. On one occasion she, Virginia Grey, Helen Grayco and I were motoring toward the new Century Plaza restaurant overlooking the lantern-spangled City of Angels. Suddenly Jane voiced a sergeantlike command: "Tip your hat, Father Bob." I obeyed unquestioningly. It dawned on me there was no church in sight. "I didn't see a church back there—or am I going blind?" I puzzled. "We didn't pass a church, but we did pass Mother Superior's house," Miss Wyman said grinning. "And who is Mother Superior?" I questioned her. "Oh," she giggled, "we always kid Loretta Young calling her 'Mother Superior.' "

In the spacious living room of her Beverly Hills home hangs a hand-painted portrait of Jane as the speechless, frightened young lady of *Johnny Belinda*. In my solitary room hangs a photographed portrait of the same subject—a gift from Janie. It's hard to believe that this fast-talking, fun-loving doll could spend half a year in a school for the deaf, learning the language of the deaf-mute. She still can speak with her hands, if the occasion arises.

Even winning the Oscar was a freak occurrence. The upper echelon at Warner Brothers decided not to distribute the film—it wasn't good enough. But then, what's expected of a Beautiful Lady who calls herself "Jeannie Weenie" and philosophizes to one and all, "Play it by ear, honey"?

WE
CALLED
HIM
"JOHN"

What was the greatest thrill of my life? Meeting Pope John. My sister Jo, diabetically and totally blind for twelve years before her demise, and I made the trip to Castel Gandolfo, the papal summer residence. The journey to Italy was made for only one reason: she wanted to "see" and talk to the greatest Pope of modern times.

His Holiness was late for the audience, which we were told was a consistent Johnine trademark. He could never say "goodbye" to people. As he made his entrance into the grand salon of the Castle, an aide clapped his hands and announced: "His Holiness, the Pope." In my excitement, I left my sister for a fleeting moment to get a better view of the Man. Upon my return, I found my helpless sister blocking the passageway of the papal entourage. Two monsignors—one Italian and one Irish, who spoke Italian with a brogue—were both gesturing for Jo to move. When Pope John asked what was wrong, Monsignor Joseph DeMarco, a family friend, informed him that she was totally blind. Placing his arms around her shoulders, cocking his head to her ear, he said to her: "My daughter, you are blind, but don't ever be discouraged. Someday you will see Light Eternal . . . you will see God forever." As this occurred, my poor sister was still ignorant of the identity of the speaker. She called out to me, "Who is speaking to me, Bob?" "It's Pope John!" Her only response: "O my God!"

At the very outset, the Pontiff apologized to all the pilgrims for the inconvenience he caused us: traveling in the hot Mediterranean sun all the way from Rome. However, he enlightened us: "They tell me this is where the Pope is supposed to be at this time of the year, and here I am." It was a semiprivate audience; about fifty people were present. Now the photographer appeared and the Pope signaled me to place my sister next to him for a photograph. This accomplished, he inquired about my apostolate. My reply was that I had been for many years a home-missioner, an advisory member of the Actors Youth Fund and national chaplain of the American Guild of Variety Artists, a theatrical union. "When you return home, tell all your artist friends that Pope John blesses them."

Pope John and Sis began conversing anew. He asked her name, where she lived, if she had a family. When she told him her name was Josephine, he immediately reminded her, "My name is Joseph also—Angelo Joseph Roncalli." Nugging his elbow against her arm as though she was about to become the recipient of a trade secret, he whispered into her ear: "Do you know, Josephine, people tell you to pray to one saint for this and to another for that. Listen to me: pray to your patron and mine, Saint Joseph. You know, after the Madonna, he is boss up there."

The forty-five minutes vanished. It was time to leave. Once again he turned to Jo, greeting her with the most beautiful, the most inspiring, the most prayerful farewell my ears have ever heard: "Goodbye, Mama Josephine." Speaking to me momentarily, he said: "I know she's your sister but she's also a mama: she told me she has a family in New York." Again his attention was directed toward her. *"Giuseppina, ci vedremo in Paradiso"*: "Josephine, we will meet again in Paradise."

As we were leaving the heavily draped walls of Castel Gandolfo, Jo had one last gem of wisdom to pass on to Monsignor DeMarco and her kid brother. In her finest New Yorkese dialect, she told us: "If I were to drop dead in this room, on this very spot, I couldn't care less. Today my life has been fulfilled. I have spoken to a Saint." I buried Jo exactly one year to the day after she received that heavenly offer from good Pope John. I can visualize the both of them in heaven—John nudging her with his elbow and saying, "Josephine, what did I tell you about Saint Joe being Boss Man here?"

THE
BEAUTIFUL
BUFFOON

On the manicured lawn of the Lewis estate in Beverly Hills, one can expect to find the unusual. To know Jerry Lewis, nothing is unusual. A statue of Moses faces a statue of Saint Anthony of Padua. Moses was a gift from his wife, Patti; St. Anthony was a gift from her husband, Jerry. "It's just insurance, Padre," Jerry observed. "I'm playing it safe—both ends against the middle." Seriously, Jerry has developed a great devotion to the brown-robed Saint of Padua, notwithstanding the fact that he is a faithful member of the Jewish faith. This devotion was due to the influence of his dearly beloved mother-in-law, Mrs. Maria Farina, who lived with the Lewises for many years.

Jerry is a kook. A compassionate, charismatic, sympathetic kook. He will virtually kill himself for a worthy cause, as is evidenced in the annual Muscular Dystrophy campaign. Almost singlehandedly he has sustained the life and growth of this organization. An idealist who knows not the meaning of failure or defeat, an indefatigable worker, Jerry Lewis has raised in the past twenty-one years the awesome sum of eighty-two million dollars for child victims of muscular dystrophy. He is not involved with this organization only one day a year via his Labor Day telethon; rather, he is a part and parcel of this humanitarian crusade to wipe out this crippling disease from the face of the earth. Jerry is as truly and sincerely dedicated to this cause as any priest is dedicated to his God. In recognition of his tireless giving of himself, he was honored with the title "Man of the Year." When the comic first started his crusade against muscular dystrophy in 1951, the challenge to fill a twenty-hour period with celebrities and guest stars was practically overwhelming. Today it is recognized as the outstanding telethon of the year. It is no longer necessary for Mr. Lewis to beg and implore entertainers to make an appearance. Today, the artists themselves, of their own volition, want to be seen in a telethon that is viewed coast to coast by at least forty million people. In fact, some who might be working out of town will gladly suffer the inconvenience of traveling hundreds of miles to make their appearance. I say this with no intent to defame the artists or to accuse them of ulterior pragmatic motives. They give of themselves because they love a worthy cause, especially a cause involving children.

Mr. Lewis has six sons and a lovely, attractive Italian wife, named Patti. I love to call her "Pasqualina," which is the Italian for "Little Pascal," or "Patti." For a period of her single life, she was a band singer in and around the Detroit area, where she was born. Six sons! If money can buy almost everything, it couldn't buy Jerry a baby girl. This one frustration Jerry and Patti suffered for many years. They wanted a girl desperately. On several occasions when Patti was pregnant and about to give birth, Jerry sent notes and even telegrams requesting that I "pray Pink." Evidently, the Divine Dispenser of Babies thought differently.

It has been my privilege and pleasure to visit many of the palatial homes of well-known celebrities. Naturally, they are all beautiful. If, however, I had to choose the most beautiful of all, I would have to say without doubt or reservation, the home of

Jerry Lewis. It is a sprawling, red-brick dwelling with plenty of acreage covered with a multitude of shrubs and greens. A sizable portion of the property is occupied by a gargantuan swimming pool. Let me remind you, in Hollywood the swimming pool is a must. It is as much a visible sign and symbol of success and affluence as the ugly navel is a mark of our humanity. To purchase a house without a pool would be equivalent to buying a chair without legs.

Zany Jerry Lewis? Don't believe it. Canny Jerry? Yes. Never have I studied a more astute businessman, loving husband and tender-stern father. In his dressing room on the Paramount lot, he invited me to his home for dinner. Driving home in his open convertible, he scared the wits out of me with his rambunctious driving. At every red light, people would recognize him and shout endearing epithets. He would respond by screwing up his face and going through one of his routines. During the dinner course, his butler remained standing directly behind me. I couldn't move one eighth of an inch without the butler coming to my rescue with a little touch of this and a little touch of that. Did you know in Hollywood even butlers are judged by pedigree? This Lewis butler was the ex-butler of Jack Benny and Mary Livingston. At this time, Jerry introduced me to one of his dear friends, an up-and-coming actor, Gene Barry. Ironically, the meeting occurred only because Gene wanted his two boys to greet "Uncle Jerry" on the day of their bar mitzvah. Another of Jerry's friends, who impressed me with his quiet, grave and solemn mien, was actor Jeff Chandler. Who could believe within the span of a few years that white-haired young man would be called by his Maker? It is truly soul-refreshing to see these boys of the Jewish faith, known and unknown, stick together, work together and really extend to each other a helping hand. They are truly "God's Children."

During my visit at the Lewis residence, we sat in the spacious living room. Unbeknownst to me, the entire conversation was being taped. I soon learned that Jerry is an absolute genius in the field of electronics and photography. At one point of the conversation he asked if I would like to see a movie. I arose from my chair ready to depart for a studio or a theater. This was not the case. He touched a button and a screen unrolled from the ceiling; pushed another button and half the wall behind me disappeared into the lower wall. There stood the equipment, with an identification mark: LOUIS B. MAYER. The boyish, skinny Jerry Lewis who once worked for Louis B. Mayer as an usher in the Brooklyn Paramount was now the proud proprietor of his former boss's home.

The Lewis' telephone rang, and with a quick scoop of the hand Patti raised the phone to her ear. "Jer, it's for you. Van wants to speak with you." Whoever Van was I didn't know at the time. Jerry kept reassuring Van with affirmative answers: "Surely. . . . Certainly. . . . Why not? . . . I'll do it." Placing the receiver back into its cradle, he notified me, "We have a date tomorrow. We're doing a benefit at one of your places tomorrow—Marymount High School." The caller was Mr. Van Heflin. The reason for the request was that Miss Vanna Heflin had been elected president of the junior class. And Jerry was to entertain the entire school assembly. I sat with Van and Frances Heflin and the Reverend Mother, principal of the school. When Jerry got to the microphone, he stared at it for a few moments. Flowers and balloons beautifully adorned the mechanism. "Who in hell are you expecting this afternoon," Jerry screamed, "Gypsy Rose Lee?" When the laughter subsided, Mother Superior turned to me to politely inquire, "Who is Gypsy Rose Lee?" For one faltering moment I went blank. Then I informed her I wasn't positive of her identity but I thought she might be a leading American ballerina. How do you explain a Stripper to a Sister???

My life has not been a bowl of cherries. But I'll be the first to admit that laughs have far outnumbered the tears. Who can dispute this when one realizes I've spent a good part of my life with the likes of the Durantes, Berles and Buttonses? One of the most hilarious moments of my life occurred in an elegant suite of the Hampshire House overlooking New York's Central Park. Jerry and Patti were the occupants. Some intimate friends were visiting. Jerry either purchased or was gifted with a tiny dog. The breed? My memory fails me, and my knowledge of the canine species is very limited. Jerry placed a large newspaper on the floor, just in case; the animal was far too young to be housebroken. Nature did call, and by a bold stroke of luck and proper direction, the dog urinated on the caricature of one of New York's newspaper writers, not very popular with most showbiz gentry. This gentle outpouring triggered an outburst of hurrahs and plenty of laughter, and a kiss from Jerry's lips to the snoot of the little sharpshooter. I would love to identify the scribe, but the gentleman(?) wouldn't hesitate to place me where so many of my acquaintances are matriculating—behind bars.

When the incomparable team of Martin and Lewis played Jules Podell's Copacabana, I learned that among the zany antics they were performing, they were also selling raffle tickets. This was difficult for me to understand until Jerry explained. It seems they were approached by some Sisters of the Poor and Sick, who operate, among other institutions, an old-age residence on East Fifty-seventh Street in Manhattan. The raffle tickets were for the benefit of the Home for the Aged, and the good, pious sisters were now the employers of the two zaniest salesmen this side of heaven. They were fantastic—charging their friends twenty-five, fifty and even one hundred dollars for a one-dollar ticket. Charging even greater sums of money if the wives of the patrons wished to dance with them. At the end of the Copa run, the good sisters were ten thousand dollars richer and the team of Martin and Lewis ten thousand prayers holier. Maybe this explains their star-spangled success over all these years.

Why the catastrophic break in their relationship when their career was at its peak? Merely and basically a question of vital statistics and characteristics. Jerry was ten years younger; Dean, ten years older. Jerry, ambitious; Dean, phlegmatic. Jerry kept wanting and looking for work; Dean kept wanting and looking for golf courses. At free intervals, between shows or engagements, Jerry would search for new material for the act; Dean would search for a couch for his repose. Jerry would seriously work on new material; Dean would seriously work on new labels. Under ordinary circumstances, with so many contradictory factors involved, it's well-nigh impossible for a husband and wife to live peaceably together; how much more two grown men who spent more time together than they did with their wives and family.

Dean pontificated he would not kill himself with hard work before he reached fifty. By that time, Jerry assumed, they both would be sitting on top of the world without hard work. A glaring example of the Martinesque brand of inertia and quiescence might be gleaned from the following stories. Photographer Marty Mills, onetime husband of Edie Adams, had been appointed to photograph at Dean's home the families of Frank Sinatra and Mr. Martin for the Christmas edition of a national magazine. During the height of the Christmas party, around ten or eleven o'clock, the host furtively left his guests, returned to his bedroom and went to sleep. And Jerry expected this man to jeopardize his health, his life mores and pleasures with hard work?

In those days, Dean harbored a very peculiar idiosyncrasy: he would stroke and comb the nape of his head for hours on end. "What are you doing, Dino?" I questioned him. "Just combing the back of my head. Helps your hair grow." Believe it or not, Dean categorized this exercise as work.

Post Scriptum: Their wives weren't too crazy about each other either.

I was born heir to poverty. I constituted one of the millions God so dearly loves: the poor—because He made so many of us. Many were the times when my young friends and I would pass a deluxe New York restaurant and look in, wondering if the days would miraculously arrive when we'd be sitting in and looking out. My clothes were numbered, cleaned but patched. Jerry Lewis' young life was not unlike mine. Born into a showbiz family, his dad, Danny Lewis, entertained as a vaudevillian, and his family life enjoyed little stability. Jerry bounced from grandparents to uncles and aunts. His heritage was far from affluent. A psychiatrist might allude to both our cases as a tremendous inducement for some psychological traumas to be suffered in adult life.

Whatever the analytical results, Jerry asked me to accompany him to his dressing room. Never in my life have I laid eyes on so many clothes. Closets gorged with suits, slacks, sport jackets resplendent with colors of a rainbow. Dresser drawers crammed with shirts of every type and color, most of them still in their cellophane wrappings. "Jerry," I advised him in brotherly tones, "I've two regrets: Firstly, aside from your tuxedos, you have no black suits. Secondly, you don't wear my size."

Upon his return to the Coast, Jerry was about to move into his new home. He kept thinking about the Sisters on Fifty-seventh Street—their life of dedication to the poor and the sick, God's most forgotten children. Then he decided to do something for them. All the furniture of his old home was crated and at his own expense shipped to New York—to the Mary Manning Walsh Home for the Aged.

As I remarked somewhere in this opus, I frown upon the act of begging. However, there are times in life when the exception proves the rule. The Franciscan Fathers were contemplating the erection of a new seminary in Catskill, New York. The construction price alone would reach the one-million mark. Our superiors pleaded with us to approach our friends for any donation, regardless of the amount. He granted us permission to travel to any part of continental America in the hope of realizing some contributions. I telephoned Jerry, explained my predicament, and he invited me to come to California as his guest.

The next day I found myself in his office on the Paramount lot. "All right, let's get down to business. How much money do you want?" The question left me mute. I found myself saying, "Jerry, this is embarrassing as hell." He in turn suggested, "I'll put up fingers and you tell me when to stop." He put up one finger, then three fingers, and lastly the palm of his hand was facing me with five glorious fingers puncturing the air. "I'll take it," I screamed. I didn't know then that each finger represented a thousand dollars. If you should visit the chapel of Saint Anthony's Seminary in Catskill, New York, you will find an altar dedicated to the memory of Mrs. Maria Farina, his mother-in-law, donated by Mr. and Mrs. Jerry Lewis.

Once I was in Jerry's company, he kiddingly reprimanded me: "So you're a big deal now, you name-dropper. You forgot your old friend." He was referring to my appearance on the *Mike Douglas Show*, where I spoke about Durante, Sinatra, Como, Dino, Bennett, Jerry Vale, Julie LaRosa, Connie Francis, etc. "Only Italians, only Italians," he kept muttering. "You forgot your Jewish friend." "No, I didn't," I assured him, "I mentioned you on several occasions—and furthermore, you Jews don't have a Mafia."

My last visit with Mr. Lewis occurred a short time ago when he substituted for Johnny Carson on the *Tonight* show. His reaction was personally gratifying as he hugged and kissed me on the cheek and reminded his coterie of friends, "This is what I call an old, old friend."

Once again a demonstrable, classical example of Jerry's feelings for children is recorded in his latest business venture. To hell with the verdict of the Supreme Court, to hell with the American bleeding hearts, to hell with the purveyors of smut and pornography; he will defend and protect the American children from the avaricious pockets of the conscienceless American businessmen. Mr. Lewis initiated a chain of movie houses which will exhibit—through his organization—only family films. He stands to make a fortune; he stands to lose a fortune. Nevertheless, he stands to protect and defend the American kids. In the jargon of the business world, these movie houses are franchised by individual owners much as the Howard Johnson restaurants. I'm not particularly interested in financial results. However, I'm acutely absorbed by the spiritual effects that Mr. Lewis' endeavors will produce in America. Jerry needn't worry too much about his children today; they're grown and on their own. If I know Jerry Lewis, and I think I do, it's his grandchildren he's worrying about.

All France loves Jerry Lewis, because all France loves pure, unadulterated buffoonery. The French have always enjoyed a God-gifted propensity for comedy. I can recall as a youngster the roars of laughter and the tears of merriment when we sat in a local theater to watch a typical French-based comedy. Each plot remained unchanged. It was always the cheating wife; her lover dangling by his fingertips from a windowsill ten stories above the ground; the irate husband pounding the bedroom door with a sledgehammer; the short-skirted, leggy little room maid flitting around aimlessly; her counterpart, the innocent bellhop, accused of flirting with the irate husband's spouse, etc. The Comédie Française remains as refreshing and mellow as their exquisite champagnes. In the eyes of the Frenchmen there exists in this world only one living, breathing, genuine comic: Mr. Jerry Lewis. Their Academy of Motion Pictures declared the comic versatility of Mr. Lewis equal to and not one iota below Mr. Charlie Chaplin. To our Gallic brothers, Jerry represents the embodiment, the epitome of the Perfect Buffoon. And if I remember correctly the cliché of my younger days: fifty million Frenchmen can't be wrong. The Beautiful Buffoon!

THE GUILD

Harry Anger and Irving Chezar of General Artists Corporation felt strongly I should be affiliated with a theatrical union. It would lend prestige to my status in the business, they assured me. Mr. Chezar took it upon himself to personally call Mr. Jackie Bright, president of the American Guild of Variety Artists. A law graduate, Irving harangued the president with the tremendous possibilities and potentialities his union would enjoy with a chaplain of Father Bob's caliber. An officers' meeting was summoned and one of the items on the agenda, my appointment. Several days passed when Mr. Bright telephoned and in the most polite language informed me the officers opposed any such assignment. Nothing personal, he rigorously maintained. It seemed some officers felt the act of assigning a chaplain might be considered prejudicial. People professing a different faith might feel offended. The identical reaction would be expected if a Jewish rabbi or a Protestant minister had been assigned. Consequently, I was out of a job I never had in the first place.

THE GUILD

A few months of tomorrows passed on when I was told to visit the AGVA office. Behind a battle-scarred desk sat Mr. President, his smiling face a beacon light of good and benevolent news. "Where the officers rationalized in one manner," he related, "the membership thought differently. At our last annual convention of delegates you've been elected chaplain of the Guild. Now you are truly a unique clergyman. Your flock consists of Catholics, Jews, Protestants and even Hindus and Moslems."

Mr. Bright's tenure as leader of the union sailed on very turbulent seas. The treasury practically depleted, he called on me to help raise funds. I flipped. Here's a voluntary association of variety artists, the greatest names in showbusiness, and I'm approached to entice a Como or another name to perform a benefit for the Guild. Now should I expect a call from the Vatican to extricate a donation from Cardinal Spellman?

Mr. Joey Adams fell heir or victim, whichever you prefer, to Mr. Bright's executive post. Joey's been blessed with a magnetic and dynamic personality. He's a born leader of men. Things began to happen at the Guild. Joey's special apostolate as a union leader was the youth of America. With the aid of friends and annual dinners he accumulated great moneys to be employed for our youth. He immersed himself so totally in his new position, he completely relinquished his career as a comedian. At the time of his election, Joey Adams' name as a comic was as well known as Henny Youngman, Jan Murray, Gene Baylos. During his tenure I commenced attending the Guild's annual delegates' conventions. What a revelation I was treated to! Where supposedly quiet and serenity reigned supreme, in reality the conventions developed into puss-infested boils ready to spit out their maggots. Screams, tirades, shouts, verbal insults, cries of profanity, epithets, on one occasion two men removing their jackets ready to fist-fight comprised the litany of the "fellow workers."

What's wrong with AGVA? What constituted its vital and fragmenting aberration? The answer is simply a lack of money. Such was the desperation for the monetary, the delegates decided to open membership for strippers. "Are they going crazy?" some members wanted to know. "It's sacrilegious," others commented. "We're prostituting ourselves and our union simply for the sake of money. How in conscience can we describe a stripper as an entertainment artist, worthy to be inscribed in the same register as the Fred Allens, Jack Bennys, Jimmy Durantes, George Burnses, Abbott and Costellos, Bing Crosbys and Frank Sinatras, etc., etc. Certainly shaking a derriere from left to right and a bosom from right to left while disrobing does not create an artist. Joey Adams gave of himself selflessly and unstintingly. But like so many good human beings, his efforts were pinned to a cross.

Depending perhaps on his ability of wizardry, the membership elected Mr. Jack Haley to the presidency. My personal relationship with the union during Mr. Haley's tenure was minimal. It consisted primarily in attending a few dinners and pronouncing invocations at some of their conventions. I shall never forget the look of dismay and consternation on the faces of the audience when Mr. Haley, addressing the convention floor, referred to himself as "we stars." Try as I would, I could not contain my laughter when a gentleman seated next to me complemented that remark with a final amen: "Bullshit."

For the past number of years, Danny Thomas holds the title of president, while Penny Singleton controls the administrative helm of the union ship. She achieved victory the hard way. Courts, lawsuits and a fortune of money. The Blondie of the films is a far cry from the Blondie of the Guild. To refine the image of AGVA, now very tainted in the eyes of many members, I suggested to Miss Singleton we produce shows and entertain the servicemen abroad. In this manner we would be accomplishing a twofold benefit: providing work for our members and at the same time providing entertainment for our servicemen. Since this project was my very own creation, Miss Administrator decided I should head it. She further suggested I occupy an office in AGVA's headquarters on New York's Broadway. And also, that I submit a letter for the *AGVA News* announcing our new plans. In fact, she wrote in her own penmanship an outline of a letter I was to write to the Federal Government:

UNITED STATES GOVT—AGVA
SPECIAL SERVICES PROJECT

AGVA—Govt Special Services
Headquarters in Wash., D.C.

clearing all talent and quality of talent for service men throughout the world in order to establish and hold high the entertainment and the cultural aspect of the U.S., plus insuring the service men of top theatre entertainment and performances. [*sic*]

Another meeting with Miss Singleton and the whole beautiful, patriotic, pragmatic scheme blew up in the smoke of defeat. Miss Administrator wanted no part of it.

THE
BROTHERS
FIVE
AND
MARY

While Danny's Hideaway is my East Side rendezvous, Frankie and Johnnie's and Delsomma are my West Side hangouts. Delsomma, Italian as the name denotes, is owned and operated by the brothers five. This is the one solitary time in my life I ever heard of five Italian-Sicilian brothers operating a business . . . harmoniously. An explanation might be forthcoming for the peace and tranquillity that exists among the five sons of Sicilian parentage. Joey, Paul, Frank, Tony and Johnny Cardinale, each of them participated in the art of self-defense. All of them were professional fighters. The patrons, aware of their battle-scarred profiles, never create troubles or scenes. Hence, the peace and harmonious serenity is realized not only amongst the brothers five but also in the restaurant. Tony actually started the business, purchasing his first restaurant directly across from the present Delsomma. He acts in the capacity of manager; Paul handles the floor as floor captain; Joey covers the bar; Johnny specializes in buying and cooking and, finally, Frank fills in as bartender and cook. How's that for family know-how!

Located in the very heart of the theatrical district, as is Frankie and Johnnie's, Delsomma becomes an eating place for many theatergoers and a meeting place for stagehands and employed actors and actresses. When the brothers five completed their banquet hall, a floor beneath the restaurant, they honored me by requesting that I bless the new addition. As I sprinkled holy water around the new room, I noticed a colorful scenario painted on the wall. Among the various figures and objects decorating the wall, I spotted the tiniest painted mouse peeking through a hole. Is that portrait of the mouse to help your patrons' appetite or their digestion? I kidded the owners. One evening, just before show time, I sat alone at the restaurant, my mood pensive and meditative. The weather, hot and humid; I had no place to go; so I sat in the cool comfort of an air-conditioned room. Pleasantly, my eyes fell on a very attractive girl seated opposite me—a very familiar face. I've seen that girl; I've met her somewhere, I kept telling myself. "Paul," I interrupted him as he headed for the kitchen, "do I know that girl?" He grinned sarcastically—a sort of "You rascal, you" grin: "I can't say you know her, but I'm certain you've seen her many times. She's Lee Remick. There's one thing I can say for you, ol' Father Bob. When it comes to clothes and food and . . ." he paused; "you have fine taste."

Frankie and Johnnie's enjoyed a completely different modus operandi. Primarily it is a steak and chop house. Probably the best in the City of New York. A one-man—rather, a one-woman—operation. A one-story walk-up leads you directly into the restaurant—a rather small, sawdusted room. The open kitchen and bar face each other at the rear of the room. The only dangerous spot in the entire place: you're liable to be killed by waiters returning full trays of dirty dishes. The place first functioned as a speakeasy during prohibition days. With Repeal, they hung a sign, FRANKIE AND JOHNNIE, on the West Forty-fifth Street side of Eighth Avenue, converted the speakeasy into a restaurant and went legitimate. On my very first visit to the eatery, I met beautiful Mary

Phillips, the proprietress and widow of John Phillips. Mary and I would sit for hours as she recalled the bizarre history of her restaurant. Notorious gangsters, the biggest in the hierarchy of crime, and outstanding cops, detectives, would sit side by side. Out of dutiful respect for Mary, neither cop nor gangster would carry arms into the restaurant. She literally threw out bums and drunks. Ever a lady, she could outcuss and outscream anyone stupid enough to get entangled with her. No celebrities, be they in the realm of crime, government, films, stage, politics, finances or whatever, ever impressed Mary. You're as good as your money, she philosophized.

One day while spending a quiet evening with my sister in Long Island, the phone rang. "It's for you," Sis said as she handed me the phone. Who would be calling me now? I thought to myself. I've never given anyone my sister's phone number. Furthermore, who would know I'm here spending a little time with my sick and blind sister? "Father Bob," a trembling voice greeted me. "This is Johnnie Philips. It's unimportant how I managed to contact you. My mother [stepmother] is very sick in the Hospital for Joint Diseases. In fact, she's dying." I assured Mary's stepson the hospital was my next stop. My nephew generously offered to drive me. However, rather than return to my rectory to gather the paraphernalia necessary to administer the last rites, I borrowed them from a church closer to the hospital. As I exited from the elevator on the third floor, a nurse at a desk stopped me. "Mary Phillips," I whispered. "With all due respect, Father, you must be kidding. She threw two priests out of her room in the past two days—and they were Irish." "Let me take my chance," I pleaded.

When I entered the room, two nurses stood beside her. One made a mad dash to arrange Mary's gown, because her bosom was exposed. "What are you worried about?" Mary chided her. "Him?" she pointed at me. "He's my love." We embraced as the two bewildered girls gazed at each other in amazement. "Father, I'm going to die." "No, you're not, Mary," I lied. Because of a divorce and a second marriage, Mary had been denied the sacraments for twenty-eight years. Now that she was widowed, Mary enjoyed eligibility. But after so many years, how do you convince someone to tell you the most intimate and revealing facts of one's life? "Mary, do you love me?" "You know I love you, Father." "Will you do anything I ask?" "You know I will, Father." "Just for my sake, will you confess?" A thin smile embraced her mouth. "Why do you think I threw out the other two? I was waiting for you."

Having heard her confession, I promised her tomorrow, at the first opportunity I shall return and bring her the holy Eucharist. The following morning I subwayed to the hospital, bearing the gold watch-shaped pyx containing the sacred species. My journey was not without fear: was she still alive? It was too early to telephone. My return was triumphant when I learned Mary desperately awaited me. I requested the nurse to be at hand with a glass of water. As I placed the sacred Host upon her tongue, tears began to streak her cheeks. She squeezed my hand and kissed it. Holding back the tears, I thanked the nurses and returned home. I waited for the call. Within hours, my phone rang. "Johnnie?" I hesitantly called out, hoping against hope it wasn't him. "Yes, Father" . . . long pause . . . "she's gone." We buried her at Saint Paul the Apostle Church on Manhattan's West Side. After I celebrated the Requiem Mass and escorted the bier to the hearse, I returned to the sacristy to divest. A Paulist Father remarked to me: "I've never seen so many minks and sables at a funeral in my life. Who was she?" "Just one hell of a gal." I smiled my You-can-bet-smile.

Frankie and Johnnie's still operates, with Johnnie Phillips as owner and manager. It's still considered the finest steak and chop house in the city. On any given night you'll find the likes of Paul and Joanne Newman, Bob Goulet and Carol Lawrence, Robert Preston, Mitch Miller, Sandy Dennis, Anne Bancroft. These people you'll recognize. There are many more, also celebrities, you won't recognize.

I WANT
YOU ALL
IN HEAVEN
BECAUSE
HEAVEN
IS A
SWINGING
PLACE

I went to Broadway's Palace to see a Queen: Judy Garland. It was a two-bill affair: comic—intermission—star. The comedian was a young, new entertainer. I say "new" because it was the very first time I had ever seen or heard of him. He was fantastic. Stories about his home, wife, kids, maids, family problems, etc. Every line a belly laugh. No blue lines, no double-entendres: just pure, simple comedy. Another Durante! Impressed by such gifted talent, I penned a note telling him that I had gone to the Palace to see the Queen of Songs and discovered the King of Comedy. His first name is Alan.

One of the strangest missions I have ever undertaken was my role as a private detective. A male superstar of Broadway, London, Hollywood and television, married but separated from his wife, was now seriously dating a very popular vocalist. She called one evening and in between tears and sobs informed me of her qualms of conscience and feelings of guilt. It seems the wife of her boyfriend attempted suicide. Could I possibly verify this? For three frustrating days and nights I called and visited hospitals without success. Finally we learned the whole suicidal drama was a hoax; the wife was alive and well. P.S.: The vocalist married the superstar. P.P.S.: That marriage went the way of all flesh and turned into dust.

I was ushered into the VIP room of American Airlines at LaGuardia Airport. Miss Kay Hanson, an executive of American Airlines, made this arrangement. There sat Tony Franciosa, Tab Hunter and Don Cornell. Their destination was Los Angeles; mine was Newport Beach, about fifty miles south. This distance created much concern among the three of them. Why don't you spend the night at my home and I'll drive you there tomorrow? pleaded Tony. All I have is a hotel room and you're welcome to share it was Don's offer. Stay at my place, suggested Tab.

When we arrived at the Los Angeles International Airport, I went to retrieve my bag while they waited for me. A man, dressed in a chauffeur uniform, approached me, and I identified myself. "Miss Wyman," he said, "has told me to pick you up and take you to Newport." I sighed with relief and asked the chauffeur to do me a favor: "I'll be waiting outside with three other men. Will you please drive the limousine right up to where we are standing? When you open the car door, kindly remove your hat and take a big bow. It's an inside joke. Just like the movies."

He followed his instructions perfectly. The three stood flabbergasted, muttering to themselves. And from the movements of Don's lips, I think he was trying to tell me my parents were never married.

I met Gordon MacRae many, many years ago; in fact, it was at the time he was appearing for the very first time on a Broadway stage. Only recently have I met him again. Tommy Valando, a music executive, invited me to lunch, telling me we would pick up a very young vocalist at the stage door. In a taxicab, Mr. Valando began the ritual of introductions. "Gordon, this is Father Bob. Father, this is Gordon MacRae." Kiddingly, Gordon wisecracked, "You're not going to ask me to do a benefit, are you Father?" Kiddingly, Father answered, "No, Gordon, I only use stars for my benefits."

Michael O'Shea, Virginia Mayo and I walked into Toots Shor's one night after Mike's performance in a Broadway show. Toots is a lovable clown, always kidding and lovingly degrading actors and athletes. If he knows and loves you, the greeting will be "Hi, yu Crum Bum!" This particular night, he told O'Shea, "I've seen your show, and as an actor you stink." Mike reminded him, "I've tasted your steaks, so I wouldn't talk if I were you."

Rocky Marciano was the undefeated champion of the world and the gentlest man I have ever encountered. To have known Rocky is one of the colorful rainbows that has streaked across the skies of my life. Many were the times Rocky and I walked the narrow, winding streets of Greenwich Village or the tree-lined avenues of Boston's Back Bay. He was the champ of the world. From his appearance you could never guess who and what he was. He would raise the collar of his overcoat high against his face so no one could recognize him. His love of God and respect for others inspired all who were fortunate enough to call him "friend."

His life in and out of the ring appeared an absolute contradiction. How can anyone be so meek and so savage, so considerate and so ruthless, so kind and so murderous? On one of our neighborhood strolls, he transgressed one of his rules of life: he spoke about himself. After the twelfth round, he returned to his corner, his nose practically split wide open, and was informed by his trainer the fight was lost. He had to knock out Ezzard Charles or lose the decision. "So I kept repeating to myself, 'Kill him! Kill him. Kill him!,'" he confessed. Charles was pulverized in the following round.

Ed Sullivan managed to contract Rocky for a personal appearance on his Sunday TV show after his fight with Jersey Joe Walcott. Como settled for second best—Jersey Joe. When I met Walcott after his fight with the Rock, I suggested he looked well and healthy. "I'm just glad to be still alive" was his prayerful comment.

Rocky took the count of ten only once in his life—for the Person he so loved and revered: his Maker.

At the Amalfi Restaurant, Barbara Hammond sat forlornly alone. She sang with the Johnny Long band and was now trying to make it as a single. She was a lovely girl—a young Barbara Stanwyck look-alike. Whenever Barbara Hammond found living a little burdensome and felt depressed about the "Don't call me, I'll call you" routine, she would drop in the restaurant and chat with Jimmy Toriello, the Amalfi manager, and some friends. One day a big-name movie producer and his New York representative visited the eatery and spotted Barbara. The representative waved the maître d' to his table to ask if he knew the young attractive lady. Receiving an affirmative answer, he sought an introduction so that the big-name producer could enjoy a pet-mate over the weekend. With an Oh! you little devil grin, the maître d' told them: "Gentlemen, I want you to know a few facts. Firstly, she's not that kind of a girl, I can assure you. And secondly, she belongs to Father Bob's stable, and that could spell trouble."

P.S.: Some years ago I received a letter from Endicott, New York. It was from Barbara's mother, telling me her daughter had been fatally stricken by pneumonia. "He called her."

The ironies of life are sometimes incredibly frightening. Elsa Maxwell was indeed a part of the broad facade of showbusiness. She was the one person welcomed everywhere. A friend of royalty, presidents, heads of state, potentates, titans of industry, the greats and near greats, her life portrayed the very epitome of La Dolce Vita. She held the title as undisputed world's greatest party hostess. Only the most influential, the wealthiest, the most important people on earth could elicit an invitation to one of Elsa's parties. When she died, her body remained for many days in the city morgue . . . unclaimed, unwanted.

A flair for trouble? That spells my name! I assisted at the Jimmy Durante–Margie Little wedding at Saint Malachy's Actors' Chapel in the late afternoon. A reception was held at the Copacabana lounge. After three hours waiting for food, I was informed dinner would be served in another restaurant, since the Copa had to accommodate its regular patrons. By this time I was famished. Connie Francis was appearing at the Copa. It was her dad, George Franconero, who extended the invitation for me to join his party downstairs and get some food.

Suddenly all hell broke loose. Connie hired a photographer to take some shots of her for her new album cover. Mr. Podell, the Copa owner, unaware of the arrangements, had the photographer ejected. Connie and Podell had some sharp words and she walked off. The next day in an interview Connie expressed only one regret about the unfortunate melee: She couldn't sing for Father Bob and his party. The notorious party-thrower made every paper in the country, including the one my boss reads.

For many years—longer than I care to think about—I held the position of Director of the Franciscan Mission Band. A mission band is composed of a group of priests who specialize in public speaking, preaching missions, novenas, retreats, etc. At a public dinner I was introduced as the Director of the Franciscan Mission Band. A woman approached me and excitedly informed me: "Sir, you're wonderful. Not only are you a fine public speaker, but you're also a musician and a bandleader."

We sat in the Roncom Music Publishing office in one of the buildings of the Rockefeller Center complex. Roncom is the abbreviation of Ronald Como, Perry's oldest child. Dee Belline, the singer's brother-in-law; Mickey Glass, the music firm's manager, and I formed the trio. Into the office walked Colonel Tom Parker, one of the greatest managerial names in country-Western music, and opening his briefcase, he presented us with a photograph. It was the picture of a young, handsome man holding a large guitar. He was Parker's latest acquisition, we were informed. An unknown, unheard-of quantity. Tom kidded: "Would you like to buy a piece of his contract? It's for sale, you know." After so many years, I still cannot disassociate the singer's name from an anatomy chart: Elvis Presley.

We were honoring a buddy, Mario Biaggi, the most decorated policeman in America and presently a Congressman from the Bronx. The site was the Boulevard Club in Queens, where the Jewel Box Revue was appearing. The Revue consisted of a dozen female impersonators, heavily made up and endowed with figures that would make most women feel masculine. They always wear pearls with a basic black. Two dear friends, Phil Foster and June Valli, were booked to perform at the testimonial show, while the Revue waited for us to leave the premises and complete the night by appearing at the two A.M. show. Phil and June learned I was in the audience and sent word for me to visit with them. The narrow passageway to the dressing rooms was clustered with the "boys." I was always considered a very slow, awkward runner; in school days I had to hit a double to rate a single. That night I bunted and made first base safely—in fact, by a mile.

Were I to introduce Joey Adams, I would describe him as America's Goodwill Ambassador, comic, author, raconteur, world traveler. To this litany we must add a few new honors and titles. Pope Paul, in the person of Cardinal Yu-Pin of Taiwan, presented Joey with a gold medal and an autographed picture. This prestigious honor was conferred upon Mr. and Mrs. Adams in recognition of their many charitable works in Taiwan. He was further honored with an honorary doctoral degree by the Fu-Jen Catholic University, whose library now bears the distinctive title The Joey Adams University Library. To think it was Joey who initiated my first faltering step into showbiz! I'm proud to call him Friend.

How long does it take to write a hit song? Years, months, days and sometimes minutes. Georgie Weiss, Benny Benjamin and I sat in an office in the Brill Building, known as Tin Pan Alley. Georgie and Benny were toying with an idea about a song for several days. On this particular day I witnessed the birth of a hit song. Georgie sat at a piano while Benny banged the top of the piano with the palm of his hand in perfect rhythm. Suddenly the lyrics were perfect, the music grand, and there was born a song hit of many moons ago, still heard regularly today: "It Was Only a Summer Romance, but Oh What It Seemed to Be."

A popular singer of a few years ago, still in the limelight, possessed a strong penchant for blasphemies. It was always Jesus this and Christ that. One evening it was my unfortunate lot to be seated at a table next to his. For no obvious reason—he was merely participating in a friendly conversation—the litany began. Finally, in an outburst of anger, I strongly suggested, "Why don't you mention the name of someone you know, or maybe talk about a friend?"

On my first visit to Rome, some twelve years ago—I've made two trips in my lifetime—the phone rang in my room at the Hotel Victoria. It was my buddy Harry Guardino, inviting me to visit the countryside location where he was working. Harry introduced me to Martin Ritt, the director; Dino de Laurentiis, the producer, and his costars, Silvana Mangano and Richard Basehart. It was a film of post–World War Two and the punishment inflicted upon Italian girls who had fraternized with the Nazis, shaving their heads down to their scalps. Miss Mangano didn't quite understand my friendship with Harry or my presence on the set. "Who is that priest, Harry?" she questioned him. "He's Perry Como's personal chaplain," he advised her. "I've heard of personal secretaries, valets, managers, representatives, but I've never heard of this. Things must be pretty good in the States when an entertainer can afford to pay a priest to be his personal chaplain," she commented.

The lovely ladies to whom this book is dedicated: my mother and sister Jo, circa 1910.

Perry preaches to a preacher.
Acropolis Photo Studio

"Mr. Nice Guy" and "Miss Nice Girl": Perry Como and Patti Page.

"Come on-a My House," says Rosemary Clooney.

The "King" and I. *Acropolis Photo Studio*

Long ago and far away. *Harry J. Fields*

Seeing eye to eye with Eddie Fisher.
Acropolis Photo Studio

The master of the keyboard, Liberace.
Fay Foto Service, Inc.

The Schnozz.

The "Tennessee Waltz" chanteuse, Patti Page.

With Dorothy Kilgallen and Jerry Vale at the San Gennaro Feast. *Harry J. Fields*

At LuAnn Simms's wedding. Can you spot Merv Griffin?

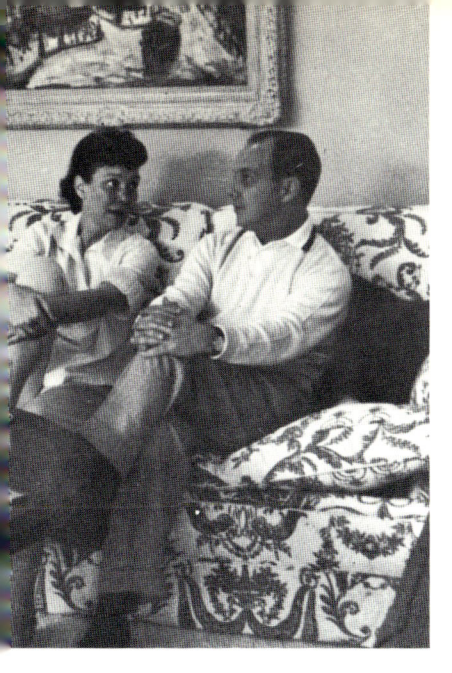

At home with Jane Wyman.

At the Lewisburg Prison benefit with Tony Martin.

Onstage at Lewisburg with Corbett Monica and Tony Martin.

A gathering of funnymen at Marty and Frenchy Allen's wedding.

Let's sing along with Mitch Miller, Pam Drake and Dick Roman.
Peter Chan, A.G.V.A. Fotos

"Pal" Joey Adams, Louis Armstrong and Virginia Graham.

A salute from the Agva Youth Fund to Danny "The Hideaway" Stradella.

Smiling for the camera with Ed Sullivan and Dagmar.   *Peter Chan, A.G.V.A. Fotos*

Sharing the spotlight with the handsome Harry Belafonte. *Photo by Tim Boxer*

Filming on Mulberry Street: Marlon Brando in *The Godfather* and Red Buttons in *Who Killed Mary What's Her Name? Paramount Pictures*

A table full of Hope—Bob and family.

Francis Albert Sinatra. *Joseph LaBella*

With songbird Connie Francis.
Joseph LaBella

There's always laughs when you're with Rocky Graziano and Godfrey Cambridge. *Joseph LaBella*

Backstage with "Engela."
Jack Winer

From left to right: Pat Henry, Ed McMahon, Jerry Vale and Robert Coe. *Joseph LaBella*

Frank Sinatra, Toots Shor and Vic Damone.   *Joseph LaBella*

Richard Conte dressed for his role in *The Brother*. *Michaelangelo Ferro*

Margie Yvonne Theresa Reed, alias Martha Raye. *Morty Morton*

Doing our part at Willowbrook with Ben Vereen, star of *Jesus Christ Superstar* and *Pippin*, and Joey Adams.

Robert "the Animal" Strauss.
Morty Morton

The beautiful buffoon, Jerry Lewis.

At the Rainbow Room with New York's Governor Nelson Rockefeller and Attorney General Louis Lefkowitz.

The handsome and talented James Darren.

The beloved Jack E. Leonard.
Richard Adler, Cashman Photo

Academy Award winner Liza Minnelli and musician Rex Kramer.

"Scooter" Phil Rizzuto and "That's-a Nice-a" Enzo Stuarti.

Frank, Jr.

Tiny Tim and Miss Vicki.

"So, what's the story?" asks Richard Castellano. *Paul Schumach*

President of the MPAA, Jack Valenti. *Paul Schumach*

America's "Toastmaster General," Mr. George Jessel, at his seventy-fifth birthday party. *Whitestone Photo*

Portrait of Jane Wyman in *Johnny Belinda*.

Now I'll take my bow.   *JoAnn Lutrario*

She is Irish, stunningly beautiful and an internationally known movie star. She decided to live in the Eternal City for a while. During this interim, the Beauty started dating a Roman restaurateur who spoke excellent English. She began to suspect his roving, continental eyes were concentrating on her attractive, teen-age daughter. The legend of the Latin Lover has been hailed in prose and poetry, but it doesn't mean a hill of beans to a spitfire Irish lass. In the heat of a name-slinging, catcalling argument, she threw a large bread knife, missing his face by a hair.

When the culprit related his story to me, I questioned his reactions to such an ordeal. "I left Rome for two months and didn't dare return until I was reassured she and her daughter were on their way back to America. Do you know, you can't fool around with these Irish broads," he stammered.

I escorted Mrs. Perry Como to the wedding and reception of comic Marty Allen and his lovely bride, Frenchy. They chose the towering Concord Hotel in the Borscht Belt as the site of their festivities. The choice was wise for two reasons. Firstly, Frenchy worked there in public relations for many years and the reception party was on the house, compliments of the Concord. Secondly, it was the largest wedding and reception I've ever attended. Three thousand friends crowded into the hotel's theater to witness the wedding ceremony. And about twenty-five hundred attended the reception in the main dining room. It looked like comedy's celebrity night: Buddy Hackett, Hal March, Jan Murray, Henny Youngman, Steve Rossi, Martha Raye—everyone was there. When the exuberant Marty asked what I thought of the Concord, I told him the place looked like a mink farm.

The Mayor of New York City, John V. Lindsay, and his wife were invited to an American Guild of Variety Artists testimonial dinner. Hizzoner's party arrived rather late, and Joey Adams, the master of ceremonies, caught sight of him. "Mayor John," Joey declared seriously, "we, the citizens of New York, love you; we hold you in great respect and esteem. In fact, such great respect and esteem that we named four hundred rooms in this hotel in your honor."

Lunching at Delsomma's Restaurant with Joe Lombardi, long-time bandleader at the defunct New York Latin Quarter, the maître d' sat four lovely, well-dressed women at a table directly in front of ours. One of them recognized Mr. Lombardi and called out his name. He in turn introduced me, and at the mere mention of my name, one of the fair creatures excitedly cried out: "Oh! you helped me to get married. I'm Mrs. So-and-so."

It's a small world, getting smaller by the missiles. Some years ago I was stationed in an upper New York parish. The phone rang and the long-distance operator told me there was a person-to-person call from New York City for Father Bob. The caller, his voice quivering with mixed emotions, glad to be speaking with me and angry because of the nature of his call, says: "Hi, Father. I'm having one hell of a time trying to get married down here. There are a couple of your fellow workers giving me nothing but trouble."

The phone bill must have been a healthy one. The conversation seemed interminable. I calmed him down and proceeded to explain step by step the procedure he must follow. His second call informed me that all went well and wedding bells would soon be breaking up that old gang of mine. Today Dottie and Don Adams are happily married and are parents of two youngsters. Yes, it was Dottie who called out, "Oh! you helped me to get married."

It was the Christmas season. Rosemary Clooney phoned to inquire if any large outdoor mangers were in my vicinity. Her children wanted to see the Baby Jesus in His crib. I told her there was such a crib in Greenwich Village. When we arrived at Saint Anthony's Church, we started our pilgrimage by viewing the outdoor manger and then visiting the church. Upon leaving, Rosemary spotted an Italian cheese store directly opposite the church and decided to do some shopping. The scent of such an establishment is not always too inviting. Her youngest son, obviously offended by the smell, cried out: "Let's go home, Mom. It stinks here." Rosie's face flushed with the redness of the flower whose name she bears.

Steve Lawrence called. We discussed the possibility of using the intricate, lacelike electrical fixtures that span from one side of the street to the other, annually employed during the San Gennaro Feast on Mulberry Street in Manhattan's Little Italy. Such a scene would make a perfect background for one of his weekly television shows. Steve appeared on Mulberry Street with his crew and guest stars including Connie Francis; Louis Prima; his wife, Gia; Sam Buttera and the Witnesses. The entire show reflected a kaleidoscope of things Italiano—even a chariot driven by a Roman gladiator and ridden by Miss Francis. The entertainers wore tuxedos and evening gowns. When Steve suggested lunch, I recommended Luna's Restaurant, directly across from the rectory. Visualize the scene: Wednesday afternoon, around two-ish . . . men in tuxes . . . women in gowns . . . followed by some twenty technicians . . . all tramping into a small, neighborhood Italian restaurant. At the sight of this procession, Annie D'Onofrio, a local waitress, yelled out in an exasperated voice, "Don't tell me it's another Puerto Rican wedding right in the middle of the week!"

I sat in one of Rudy, the barber's, chairs in the Warwick Hotel. He suggested that I and the gentleman seated next to me should meet—we have so much in common. He was Billy Rosen, the proprietor of the famous East Side steak house, Gatsby's. As I was about to leave, Mr. Rosen asked if I had a moment to spare—he wanted to speak with me. He was dating an Italian girl from Los Angeles, the widow of a bandleader and mother of a large family. Because he was of the Jewish faith, would he have any trouble marrying in the Catholic Church? "No trouble at all," I encouraged him, "unless there exists some impediment of which I am ignorant. Incidentally," I conjectured, "would this young lady be Miss Helen Grayco, the widow of Spike Jones?" "My God, this man is clairvoyant," was his startled reply. Not really; you see, Helen asked the very same questions when I first met her at the home of Jane Wyman.

The motion-picture industry tendered a testimonial dinner to Joseph E. Levine and appointed Cary Grant to be the principal speaker. The locale of this glittering assembly was the Main Ballroom of the Americana Hotel. I was flattered with the reception of two complimentary tickets.

Beautiful, red-haired Louise O'Brien of the Mitch Miller Show had generously accepted my offer to sing for the Dominican Sisters' benefit at the Gun Hill Manor in the Bronx. The entire cost of the benefit is absorbed personally by the proprietor, Joseph "Sonny" Ventola. Because of her graciousness, I thought Louise was deserving of a good dinner and a night on the town. I invited her to the Americana, and she accepted.

That evening I waited for her in the spacious, marbled lobby of the Americana. I noticed two young men in their early twenties leisurely taking in all the sights, including a good amount of girl-watching. When Miss O'Brien made her entrance looking like something out of *Vogue*, the two men reacted with a single word: "Wow!" Louise approached me, pecked me on the cheek, asked about my well-being while the men were getting bug-eyed. As we passed them, I politely greeted them with a single line: "Eat your hearts out, fellers."

While engaged in a conversation, Harry Belafonte was excoriating a white musical conductor. "Where in the hell were you when my people were on the cotton fields?" Harry demanded. The conductor pondered the question for a few moments. "Let me give you a bit of information, Harry," he began. "If you're talking about That Garden near Jerusalem and That Crown made of thorns, I'll plead guilty. But when it comes to cotton fields, leave me out."

The locale is Venice, California. The household, modest and nondescript. As I made my entrance into the dwelling, it seemed as though a cyclone had struck. Welcomes, kisses, embraces. One young girl transferred her baby brother into the arms of a younger sister and put the coffeepot on the fire. Another prepared the table. Still another sliced pieces of cake and placed them on a platter. The family that prays together stays together. I was in the home of Bill and Ciss Lennon and their wonderful family: eleven hardy, healthy, handsome children. The younger members of the brood, the professionals, sang a number of songs for me a cappella. When I asked Bill what his plans were after the older TV Lennon Sisters married and had their own families, with his twinkling Irish eyes he winked a fast answer: "I've plenty of help in the dugout."

What a senseless shame, what a priceless loss that the life of such a devoted husband and loving father should be snuffed out by a maniac.

It was ten minutes before the curtain-opener of the Vic Damone–Pat Henry concert at Carnegie Hall. "Do you have tickets?" Pat inquired. When I gave a negative answer, he presented me with his last two tickets. "Keep one for yourself and give the other to someone," he suggested. I met a young boy about fourteen, standing on Fifty-seventh Street, dressed rather shabbily, wearing white sneakers. At first he refused the ticket, thinking I was depriving myself. When I assured him it was an extra from Mr. Henry, he accepted. He went to his seat; I returned to the dressing room. It was curtain time when I presented my ticket to an usher and he jockeyed me to my seat, front row, center. There sat the young boy, his face beaming and radiating with joy. "Hey, Father," he exclaimed, "I never had a seat like this in my life. I should be wearing a tuxedo! And look at me, with a broken-down lumber jacket and dirty sneakers." "Where did you get the jacket and sneakers?" I asked. "I bought them with money I made shining shoes after school." "In other words, you got them honestly," I reminded him. "I had to polish a hell of a lot of shoes," the youngster advised me. "Do you know, son, there are many people here this evening dressed in silk-mohair suits, embroidered shirts, imported ties and handmade alligator shoes who cannot make that same statement about honesty?"

Jackie Gleason was in his typical gay, boisterous, painless mood as Father Michael and I entered Toots Shor's restaurant for dinner many years ago, long before the Great One decided to live in Florida. Mike was a young lieutenant in the United States Army; today he is a lieutenant colonel stationed somewhere in Italy. Jackie invited us to his table for a drink. Joe DiMaggio had just left. It seems the waiters were all so preoccupied, Gleason couldn't catch the attention of one of them. In a burst of understandable anger, he shouted loud enough to be heard five blocks away, "Hey waiters, how about some booze for these two good priests?" Jackie reminded us when a waiter dies the gravestone's inscription should read, THE LORD FINALLY CAUGHT HIS EYE.

The world of magic has always fascinated me. The great Houdinis of the stage have always held a special spot in the heart of audiences everywhere. Now, I'm aware of the wisdom of stage directors in placing the magician at the top of the bill. There is hardly an act that can captivate an audience with greater precipitancy than the magic-man. Some possess such dexterity of hands and concentration of mind, they're capable of breaking the magic spell of a diner and a luscious filet mignon. This is precisely what occurred at Gallagher's restaurant in New York. The svelte of hands is Doc Marcus. He presented me with a deck of cards, telling me to take one card, show it to my dinner companions and return the card into the deck. I removed one card, decided against it and asked for another, unseen by Doc. I drew the ace of spades. Now he had the entire deck in his hands. Then he threw the fifty-two cards against the wall. All came tumbling down; only one remained hanging on the wall: the ace of spades.

It would prove a much easier task to group-psychoanalyze any other strata of humanity than the entertainer. He is unpredictable. He is impossible. Al Jolson is probably more deserving of the sobriquet "Mr. Showbusiness" than any other artist who ever walked, talked or knelt across a stage. In death he willed a massive fortune to the three great religions, Catholic, Protestant and Jewish. Yet, I'm told, he suffered from an intense jealous phobia, almost bordering on the psychotic. A tremendous ovation for another artist would create the sound of a death rattle to his ears.

Take the case of another talented artist, Woody Allen. He has participated in every phase and facet of the entertainment world —movies, TV, concerts, nightclubs, etc. Music is also his forte. Nowadays Woody joins a band two and three nights a week, playing his clarinet, in some of the worst honky-tonks in the city, without pay. One hotel offered him a staggering price to play their main room and he refused. But he continues to play the honky-tonks two and three nights a week—for free!

Robert Strauss is a prodigious performer, having worked in numberless films, notably in the role of a character actor. In *Stalag 17*, in the role of "Animal," he reached the zenith of his professional ability with the rewarding accolade of being chosen a contender for an Oscar as best supporting male actor. Bob suffered one insufferable problem. Another actor, a has-been on the road of the ethereal comeback, enjoyed the same, identical recognition. His role in *From Here to Eternity* was that of a smart-aleck Italo-American soldier fighting and dying in World War II. After the final count, Mr. Francis Albert Sinatra enjoyed the winner's post.

I have been in Bob's company on countless occasions. On one of these, he described me as the Goodwill Ambassador of the Church to Showbiz. He further extended the good-natured tirade by informing the audience I attended so many theatrical banquets, he was convinced I only heard the confessions of waiters, cooks and hatcheck girls. When someone observed Strauss was the only person of the Jewish faith in the entire assemblage, he cautioned them, don't knock it. "Without my people, you wouldn't even have a God to pray to."

The scene was very much Hollywood-ish, except for the fact the locale was Las Vegas. Eight hundred guests, biggies and nonbiggies, gathered around the giant swimming pool of Caesar's Palace. The occasion was a barbecue party in honor of Nancy Sinatra's opening. A short distance away a Latin band filled the torrid Nevada air with the sounds of mambos and cha-chas. The music sounded strangely familiar. Could that be Pupi—Pupi Campo? "That's precisely who it is," someone reassured me. The sight of the ubiquitous straw hat removed all doubts. "Do you recognize me, Pupi?" I questioned him. "Should I?" was his reply. "I think you should." Again he inquired, "Why should I?" "Because it was I who put you and Betty Clooney together in marriage." Clutching me in a typical Latin bear hug, he cried out: "Oh yes! You're Father Ba . . . Ba . . . Ba . . . Baaba," in his finest Cuban accent.

My sister Jo called asking me for two tickets to see Rex Harrison and Julie Andrews in *My Fair Lady*. The fact she was totally blind did not alter the situation one iota. She wanted to "see" *Fair Lady*. Her zest for life was prodigious! The remaining ticket was for her husband. My brother-in-law spent a lifetime as a hardworking, superbly gifted tailor. In an entire lifetime he worked for only two firms, Hattie Carnegie and, when it closed, Christian Dior. Notwithstanding the many years he spent in America, having left Italy as a young man, he could never master the English language. He spoke with a heavy-accented dialect. On the day of the matinee I cornered him and strongly suggested he explain to my sister the different events occurring onstage. After the performance, my sister exited from the theater with a broad, smiling face and he with the look of helpless chagrin. "He was supposed to help me," she taunted him. "He went crazy with Julie Andrews' Cockney accent; he didn't understand a word she spoke."

We were enjoying a congratulatory cocktail at Danny's—Bobby Vinton; his pregnant wife; Lee Solomon of the William Morris office; I and a few friends. Lee had just conveyed the happy tidings: Bobby was accepted to play a role in John Wayne's next picture, *The Million-Dollar Kidnapping*, to be filmed in Durango, Mexico. He would portray the role of Wayne's youngest son who is kidnapped at the very inception of the film. "Too bad, Bobby," someone complained; "your part will only last about thirty minutes." To which I interjected: "Making a picture with Wayne, even if the part is only thirty minutes, would be equivalent to a role of three hours with any other character in the business. That's how great the Duke is!" Bobby expressed his assent with a nod of the head and a single word: "Amen."

Miss Jacqueline Petite is a ballerina, a darn good one at that. She's traveled the world, pirouetting her way through life. A few years ago she moved to Mexico—Acapulco, to be specific. Jackie is one-hundred-percent girl: delicate, refined, feminine, a veritable Miss Petite. Yet some of her escapades are incredible, the antithesis of anything delicate, refined, feminine or petite.

There is an area in Acapulco called La Quebrada—a wooded, mountainous spot where young men dive one hundred thirty-five feet into a shallow inlet body of water. The peril of this particular brand of diving is not so much the height but the jutting, jagged rocks and the undulations of the seawater. As the waves roll in, the water reaches its fullest height; seconds later, as it recedes, it measures its lowest. Hence, it requires absolute perfect timing; otherwise, outside of death, the least calamity to be suffered would be a fractured neckbone or a broken back. Jackie had some natives teach her, starting from the lowest possible height, ascending each day until she reached the pinnacle. She made the La Quebrada dive on a thousand-dollar bet. It wasn't the money, she assured me; it was the challenge. "What's next, Jackie?" I inquired. "Bullfighting," she oléd.

At a benefit show held at the Felt Forum of the new Madison Square Garden, I passed by one of the dressing rooms. There was Toots Shor posing for the photographer with the PJ's, Paula and Jean, his arms gingerly wrapped around waists. At the sight of me, Toots yelled: "Forgive me, Father. I just happen to love beautiful women." It was about a half-hour later in the same dressing room that I and the PJ's were posing for the same photographer with my arms gingerly wrapped around them when Toots passed by. This time I was the culprit who yelled: "Forgive me, Toots. I don't hate them either."

Jack E. Leonard and I taxied to Doctors Hospital. The journey was intended for a dual purpose: to visit LuAnn Simms and her newborn baby girl and Eydie Gormé and her newborn baby boy. Loring Buzzell and Steve Lawrence, the proud fathers, were dispensing cigars. As I placed my hand into my inside jacket pocket for my cigarette pack, Eydie gently pointed to a printed sign above her bed: PLEASE, NO SMOKING IN THE ROOM. It was signed: MR. DAVID. I was befuddled. "I just came from LuAnn's room and don't recall any such prohibiting sign. How come?" Eydie proudly pointed to her son and said, "His name is David."

Joe and Rose's is a great eatery on New York's Third Avenue. It is managed by the brothers two, Freddy and Rusty. Mama Rose supervises the kitchen. Papa Joe died many years ago. This was our hangout every Saturday night after the Perry Como TV show. We would gather there, Perry, Dee Belline, Mickey Glass, Mitch Ayres and some friends, usually golf greats. One evening we were discussing Perry's new contract with Kraft involving astronomical figures. After dinner, we proceeded through the usual Saturday ritual: a handshake with Freddy and Rusty, a kiss on Mama Rose's cheek, a few parting words outside the restaurant and the gang would step into Como's Caddy and off to home. This particular evening, when I put my hand into my pocket for cab fare, I found I had only forty-five cents. I walked to Forty-second Street and Third Avenue and took a crosstown bus for fifteen cents to Saint Raphael's, located at Forty-first and Tenth Avenue. What is the moral of this story? You don't have to be a millionaire to live like one!

Paul Newman is not aware of this incident. He; his wife, Joanne Woodward, and another couple sat at a table directly in front of ours, not three feet away, at Frankie and Johnnie's restaurant. Mr. Newman was furious, shouting obscenities. It seems the box office of the theater at which he was appearing ignored or forgot to reserve two tickets in his name. We were not eavesdropping; the room is tiny, and Newman's voice was loud. I sat with three friends who are completely unimpressed by glamour dolls or movie stars. They bitterly resented the actor's language because, they thought, his proximity to the Roman collar demanded more common courtesy and respect. Their tempers were escalating so rapidly I literally had to plead with them not to create a scene. I transgressed every proper technique of eating; very little mastication, very much swallowing. My ultimate goal was to leave the premises as soon as possible. Otherwise, Mr. Newman would have found himself in another Hollywood barroom brawl, but with a few exceptions: no script and no stand-ins.

Louis Armstrong was King for the night. Carnegie Hall was his domain. The American Guild of Variety Artists had chosen Louis as the outstanding performer of the year. Every star within striking distance of New York made an appearance to honor Satchmo. Among them I met a new artist from England, at that time appearing at the Copacabana, dressed in a belted white jumpsuit, matched with white boots, and his long hair knotted into a pony tail. "How are you, sir?" he greeted me. "My name is Tom Jones."

The theatrical critic is a surgeon; he holds the power of life and death in his scalpel, the pen. It is unfortunate that one man must decide for so many; even more unfortunate that the public cannot decide for itself. At first I was skeptical about this pseudo power until I personally witnessed a first-class surgical homicide. Gloria De Haven invited me to an opening of an Off Broadway play in which she had the lead. It was an innocuous, small-priced musical entitled *Have I Got One for You*, wherein each actor impersonates an animal and, love conquering all, two croaky frogs fell in love, married and lived happily ever after. It should have been a perfect vehicle for children from seven to seventy. After the performance the entire cast and I waited patiently in a restaurant for the eleven o'clock news with its drama critic. He appeared just as I occasionally do—at the graveside with the purple stole of mourning around my neck, the black funeral prayerbook in hand, ready to lay someone to their eternal rest. *Requiescat in pace!*

Tommy Valando, music publisher, is a winner. In the world of music they say Tommy has a "nose" for picking hit songs and great talent. Thirty years ago he was one of the few to recognize the tremendous potential of young Perry Como. He exerted much influence in the career of Gordon MacRae. Today he hasn't lost one iota of that intuitive, indefinable quality that qualifies him to predict, "It's a hit song" or "He'll make it big." Many were the names Tommy prognosticated for stardom and many the names he prophetized would never reach the heights.

Some years ago, Tommy met two writers, one a musical composer, the other a lyricist. He signed them immediately to a contract. Why the urgency? They hadn't written any compositions of worthwhile value; they were merely two names in the vast and turbulent sea of Broadway's composers and lyricists. Intuition! That sixth sense that makes Tommy tick. Years passed and the two gentlemen were neither productive or very successful. Nevertheless, his faith in these two men remained totally blind and unshakable. He knew something would happen—someday. It did! On September 22, 1964, at the Majestic Theater, Sheldon Harnick, composer, and Jerry Bock, lyricist, presented for the first time their musical composition *Fiddler on the Roof*.

Virginia Mayo is a very beautiful woman today. Can you imagine her beauty fifteen years ago? I met Virginia through her husband, Michael O'Shea, who at that time enjoyed nationwide popularity. Mike had starred in a powerful Broadway vehicle, *The Eve of St. Mark,* and as a result Hollywood picked up his option. One day I was strolling along Park Avenue and ran into Virginia and Mike as they exited from Delmonico's Hotel. "Where are you heading?" O'Shea inquired. "No place in particular; I'm merely exercising," I small-talked. "Good," he impatiently gasped. "Will you accompany Ginny? I have an appointment with my agent." I suddenly find myself the escort of this lovely baby-blue-eyed blonde.

I asked Ginny where we were heading as we made ourselves comfortable in a taxicab. Abercrombie and Fitch, she directed the driver. Once we arrived at that venerable emporium, Miss Mayo walked a few steps in front of me into the sweater department. Not until that moment did I ever realize how women test the size, color and attractiveness of the article. They place the sweater across their shoulders and let it gently fall over their chests. Nothing risqué about that! Except each time Ginny tried a sweater, she would ask, "How does this pink look on me, Father?" and "How does this blue look on me, Father?" Suddenly I realized the whole place—managers, clerks, customers and maybe Messrs. Abercrombie and Fitch—were looking at Father. Even my collar turned red!

A star-sprinkled dais with Lauren Bacall, the music-writing team of Betty Comden and Adolph Green, movie mogul Spyros P. Skouras, song-spinners Jule Styne and Harold Rome, columnists Earl Wilson and Louis Sobol, Corbett Monica, Robert Alda, Lionel Hampton, sport figures Jack Dempsey, Jake LaMotta and Elston Howard, with M. C. Joey Adams . . . all gathered together to honor Mr. Joe Kipness, producer of the Broadway smash hit *Applause* (Best Musical of 1970 and three more Tony awards) and another hit of the past, *High Button Shoes.*

Each of these celebrities took a turn at the microphone with a rating of great, good, fair, indifferent. However, Elston Howard made the biggest hit of all as he unwittingly perpetrated the biggest faux pas of the evening. Facing a pitcher with a bat on his shoulders and seventy thousand rabid fans in the Yankee Stadium was all in the course of a day's work for the ex–Yankee catcher. But facing an audience of fifteen hundred in black tie and evening gown is quite a different story. When introduced, Elston faced the gathering and nervously began speaking. He had come to the Americana Hotel to praise Joe Kipness. He and Joe were very close, dear, intimate friends. In fact, he recalled only a few nights ago, attending the Muhammad Ali–Oscar Bonavena fight at the Garden, in the company of his own wife, Joe Kipness and his wife, and Mr. So-and-so and his . . ." Elston stopped. He was groping for a word which mysteriously escaped him. "Mr. So-and-so and his . . ." He stood at bat with two strikes and no balls. Finally he struck out. "Mr. So-and-so and his MISTRESS." Joey Adams quickly came to the rescue, informing the shocked audience the word "mistress" was a slip of the tongue. What Elston originally intended to say was "governess."

The Troy, New York, Police Department approached me with the hope of packaging a show for the benefit of their Police Benevolent Association. They were willing to pay the artists. However, they felt employing me as the liaison man would save them a few dollars. We managed to contract Tony Bennett; the beautiful songstress of the Mitch Miller show, Louise O'Brien, and an up-and-coming Como regular, Don Adams. With a lineup so potent in talent and magnetism, it caused practically every member of the police force to fall victim to the dual French epidemic of laissez-faire and ennui. On the day of the attraction only one-half or one-third of the entire house, seating seven thousand, was sold. It reminded me of the old gag: I know you're out there; I can hear you breathing. Of all the shows I've ever seen, this was the most tragic. While Don was entertaining the audience, a large, deafening, almost catastrophic-sounding crash occurred backstage. For a moment, there was a deadly silence, everyone fearing the worse. Don faced his audience and wryly informed them, "I want you to know some cop just shot himself backstage."

The cameras were grinding; huge spotlights flooded the set. Terry Moore was in the throes of impersonating a girl who was about to leave her jail cell and walk the long last mile to the electric chair, as I sat with Al Simms on the American-International Films lot. At this point an actor enacting the role of a priest was supposed to enter the cell to offer her the solace and comfort of religion. "O.K. We're ready," someone yelled at me. The remark went completely over my head. "Hey, we're ready," came the second blast. Then I realized he mistook me for the actor who was to portray the priest. "You're mistaken, sir," I quivered. "I'm for real."

Mention Radio City Music Hall and practically everyone will tell you it is located in Rockefeller Center. Most people, however, are unaware there was another theater in the original construction of the Rockefeller Center complex. It was called the Centre Theater, located on the southeast corner of Forty-ninth Street. Unlike the Music Hall, the Center presented lavishly costumed ice shows. When this project failed, the theater was converted into a television studio.

It was here, in the company of Jimmy Durante, that I first met Danny Thomas, who had just completed one of his initial NBC-TV appearances. And it was Danny who referred to this new medium as the "bloodshot, one-eye monster." On another occasion at the same theater I sat backstage with Durante. The show had ended, and I found myself congratulating the irrepressible, lovable Miss Martha Raye, who at the time was enjoying a well-deserved drink. The moment she spotted me, she laid the glass down and absolutely refused to drink in my presence. Nor could I convince her otherwise. Moments later, someone handed me a drink. With glass in hand I visited Martha's dressing room. The sight of me standing there with a Scotch-

and-water in my hand caused Martha to grab her glass. "Well, if the Pope can drink, so can I," she blurted out, twinkling her laughing Irish eyes.

Charlie Rapp, the high priest of theatrical bookers in the mountain resort area, arrived at Danny's Hideaway with a gorgeous black-haired beauty hanging on his arm. I was reminded of this meeting when I caught a TV rerun of James Coburn in *Our Man Flint*. This young lady enjoyed the co-starring female lead in that flick. As we sat in Danny's bistro—Charlie, Gila Golan and I—the conversation meandered to religion. A Kent rested between my fingers, a Dewar's-and-water glistened before my eyes, as Miss Golan began the interrogation. "Are you permitted tobacco in your religion?" "Yes, with moderation," I replied. "Are you permitted alcohol?" "Yes, with moderation," I repeated. "But you are not permitted marriage and sex as a priest?" "No, not even with a little moderation," I regretfully informed her.

The Monticello is a sprawling, attractive supper club in Framingham, Massachusetts. When I arrived in Boston, on a speaking engagement, I learned Caterina Valente and her brother, Silvio, were appearing there; in fact, it was the night of their final appearance. This lovely, vivacious young lady, who lives in Switzerland, is a Talent. She is a singer, musician and dancer par excellence. Very few artists, male or female, can top her. She also speaks a half-dozen languages. As she was signing off with her final number, walking the semicircular stage, she sang "Auf Wiedersehen" in a variety of languages. I sat at a table alone, completely segregated from the others, courtesy of the management. When she arrived directly in front of me—there was no other person in sight—she transferred the microphone from her right to her left hand and threw a kiss, greeting me, "Ciao, Padre" —"Goodbye, Father." One thousand pairs of perplexed and bewildered eyes were focused on me. It was then I wished the management had not been so courteous.

On the same sojourn, another friend was working the opposite end of town, Revere. I asked a priest friend to drive me to the club. When we arrived, Janice Harper was rippling through the scales. A knock on the door and I was embraced in an outburst of enthusiasm. She suddenly turned and said, "Please zip me up." Perplexed, the priest whispered, "I didn't think you knew her that well." "THAT well I don't know her," I reassured him.

Trying to be a nice guy often spells trouble. I've had many such incidents. Here's one. Jewish boy, Catholic girl want to be married. Jewish parents demand the rabbi; Catholic parents demand the priest. Why not compromise? I suggested. Be married in church by a priest; be blessed at the reception by a rabbi. "But we don't know any rabbi personally," complained the Jewish parents. "Maybe, Father Bob, you can get us a rabbi?"

I have been asked many favors, but never to go rabbi-hunting. I called the Actors' Temple unsuccessfully; tried a few other channels and failed. Then the miracle occurred. Seated at a table at Danny's Hideaway, I found my neighboring diner to be Totie Fields. When I asked if she knew of a rabbi personally, she practically screamed, "Father, have I got a rabbi for you!" The finale of this "Abie's Italian Rose" love story: The Jewish boy and the Catholic girl are man and wife. They were united by me in marriage in a church; they were blessed by Rabbi Arnold Kaiman at the reception. I wonder if they will name one of their kids "Totie."

Andy Williams' career was about to burst wide open. He had been called to California, with a film career only a signature away. Learning of the impending journey, I telephoned him and asked a favor. "Would you kindly carry a book with you and give it to Nancy Sinatra, Jr., with all my love?" I politely requested. He said he would. Returning to New York, it was his turn to call. "The next time," he reminded me, "you ask me to carry a book to California, I'm going to charge you by the pound." The book referred to was a Bible containing well over a thousand pages and weighing a ton.

We sat at a table in Max Asnas' Stage Delicatessen, Joey Bishop and I, tasting Jewish delicacies. Max was a delightful, patriotic man. He hated two things in life: Communism and Communists. Where but in America could an uneducated, immigrant bum like me make such a fortune? he would inform anyone willing to listen. Joey and I lunched at this eatery frequently. On this occasion a man spotted Joey and came to our table to say hello. He then noticed my Roman collar and did a double-take. "What are you doing with a priest?" he asked Joey. To which Joey replied, "What's so unusual about a Bishop talking to a priest?"

Nancy Sinatra, Jr., swears till this very day that I was responsible for Tommy Sands's proposal of marriage. Whenever she visited New York I would act as her chaperon. It usually entailed a round of theaters and restaurants. Tommy knew there was another gentleman involved in this triangle but couldn't figure out his identity. One afternoon, after a matinee, Tommy called from the Coast, when Nancy told him she had been to the theater with a friend, Tommy popped the question. Later she informed him her New York escort wore a Roman collar. Unfortunately, Nancy and Tommy's union was dissolved, but Nancy is now happily married to Hugh Lambert.

At Cindy Adams' birthday party, tendered by her husband, Joey, I met an attractive Italian vocalist who originates from South Africa and is married to an Englishman. "This is Donna Valery," Mrs. Adams introduced us. The name sounded vaguely familiar. Then it struck me: "Oh, yes—you're the sister of Sergio Franchi." "Oh, no," she responded; "Sergio Franchi is my brother."

I like the boyishness of Eddie Fisher. I have always found him to be a very respectful young man. As often as we meet, his greetings are always warm and affectionate. During his marriage tenure with Elizabeth Taylor, we met many times in various places, even in the home of Jerry Lewis in Beverly Hills. On each meeting, Eddie would put his arms around me and inquire of his beautiful wife, "Honey, you remember Father Bob?" No, she didn't think we had ever met. Once, twice, three times; it became a story with the same monotonous ending. Finally we met again one night at Danny's restaurant. Seated at the celebrity table were Liz and Eddie, Natalie Wood and Robert Wagner. At a table next to them sat Dinah Shore and George Montgomery. Dinah greeted me with a big cheeky kiss. Eddie jumped to his feet, again put his arms around me and on this occasion asked *me* if I knew his wife. "I don't think we ever met before," I lied. "Certainly we did, Father," Liz reminded me. "The time was at Jerry's home in Beverly Hills." A diabolical grin crossed my face as I bade them, "Good night, friends."

It was past midnight and I was fighting drowsiness. I wanted to stay awake to watch my buddies, Tony Bennett and Don Adams, on the Johnny Carson show. I succumbed and fell gently into the tender arms of Morpheus. In my sleep I kept hearing the name "Father Bob . . . Father Bob . . . Father Bob." I awoke in a jolt, beads of sweat caressing my face. For one fear-packed moment I thought it was the Almighty calling me home. I looked around the room in a daze. My only companions were the darkness that engulfed me and the tiny glow of the night light. As the stupor of sleep went, I realized it was the TV set with Tony, Don and Johnny talking about Father Bob, Father Bob, Father Bob.

Andy decided to leave the Williams Brothers and do it as a single. Maybe the chances were better. There were quite a few groups making the scene, such as the Ames Brothers, the Mills Brothers, the Four Lads. Andy's route was typical of most vocalists: the broken-down run-of-the-mill roadhouses, usually referred to as "toilets," to the more sophisticated nightclubs and supper clubs. Then on to the hottest of all media, television.

It was as a guest star on the Como show that I first met collegiate-dressed Andy Williams. Two young ladies, friends from Worcester, Massachusetts, were my guests at that particular show. They were avid Como fans. There wasn't another singer in the entire world, only the Canonsburg Camelot. I asked if they were interested in meeting Andy and their reply was vehemently negative. Andy either caught the scene or sensed it. He called me in his typical soft manner of speaking, predicted, "Someday I'm going to step right into your buddy Perry's shoes." The fit was perfect.

Flying is part and parcel of showbiz life. I mean flying by airplane. Such was the mode of transportation employed by two dear friends. They were on a coast-to-coast flight, New York to Los Angeles, for business reasons. One was a music publisher, the other a theatrical agent—in fact, a vice-president of General Artists Corporation. In those days a part of the flight procedure was for the stewardess to ask the name and city residence of each passenger. When the stewardess approached my friends, she asked for their names. "J-O-Y," he alphabetized; "Eddie—Eddie Joy." The pretty little "coffee or tea" gal looked at him in disbelief. "You're putting me on," she giggled, "I've never known anyone with the surname of Joy." "If you think he's putting you on, just wait until you hear my name," interjected the agent. "May I have your name, sir?" came the gentle request. "A-N-G-E-R; Harry—Harry Anger." Joy and Anger were quite a team.

At the annual dinner of the Actors Youth Fund, headed by Joey Adams and attended by a galaxy of show personalities, it was Jackie Mason's turn to face the microphone. In his staccato style of speaking, he gazed at me and said, "Father, you people confuse me." A roar of laughter emanated from the audience. Cognizant that I was about to become the butt of a joke, I was smart enough to keep my mouth shut and not attempt to buck a pro. He continued, "A rabbi goes into the world, plays the field, finds a girl, marries, has a family—him we don't call Father." I immediately sensed the nature of the joke. "A minister plays the field, finds a girl, marries, has a family—him we don't call Father. But you, Father Bob—no girl, no marriage, no kids—you we call Father?????"

Frank Sinatra, Jr., was appearing at the Rainbow Room at Rockefeller Center, some sixty-five stories above the ground. For his opening night he invited some close, intimate friends including myself, Jack E. Leonard and his new bride. While Junior was performing, it suddenly began lightning. Not the ordinary natural phenomenon: this event might be described as extraordinary, with continuous bolts and bolts of lightning streaking the sky. As this heavenly orchestration was taking place, Jack E. turned to me, his hands gingerly resting on his huge stomach, and commented, "I think your Boss is taking pictures again, Father Bob."

There is a rather plush restaurant in New York called Chandler's. The founder was Lou Rubin, a dear friend and a restaurateur par excellence. One of the outstanding features of Chandler's is a large mahogany-glass divider separating the bar and the dining area. It stands about eight and a half feet high by ten feet wide and each block contains an oval piece of glass with the imprint of every United States President.

Chandler's was visited one day by a group of men—four to be precise—who examined every nook and corner of the establishment, including the bathrooms. The following day these same gentlemen reappeared and repeated the investigatory procedure. That afternoon the sleuths made their third appearance, this time in the company of the Vice President of the United States, Lyndon B. Johnson. After the Vice President and the secret agents had their lunch, Mr. Rubin introduced himself and, pointing to the glass divider remarked, "Mr. Vice President, I hope some day to have your portrait on one of these glass blocks." Mr.

Johnson studied the caricatures with sad, mournful eyes and as though talking to himself, repeated: "It will never happen! It will never happen!" Only months later President Kennedy was assassinated.

Mr. P. J. Moriarty is a legend. Unlike so many nouveaux riches, P. J. has remained the same unassuming, genteel, democratic bourgeois. The proprietor of four successful restaurants—P.J.M., Mrs. P. J., Moriarty Chop House and P. J. Moriarty—Pat bounces from one establishment to the other sputtering out orders in his rich brogue baritone. One of the most hilarious sights anyone could ever hope to witness is P. J. in the swimming pool of the New York Athletic Club. With a bathing cap securely fastened, in a corner of the pool, he hangs on for dear life and kicks and slices the water with his legs as though they were the blades of an outboard motorboat.

One of Pat's original restaurants was located on Sixth Avenue in the shadows of Radio City Music Hall and the Ziegfeld Theater. This was one of our—Como and Company's—hangouts after each weekly TV show. Invariably, we were greeted first by "Susie," a cocker spaniel, and then by her master, P. J. In order to provide Susie with a plaything, Pat purchased a life-size rubberized water hydrant. One day he placed the hydrant in front of his establishment, beside a parked car. A police officer passed by and gave the unoccupied car a ticket. In the meantime, the hydrant was returned to the restaurant while the driver of the ticketed car was trying to figure out the enigma. The driver found the cop who issued the summons, and the poor gendarme thought he had become the victim of a myopic condition when he found the hydrant gone. The following day, the hydrant reappeared again—in the exact spot he found it yesterday. Upon police inspection, it was Mr. P. J. Moriarty who received the summons.

"This is going too far!" was the solemn, angry verdict of my superior. The denunciation referred to a horse named "Father

Bob." He believed the thoroughbred was so named in my honor. The truth of the matter is, I'm told, the beast came from a New Jersey stable owned by a Mr. McGee, whose son, Robert, was studying for the priesthood. Obviously, the horse was named after the youngster. Most of my Doubting Thomas friends believed this story apocryphal. They contended it was I who was honored. A young hatcheck girl at Chandler's Restaurant realized a small fortune betting the horse across the board on many occasions. Others did not fare as well. In fact, while stationed in a city in upper New York State near Saratoga, we visited that shrined raceway to catch "Father Bob" in the seventh. Practically the entire parish made the pilgrimage. The results of the race were obvious judging from the collections on the following Sunday. "Father Bob" ran dead last.

Nino Maggio is a personable young man born and reared in the borough of churches and taverns, Brooklyn, U.S.A. A boyhood chum of Julius La Rosa, he was affiliated with the singer as a road manager. During that time we enjoyed many opportunities to get together, dine together and converse on many topical subjects. Once we discussed astrology and the horoscope. He asked me under what sign did I make my first earthly appearance and I informed him it was Cancer. "Me too" was his reply. "What month?" "July." "Me too." And finally, "What day?" "July first." The very sound of that numeral caused him to squeal, "ME TOO!" Then and there he decided we should celebrate our next birthdays together. The Day finally arrived and we enjoyed an early-evening dinner. "It's too early to go home," Nino nonchalantly observed. "Where do you want to go?" "I don't know; where do you want to go?" came my *Marty*-inspired line. "How about catching Roberta Sherwood's first show at the Copa?" We arrived just as the lovely "Cry Me a River" lady with a sweater casually resting on her shoulders, a drumstick and cymbal in hand, finished her first number. After the show Roberta approached our table very surprised to find the two of us at the Copa. "What are you two doing here?" the chanteuse inquired.

"We came for two reasons," Nino explained: "firstly to see you and secondly, to celebrate our birthdays." "Make room, fellers—it's my birthday, too," said Roberta as she sang "Happy Birthday" to us all.

Every boxing fan recognizes the name Johnny Addy—the ring announcer of the Madison Square Garden and other ring sites. His high-pitched voice announcing, "Ladies and Gentlemen, in this corner . . ." was heavenly music to my ears. As often as the Garden presented a match, I would find some sort of excuse to attend, never telling my superior my exact destination. Inwardly I felt my boss, a very old man, would never approve. The very nature of boxing in his estimation ran contrary to the basic norms of Christianity. Hence, my excuse would sound like this: "I'm going to a social gathering tonight," or "I think I'm going to an assembly meeting this evening."

One torrid summer evening the Fathers of Saint Anthony's Church were invited to attend the Midget Boxing Matches staged by a settlement house on Macdougal Street in the Village. Local youngsters with oversized, stuffed and padded gloves were going to demonstrate their fighting prowess before the proud and anxious eyes of their families and friends. All the clergymen accepted the invitation, including my superior. Johnny Addy and a number of sport celebrities were also present. Johnny introduced them and then spotted me. He thought, he told the audience, he would be remiss if he did not introduce one of the spectators. He continued, "This man is not just a spectator but a man of the cloth, a fight enthusiast and a red-blooded fan, a priest who visits the Garden every Friday night to see the fights. Father Bob," Johnny magnanimously offered, "won't you please take a bow?" I took the ten count instead.

Anthony Caruso is a name very few people will recognize. His face, however, is known to all cinema addicts. He always portrays the tough guy, the wise guy, the crook, the prisoner, the racetrack tout, the nightclub proprietor. Naturally, when Al Simms of

American-International Films advised me we were visiting Tony Caruso, I did a double take. "Who the hell is Tony Caruso?" I muttered. "He's a character actor. You'll know him when you see him," he forewarned me. Truer words were never spoken. A mere glance of that hard and rugged face and I visualized the tough guy, the wise guy, the crook, the prisoner, the racetrack tout, the nightclub proprietor. Tony complained he had a serious problem. In a few days he would appear as master of ceremonies at a diocesan Holy Name breakfast at the Ambassador Hotel in Los Angeles. The guest of honor, no less than His Eminence, James Francis Cardinal McIntyre. "Father, do you have a good, strong religious joke for an opener?" he pleaded. "Do I have a joke for you, Tony," I kidded him. "Tell them a friend of yours, Father Bob, always staunchly defended the celibacy of the priesthood. Now he's changed his mind and thinks priests should be married. However, not for the obvious reasons. He wants married priests because there are a couple of bishops and perhaps a cardinal he wants to see stuck with a mother-in-law."

In a corner table of a plush New York restaurant I sat with Gary Morton and his stepson, Desi Arnaz, Jr. Lucy Ball and daughter, Luci, had left moments before. Gary was the typical struggling comic, playing the honky-tonks, spending the better part of his life on planes, trains and buses. Through Jack Carter, he met and married Lucille Ball ten years ago. For the occasion I wore a black suit with very thin gray stripes.

Shamefully I admit being an inveterate smoker; proudly I boast not inhaling. The perennial cigarette flickered between my fingers as Gary's proffered drink rested before me. Young Desi looked at Mr. Morton puzzled. "Did you say he was a priest?" Gary was wonderful as usual. He explained to his stepson that priests were human; there's nothing wrong with anyone, priests included, smoking, eating and drinking in moderation. Now I was puzzled. A cigarette flickered between the fingers of the youngster; a drink rested before him. And he was only sixteen. Do some thin gray stripes make that much difference???

Mr. Pat Henry is a madman. If he thought jumping from the George Washington Bridge or Boulder Dam would produce a laugh, he wouldn't hesitate. At a poolside party for Nancy Sinatra, Jr., there were eight hundred guests. Names, names, names! I was seated at a table with Pat, John Saxon, Anne Jeffreys, Robert Sterling, Don Costa and Connie Stevens, among others. Suddenly, Pat was standing on his chair, with a lantern that he removed from the table, and facing the hotel he started swinging the lantern from right to left, left to right. Since he sat next to me, I inquired, "Pat, what the hell do you think you're doing?" Came the bomb: "Trying to tell the broad to get out of my room. My wife is going up there in five minutes."

"You're Father Bob?" I assured the inquirer I was. "I want to shake your hand, Padre, for doing me a great favor." When I asked about the nature of the favor I had performed, he told me it concerned an interview I had on the *Mike Douglas Show*. "You see," he informed me, "I am the sole national distributor for the J & B Scotch company. And when you told the coast-to-coast audience that J & B was the brand you drank, it was a free million-dollar plug for me."

This was heartening news. My minute business acumen led me to believe I would make the gentleman's Annie Oakley list. However, he did not ask for my address or my telephone number, which automatically disqualified any cases, bottles or freebies. As of that moment, I changed my brand. Living in Chinatown for the past eight years has taught me an important lesson: no whiskey, no pluggie. You can't drink "Thanks," and you can't eat "Hail Marys."

The barometer of success or failure in showbiz may invariably be found in reviews, be they in newspapers, trade papers or any form of the media. It is not so at the world-famous New York Copacabana. Its major domo is Mr. Jules Podell. This man is absolutely blessed with an uncanny eye for talent. For many, many years he has discovered the undiscoverables, and for an equal amount of time he has separated the talented from the non-talented. One of his most demonstrable idiosyncrasies is to repeatedly bang the stone of his ring against the top of a table. This alarm produces miraculous results. Maître d's, captains, waiters, busboys, musicians scurry all over the place. "Did he take you into the kitchen?" is a question without significance to the ordinary layman. But ask an entertainer. Once a newcomer is booked into the Copa, comes opening night, the second show, if the neophyte is a tremendous hit, this is the procedure that follows: Mr. Podell will take the newcomer into the kitchen, bang the table with his ring and tell the kitchen help to applaud and enjoy a drink on the house because a new star is born.

Baby-sitting is not my domain. However, my one and only such experience did provide some exhilarating moments. I ran into Vic Damone in the lobby of the Riviera in Vegas. Vic introduced me to his date, a strikingly beautiful blonde. After the introductions, I learned that her name was Miss Becky Jones from Forth Worth, Texas. This knowledge was supplemented with the fact that she was the daughter of the oil-magnate zillionaire Mr. Available Jones. The nomenclature is not a mistake. The name is Available. The time arrived for Damone to join Don Rickles and entertain the customers in the Lounge. Before departing, Vic asked if I would mind sitting with Becky until he and Don finished their show. I assured him it would be a pleasure. Let's face it, it's not every day a priest can sit with anyone so beautiful and anyone so rich. As the old song says, I found my million-dollar baby—but not in the five-and-ten-cent store.

Tempus fugit! This anecdote covers so many years I feel it belongs to the era of the brontosaurus. The pre–teen-age girl about whom I will write is today probably married with a family. As I repeatedly assert, the priestly labors are not necessarily confined to religion or anything of an ecclesiastical nature. I personally found myself in unemployment offices, real estate offices, Internal Revenue Service offices, seeking employment for a hoofer out of showbiz work, an apartment for a newly arrived thespian and trying to square things with the United States Federal Government for some idiotic actors.

This story wears a new coiffure. "Father, could you get my daughter into a private Catholic school?" pleaded a young actress. "I'm not Catholic, but would that make any difference?" Actually, religious affiliation played a major role in the acceptance or nonacceptance of a pupil. The young actress enjoyed a smattering of popularity on her own, but mostly she was known as the sister of a famous burlesque queen. June Havoc and Gypsy Rose Lee. In those days, the word "burlesque" connoted every luxurious, hedonistic, sensual human depravity. How do you tell a Mother Superior that the child's mother is a Broadway stage star? Her aunt a burlesque queen? Not in those staid, puritanical days when a woman of the stage was immediately and automatically relegated to a woman of the street. What a terrible dilemma. I wanted to help, but how? Could I attempt to circumscribe the case and at the same time be as circumspect as possible? The case suddenly, miraculously was resolved: June and her daughter moved elsewhere.

Tragedy can strike at the lives of stars as well as the masses. Pier Angeli was such a tragedy. Vic Damone had asked me to perform the marriage ritual between Pier and himself and asked Como to be his best man. Neither Perry nor I could negotiate the trip to California because of previous engagements. Nevertheless, they did name their only child Perry. Some time ago Anna Maria, her true name, died of an accidental overdose of barbiturates. She was mentally and physically a very sick girl. She and her sister, Marisa Pavan, were the products of an overwhelmingly ambitious stage mother.

Now I've heard that Mrs. Pierangeli possesses a manuscript supposedly containing the names of Hollywood men with whom Anna Maria had some torrid affairs. This is not believable as far as I am concerned. This is not descriptive of the girl I had known for years. During her infrequent trips to New York, I would visit with her at the Navarro Hotel and dine with her at Lou Rubin's Chandler's Restaurant. She was always kind, sincere and modest.

One Saturday afternoon, the day before Easter, I was informed of a person-to-person long-distance call from California. "Hello, Father Bob," a soft voice greeted me. "This is Anna Maria." "Alberghetti?" I ventured. "No," was the quick retort, "Pierangeli." "Why are you calling me all the way from Los Angeles?" Hesitantly she replied, "To wish you a Happy Easter." "Why a happy Easter," I kidded her, "when you don't call me for Christmas?" Now she began to stammer, asking about my health and well-being. Suddenly I realized she did have something to tell me but grew reticent. Several days later, the newspapers printed the story: she had taken her son and run off to Europe. It was the last time I heard from lovely Anna Maria. May God be good to her.

I was standing in the lobby of a hotel and being cussed out, in no uncertain terms, by the mother of a dear friend, Anna Maria Alberghetti. She could not understand how any person wearing the frock and working for The Man with headquarters in Rome would be guilty of the crime I had committed. How can you justify my daughter marrying a man who is already married and the father of a child? was the puzzling issue. I did not advocate this marriage. However, it is possible to achieve such a union within the context of canon law, I explained. After being informed that we, the American priests, are all the same, I was further queried as to the identity of my Boss—God or the Devil? Patiently I tried to unravel what-God-puts-together-let-no-man-put-asunder: "Your daughter is single and marriageable. Her fiancé, a Catholic, married a divorced woman; consequently, in the eyes of the Catholic Church, that marriage is null and void: there is *no* marriage. The divorced woman and her first husband were both Catholics and married in church. Hence, your daughter's fiancé is single and eligible for marriage within the Church." We terminated our tête-à-tête on an inspirational ethnic level. She would prefer seeing her lovely daughter married to a nice young Italo-American boy. With some Ragu' on the side.

Gene Baylos is the funniest comic in the business—offstage. He is beloved by all who know him except haberdashers. And haberdashers would be pounding the doors of Catholic Charities or the B'nai B'rith for all of his purchasing power. Gene strongly believes in the ancient axiom of plying one's trade; consequently, he is "on" twenty-four hours a day, be it in the Pavillon Restaurant or Campbell's Funeral Home.

Such was the scene one evening when I visited Danny's Hideaway. Mr. Sartorial bombarded me with every religious joke he possessed in his funny satchel. Time and again I attempted to greet some friends, but all in vain: with the staccato of a machine gun, the jokes came spilling out. "Gene," I admonished him, "if you're that desperately in need of work, I'll get you a split week at the Vatican." And again he had to Baylos me. "Speaking of the Vatican, tell your Boss since he removed Saint Christopher, my car is afraid to leave the garage."

Mr. and Mrs. Enzo Stuarti and their entourage of friends visited me during the annual feast of San Gennaro, the Patron Saint of Naples, on Mulberry Street on the Lower East Side of New York, commonly referred to as Little Italy. The streets were festooned with multicolored electric lights; the venders selling their wares of food and games; the people eating sausages, peppers and onions as though the whole world was Italian. Enzo is primarily a singer—a well-versed, professionally trained vocalist. However, his claim to fame is commercials. And ironically, commercials for an Italian tomato sauce, Ragu'. He was recognized by thousands of people, many of them shouting his epigrammatic commercial gem: "That's-a nice-a." "Enzo, that's-a nice-a." We walked into a neighborhood restaurant, Paolucci's, for dinner and the entire assemblage stood up, applauded and cried out in unison: "That's-a nice-a." Many are the times Enzo must reminisce: the cold, hungry, depressing, workless yesterdays. Today he is the proud possessor of a huge house in New Jersey, a Rolls-Royce, five other sport cars plus all the goodies of life. Now I can understand why when people say to him, "Enzo, that's-a nice-a," he always responds, "That's-a right-a!"

It is an unwritten law in showbiz never to follow a great act. It's tantamount to suicide. This brings to mind the occasion Perry was invited to perform at a spectacular Broadway benefit. As we arrived backstage, Milton Berle was in the act of removing his hat and coat while Jimmy Durante stood stage center, virtually killing the audience with his fast and hilarious routine. Berle, hearing the roars of laughter, turned to Como. "Per," he whispered, "you're a singer. Why don't you follow Jimmy?" "Follow the Schnozz? I wouldn't follow that man even if he led me to the pearly gates of heaven." They reached a compromise: a dog act followed the Great Schnozz.

If you ever see Henny Youngman on TV or in person, I'll give you odds he'll tell this joke: Father Bob visited his doctor and was told he was a very sick man. "Forget your work; forget your church and parish. Go to Miami Beach for a month and relax." While at the Beach, he frequented the Playboy Club for a drink. A Bunny spots him and casually greets him with "Hello, Father Bob." "How did you know who I am?" the perplexed clergyman inquires. "Oh, I'm Sister Theresa, and I go to the same doctor." I've begged and pleaded with Henny to stop using my name. In fact, I suggested, "Why don't you give your rabbi a piece of the action?"

What is Red Buttons' favorite story? It's the one he has recently told on every national network talk show and every personal appearance. The story occurred here in our neighborhood during the filming of *Who Killed Mary What's Her Name?* Sylvia Miles, of *Midnight Cowboy* fame and Oscar contender, costars. In one scene Red takes a cab and disembarks at the corner of Mulberry and Hester Streets. This same scene was rehearsed at least fifteen times, and after each take the makeup man would comb Red's orange hair. Two local characters viewed the entire monotonous routine. Finally, Red overheard one say to the other: "Now do you see why they pay these Hollywood stars such fabulous salaries? Do you see how hard they work? Why they've combed Red Buttons' hair at least a dozen times."

Mrs. Jerry Lewis and I attended Mass one Sunday morning at the Church of Saint Paul in Westwood, California. She had specific reasons for bringing me to that particular church and that particular Mass: "Listen to the sermon and tell me what actor the priest sounds like." Merely from the greeting—"My dear friends and visitors"—I read him perfectly. Turning to Patti with an omniscient wink, I told her I could close my eyes and swear Ronald Coleman was on the pulpit. "There are a few more surprises in store for you, Father." Beautiful Ruth Roman daintily fingered her rosary while two gentlemen marched in military precision up the aisle with collection baskets in their hands. This time I became the recipient of a wink as Lawrence Welk handed me the basket for a handout. A-one-a—a-two-a—a-three-a—a-four-a.

Speak to me of Boston, the Common, Tremont Street and my mouth begins to water, my stomach begins to crave seafood. Dini's Seafood Restaurant is located on Tremont Street practically across the Boston Common. It's nationally known as "The Home of Boston's Famous Scrod." My first stop as often as I visit the Hub City is Dini's.

Meeting Louis Dini and his vivacious family germinated out of a totally fortuitous incident. A young, aspiring singer recently relieved from his army tenure sang for me and some friends. My ears refused to believe the amazing similarity of his voice to another vocalist. "Holy cow," I screamed out incredulously, "if Eddie Fisher were in this room I'd swear you were mouthing the songs for him." Lou's son, handsome Bob Dini, a bit embarrassed by the unexpected accolade, modestly explained he had succeeded Eddie Fisher as the appointed vocalist of the Official Army Band.

On one of my visits to the restaurant, my foot no sooner crossed the threshold of the door when Louie cried out, "You won't believe it: look who's here." His words were directed to four Franciscan sisters politely sitting at a table enjoying dinner. I gathered Mr. Dini had been talking about me as I made my entrée, causing the exclamation. "Sisters," he assured them in a grandiose voice, "if I can't bring Perry Como to you, the best I can do is deliver his personal confessor. Meet Father Bob Perrella." Mortified by the importance the good sisters attached to my position and hoping to evade the inevitable questions about Mr. C., I sought refuge in the person of my friend Louie. With a wave of the hand, he informed me he was on his way out—to a business call. Only one thing remained for me to do: I graciously asked for the sisters' check. Those petite, clean-cut, sanctimonious, brown-clad girls ate and drank thirty-two dollars' worth of food and drink, tips and all included. It doesn't pay to be a bigshot personal confessor, believe me!

Al "Doubletalk" Kelly was one of the funniest of the funnymen. I use the past tense because Al is no longer with us. The appellation "Doubletalk" spelled out precisely Al's hilarious talent: he double-talked. Invariably, he was introduced as a Wall Street financier, an Ambassador to Cambodia, a statesman, the president of a university, etc. He would approach the rostrum, carrying a bundle of typewritten papers, place them carefully on the podium, gingerly place his glasses on his face, study the crowd for several minutes and begin. For the first few lines, all was intelligible; then, catatonic confusion. A number of words would be understandable, and again more confusion. The audience reactions: complete incredulity, then the realization, He's putting us on.

In a restaurant with Al and some friends, the Italian waiter prepared to take our order. Al began legitimately with the antipasto and a few other items. Then he started to double-talk. The poor waiter looked in disbelief. The waiter "I-beg-your-pardoned" a number of times as Al snapped in feigned disgust, "Don't you understand English?" Then came a repetition of the entire script as the blushing waiter stared into space wishing he were back in Naples.

Another story Kelly loved to tell. He was taken to general headquarters of the New York baseball Giants on Forty-second Street to meet the president of that organization. Al was introduced as an eminent writer from the West Coast who intended to write some papers on the number one American sport. The conversation was now in Al's hands, and suddenly began the litany of incoherence. The befuddled look on the prez's face told Kelly he was making his point. Suddenly the prez suggested he would close the window; there was too much noise on Forty-second Street and he found it difficult to understand the noted writer. Having accomplished that chore, he returned to his desk and Al started all over again. The prez arose, went to the window and opened it.

The Plaza is the most sophisticated of all New York hotels, and its prices are equally expensive. My infrequent visits there were always as the guest of some friend. Actually, one visit would blow my entire monthly allowance. On one such occasion, just before Christmas, we sat in the Persian Room to see and hear the resonant tenor voice of Enzo Stuarti. The Ragu' Man sang for an hour. Because of the Yuletide season, his final number, he informed the audience, would be the Ave Maria. As the strains of that sacred song filled the Persian Room, a cross was reflected on the ceiling. For one flashing moment I thought I was back in church. The show ended. Mario, the maître d' of the room, excitedly approached me. "Father," he blurted out, "while Enzo was singing the Ave Maria I saw a number of people actually crying." "Mario," I forewarned him, "if they cried while Enzo was singing, just watch the tears when they get their checks."

My phone rang. I immediately recognized the voice. Danny Stradella asked if it would cause any inconvenience to bless his new Eldorado. In fact, we would have to drive to the showroom. He wouldn't consider placing the new vehicle on any dirty city street unless I first poured the clean, blessed water over it. We taxied to the Cadillac people and I performed the ritual. In the shining, new car, Danny drove me back to his Hideaway. With a glass in hand, we toasted Danny and the new Eldorado.

A little less than two weeks after the automotive baptismal, someone called me. "Did you hear the bad news, Padre?" offered Joe Gallart, the restaurant's doorman. Closing the restaurant, around two-thirty in the morning, Danny was on his way home. Waiting behind another car on Third Avenue while the signal flickered a bright red, some drunken driver roared into the Eldorado's rear and its bumper, likewise, into the car in front. Four thousand dollars' damage. And I just blessed the car! I realize I don't give any guarantees with my blessings, but the poor man was standing still—not even moving. What would be Danny's reaction when he saw me?

I dropped in shortly afterwards. The mere sight of me induced an instant act of thanksgiving. "Thank God you blessed my car that day. If you hadn't, I wouldn't be here talking to you."

I've professed the three vows of poverty, chastity and obedience. Georgie Jessel, the septuagenarian, has practically doubled that figure in marital adventures. One day the Toastmaster General, as he has been dubbed by the last four United States Presidents, greeted me in Toots Shor's. He held a strikingly beautiful blonde around the waist. She was young enough to be his great-great-granddaughter. "Father," he pleaded seriously, "won't you bless our forthcoming marriage?" Like a kindly old Padre, I looked Mr. Jessel straight in the eye with this bit of fatherly admonition: "Georgie, if you ever marry again, I think you're going to need the blessing." P.S.: There was no blessing and no marriage. P.P.S.: Georgie is alive and well.

I sat with Marty Allen and his wife, Frenchy. Marty, the maniac onstage, is an unbelievably quiet man offstage. We were soon joined by another gentleman. "Mike," said Marty, "I want you to meet Father Bob." Mike looked terribly perplexed. You couldn't really blame him, because Father Bob was wearing a light green sports outfit. Hesitantly, Mike turned toward Marty and squawked out, "Did you say . . ." "Yea," grinned Marty, "I said Father Bob." Still doubtful, in search for some reassurance, he again asked, "You mean he's a real—I mean, he's a priest?"

Once my identity was confirmed, Marty reversed the introduction. "Father Bob, meet Mike Connors." The name meant nothing to me. I now proceeded to pull one of the greatest faux pas of my life. "Are you in showbusiness, Mike?" The silence at the table was deafening. You see, I had never seen the Great Mannix on TV. Minutes later another man came to our table. I had learned my lesson: keep my mouth shut. "Father, this is Rick Jason," said Frenchy. A smile, a handshake and a "Hi." I had never seen *Combat* either.

Bobby Quinn is Irish. If his name does not convince you, his face would. Bobby belonged to that exclusive membership of TV technicians and stagehands. He was probably the youngest in the group. An industrious youngster, no task was too big or too small for him to accomplish. He pushed the huge TV cameras and cranes and hauled the heavy cables all over the Ziegfeld Theater stage. Quiet and unassuming, Bobby remained unimpressed by the presence, star or superstar, of any invited guest on the show. He had a job to do and he did it. In between chores, he would rush out to buy us coffee and cakes. Whatever spared him from a hernial condition I'll never know.

He must have learned his trade well. The many years of learning, working and sweating paid off well. Whenever Johnny Carson calls out, "Let it roll, Bobby!" he's talking to Bobby Quinn, the director of the Johnny Carson *Tonight* show.

I WANT YOU ALL IN HEAVEN

When I first met counselor Joseph D'Imperio, he started work with RCA Victor at their East Twenty-fourth Street headquarters. His initial job was legal adviser to that gargantuan corporation, and after fifteen years he held the title of vice-president of one of the special departments. One night I was invited to a private gathering at Danny's to celebrate his wife, Dolores', birthday. Then I learned Joe had relinquished his post at RCA and transferred to another firm. He now held the title of president of Ringling Brothers and Barnum & Bailey Records, Inc. This is the parent company with six subsidiaries, all relating to management, records and music publishing.

The name of the organization fascinated me. As a youngster I hardly went to the circus. I didn't have the price of a ticket. In those days I didn't have the price of a subway ride. I reminded Joe that my neighborhood kids were practically in the same category; please don't forget them when the circus comes to town. He didn't. There were twenty-five tickets, eight dollars per, waiting for me at Danny's. It was worth the trouble to hear eight-year-old Greg Esposito say to me, "Father, you're the bestest friend in the world."

"The phone's ringing, Bob. Why don't you grab it? Most probably it's for you." "Hello," I greeted the caller. "Father Bob, please," a very refined feminine voice politely summoned. "Speaking, Margie," I peremptorily addressed her. "Good," she commented. "We have a very sad and serious problem on our hands. Maybe you can help." At the time, Mrs. Margie Coates held the title of executive secretary-treasurer of the American Guild of Variety Artists. The sad and serious problem? A young entertainer, a girl dancer-singer, on the road, was killed in an automobile accident in San Francisco. How do we negotiate the transfer of the body from California to New York?

I had never been involved in such a transaction before. I communicated the sad and heartbreaking news to the girl's parents, and they were most agreeable that I accept the intermediary role. Blessed to be a son of Saint Francis and San Francisco blessed to be the city of Saint Francis of Assisi, I called a Franciscan friar friend, San Francisco's City Hall and a few other friends. Within three days the job was accomplished; the mortal remains of the stunningly beautiful AGVA member rested in a local funeral home. Grieved beyond description, crushed in body and soul, the parents thanked me magnanimously. Attempting to demean my efforts, I sadly acknowledged, "It's all a part of the job."

A champagne party took place on the second floor—the party room—of Toots Shor's Restaurant. Jackie Gleason hosted the party for no particular reason—just to celebrate with his many friends. A waiter brought a platter of hors d'oeuvres to our table, informing my friends and me that the food came from the Gleason party and it would be sinful to throw away. The Great One suddenly appeared as the elevator doors parted. Impeccably dressed in a light gray double-breasted suit, with the ever-present boutonniere caressing his lapel, Gleason was stoned to the gills. He jumbled a few words to Toots, put on his hat and coat and headed for the revolving door. Corpulent as ever, Jackie placed his body weight against the door, made a complete revolution and found himself back in the lobby of the restaurant. "What the hell am I doing here?" he screamed. "I've just left this damn place!"

An habitué of nightclubs I'm not. Very, very infrequently might best describe my visits. Numerically, three times a year is maximum. These infrequent visits are made purely for social reasons. If Enzo Stuarti is working at the Persian Room of the Plaza Hotel and invites me to his opening, I must go because the same Enzo Stuarti traveled nine hours to entertain prisoners at my request. If Jerry Vale—whose family now resides in Las Vegas and we, consequently, see very little of him—invites me to his closing night at the Copa, I must go because of the many favors he has performed in my behalf.

It was at this affair that I sat with Mr. Jules Podell enjoying a drink, compliments of the house. Lo and behold, nine unescorted women marched in as though the line were a church procession. I knew every one of them. It seems they belonged to a neighborhood women's club—the same area in which I spent my boyhood and was stationed as a priest. It was impossible to convince them that this visit was the first in years. "What kind of a showbiz priest are you if you don't visit clubs?" one of them wisecracked.

"Would you like to catch the Phil Brito concert at Carnegie Hall with Cora and me and some friends?" said the voice at the other end of the telephone line. "Me" was none other than the Scooter himself, Phil Rizzuto. The name Phil Brito triggered so many memories. Thirty years ago Phil headlined the show at the very fashionable Martinique while farther down the street a young unknown named Frank Sinatra sang at the not-too-fashionable Rio Bamba. Mr. Brito was enjoying a goodly measure of success on radio, on records, in nightclubs, theaters and supper clubs, when he learned about his heart. He retired from the business nine years ago and during that interim suffered three brutal heart attacks. At the pleading and insistence of the Scooter and other friends, Phil underwent open-heart surgery. The miracle was accomplished: the miracle of seeing that familiar figure, mike in hand, "singing his heart out."

It was quite a wedding. A football wedding, no less. Plenty of sandwiches, beer, wine, whiskey and goodies. Little Rita and prizefighter Tony Pellone were married by yours truly. The site of the reception was a huge loft on Second Avenue. It's inevitable such a wedding would draw a good number of pugilists. Rocky Castellani, Jake LaMotta, Rocky Graziano were there.

The Bronx Bull, Jake, was as lethargic then as he is now. The *Somebody Up There Likes Me* Kid was as crazy then as he is today. While Jake sat glued to his chair discussing the gate, the percentage, the take of each of his fights, Rocky danced with LaMotta's beautiful blond wife from the first to the very last dance. Rocky could have danced all night—and did.

Maybe Jake is not as lethargic as I thought. Over the span of years I was in LaMotta's company four times, and on each occasion I met his new bride. Number four. Feast or famine. Feast for Jake—famine for me.

Johnny Johnson is a dear friend; Kathryn Grayson, less than an acquaintance. At the time, they were husband and wife. Johnny and Kathryn were appearing at the RKO Boston Theater. A quick telephone call brought me an invitation to have dinner with the couple and later catch their show. To see Johnny and Kathryn on the screen, to hear them onstage would be the perfect portrait of true love.

In reality, things were different. We arrived at the restaurant; a table was earmarked for the "lovebirds"; we sat and began to converse. Suddenly, unexpectedly, an argument ensued. I have witnessed many arguments in my life, but this was incomparable. Johnny tossed his napkin on the table and stalked out. Kathryn, with a tearful apology to me, arose and stalked out. Johnny refused to do the remaining shows that day. There I sat . . . alone: no meal . . . no show.

It was in this same theater I watched Dick Haymes telephone Joanne Dru in California twice a day. What ever happened to the perfect portrait of true love???

Monique Van Vooren is a stunningly beautiful woman. The Belgian Beauty! The reasons she never achieved international prominence and prestige were Marilyn Monroe and Jayne Mansfield. It was humanly impossible for her to infiltrate through the reams of publicity the M & M girls gleaned for themselves while Miss Van Vooren stubbornly attempted to acquire some recognition as a sex goddess.

This same spellbinding beauty sat on the dais in the Imperial Ballroom of New York's Americana Hotel. Her attire left little to the imagination. She wore a shockingly deep décolletage, with an appreciable amount of bosom exposed to the viewers, and a completely bare back. She sat demurely as Joey Adams, the master of ceremonies, introduced the many celebrities on the dais.

Finally, Joey the Beast came to Monique the Beauty. Joey told his audience whenever he lays eyes upon the pulchritude of Miss Van Vooren, his mind automatically reverts to the Holy Scriptures. "Monique," Mr. Adams gallantly informed her, "a mere glance at your loveliness and I think of the scriptural words, 'My cups runneth over.'"

From my earliest days I always considered Bing Crosby as the kind, benign, considerate gentleman. Como spoke frequently about Crosby, publicly and privately. Bing was his idol. Perry molded his career in the wake of the King of Crooners and imitated his singing style. Because of this public acknowledgment, Bing grew very fond of his protégé. In fact, Mr. Crosby stated publicly that of all the singers he helped, Perry was the one and only to express his gratitude.

I met Crosby on several occasions and sad to say, my ideal preconceived image of the Crooner was slightly jarred. He and Fabian guest-starred on the Saturday-night NBC Como show. After a rehearsal break, Crosby and a few others left the studio through a stage door. A group of overzealous young girls rushed El Bingo, requesting autographs. He bluntly refused to sign even one. The girls were adamant in their requests; he was even more adamant in his refusal. Finally, he told the young ladies to ask Fabian for his autograph because the young Philadelphia vocalist was more their age.

Sometime later, the Protégé hosted a party in honor of his Idol at Danny's Hideaway. Since Danny made it a practice to be photographed with the celebrities who frequent his bistro, he asked me to intercede. I in turn asked Como. Perry asked Bing. Like the young autograph-seekers, we were refused. It just happened Crosby forgot to bring along his toupee. No toup—no pix!

Frankie, a Sicilian-born baker boy, and I stood in front of his pastry shop. It was about eight-thirty on the evening of a cool autumn day. Frankie's face suddenly lit with a glow of surprise, bewilderment and recognition as two people—a young man and a girl—exited from Luna's Italian Restaurant. "It's Lemon—it's Lemon!" he shouted. I couldn't quite understand if the baker referred to the young man as a fruit vender or was casting some sort of epithet. By this time their number grew to six people. I recognized no one until the companion of "Lemon"—dressed in a very short brown leather hot-pants outfit—turned in my direction. She was Yoko Ono, John Lennon's Japanese wife.

Later I learned from the Luna establishment that Annie, the matronly waitress, took a phone call. Someone wanted to make reservations for a party of six. She instructed the caller that reservations were not accepted at Luna's. The caller insisted, reminding the waitress the reservation was in the name of a Mr. John Lennon of the Beatles. Annie couldn't care less. Unimpressed by the glamour of such a nomenclature, she offered a suggestion: "Tell him to come down with his guitar and sing while he waits for a table."

I narrated this story to Tony Zoppi, the public relations man of the Vegas Riviera and a close, intimate friend of Bob Hope's. He in turn recalled a similar experience with the Groto Azzuro and evidently the same waitress. Tony begged her for a reservation, deploring the idea that Mr. Hope be expected to wait in line. "Mister," Annie reminded him, "I don't care if his name is Mr. Faith, Hope or Charity. He waits like everybody else." Mr. Hope never appeared.

An agent called informing me two of his clients were traveling to Italy and could I do him a big favor? In the order of importance, I wanted to know firstly what is the "big favor" and secondly who are the clients? "They'll be in Rome, and is it possible to negotiate a private audience with His Holiness?" "Who'll be in Rome?" "Lucille Ball and Desi Arnaz." Wow, this is really big time! was my reaction.

I immediately wrote to a monsignor friend working for the State Department of the Vatican. His negative reply and the reason for the refusal struck me as very disconcerting and improbable. Desi and Lucille, as everybody knows, were husband-and-wife motion-picture stars, and—again, as everybody knows—such marriages aren't very stable. Consequently, it might prove embarrassing for His Holiness to be photographed with such people in the event of a future divorce. However, the good monsignor promised to make other plans.

Months after their European return, I met Lucille for the first time in the Sands Hotel at Vegas. After the introduction, I reminded Miss Ball that it was I who made the arrangements for their audience with the Pope. "What audience?" she snarled. "We were in a large auditorium with ten thousand other people." As for the fate of their marriage, we all know the answer.

Henny Youngman is King of the one-liners. There isn't a comic alive who could stand in Youngman's shadow when it comes to epigrammatic routines. The jokes might be as old as Henny, but they are hilariously funny. The success of the Dan Rowan and Dick Martin *Laugh-In* is due in great measure to the Youngman style of comedy. In fact, *Laugh-In* is a one-hour one-liner comedy show.

On one occasion, Henny was performing for the AGVA (American Guild of Variety Artists) dinner at the Waldorf Astoria while the other half of New York's population was flat on its back suffering from the flu. While Henny entertained, a dear friend of Chinese extraction, Peter Chan, AGVA's official photographer, snapped pictures of other celebrities and was approaching Mr. Youngman. Spotting the photographer from the corner of his eye, Henny screamed, "Don't let that damn Chinaman near me—I don't want the Hong Kong flu!"

The massive frame of James Arness sat at a dining-room table of the Las Vegas Desert Inn accompanied by Red and Georgia Skelton. Some friends and I occupied the next table. Red talked constantly. His conversation must have been hilarious, because

Mr. Arness grinned or laughed aloud continuously while Mrs. Skelton just sat motionless.

Throughout this scenario, Mr. *Gunsmoke* occupied his time with a hefty amount of hard drinking. At one point he notified Skelton he was hungry, and Red immediately called the captain. After a short stay, the waiter brought Mr. Arness a double steak and, of all things, a large pitcher of milk: plain, unadulterated cow juice. The meat consumed, the pitcher emptied, the waiter presented the gargantuan Cowboy with a fifth of golden drops of Scotch.

Such are the inevitabilities of life. On a Friday night I sat on the dais of the International Film Awards Dinner tendered by the International Film Importers and Distributors of America. I sat in the midst of such personalities as Jack Valenti, Otto Preminger, Carol Channing, Joel Grey, Godfrey Cambridge, Sylvia Miles and many more. The following day, midafternoon, I found myself in the auditorium of the Willowbrook State School for the Mentally Retarded. The purpose of this visit was a benefit show hosted by the Actors Youth Fund for six hundred of its inmates, young and old. Mr. Joey Adams, God bless him, put together eight visual, entertaining acts: vocalists, acrobats, puppeteers, ventriloquists, etc. It inspired me to see the reactions of the children and grown-ups as well from the very first note of "Let Us Entertain You" to the closing, final act. The large room was drenched with laughter, glee and merriment. Four times a year the Actors Youth Fund performs this noble and selfless act of love.

During this visit, I heard one incredible story. It seems some time ago, during another benefit show, a resident psychiatrist told the entertainers about the plight of a young girl. Deeply disturbed, she refused to communicate in any manner with her parents, family, doctors or nurses. The ventriloquist-puppeteer man offered his own brand of therapy. The little sick girl ignored him, the psychiatrist, her parents, but spoke to the puppet for hours.

Never play the game of repartee with Milton Berle. His tongue is razor-sharp; his mind, a thesaurus of jokes. When the Lincoln Hotel was rechristened the Manhattan Hotel, a new supper-club room opened called The Carnival. Berle enjoyed the prestigious privilege to be the first big name to play the new room. While the Texaco Kid performed his routine, a middle-aged woman, well in her cups, became boisterous and started heckling the Star. Evidently, she knew his routine by heart. He told his stories and jokes and she anticipated each of his punch lines.

Berle became infuriated. "Lady," he fumed, "this is not a hobby of mine. It's my livelihood. It's my bread and butter. I get paid to tell funny stories and funny jokes. Why do you interfere with my work?" Now, feigning a little compassion for the startled and embarrassed woman, Mr. Television confessed, "I would never think of going to your home and removing the two big red electric bulbs from the front of your house." She left the Carnival Room in tears.

Some time ago the country was plagued with an incredible amount of trivia about the Howard Hughes "autobiography." The names Howard Hughes, Clifford and Edith Irving, McGraw-Hill, *Life* Magazine, Ibiza, Nina Van Pallandt suffused every news media imaginable. Much ado about nothing! What is so significant and important about meeting Howard Hughes?

I met him personally about twenty-five years ago, and he probably looks the same today as he did then: an unmade bed. His attire wasn't exactly chic. He wore white sneakers, white slacks, an open-collared shirt with a black double-breasted jacket. His whole appearance conveyed a sense of uninhibited shabbiness, as though he slept in his outfit for a week or so.

It happened on the sixth floor of Rockefeller Center's RCA Building. Mr. Hughes stood with a foot resting against a wall as Mr. Como, I and some friends were heading for Studio 6A—the *Chesterfield Supper Club* habitat. As he approached us with a mutual friend, my first thought, not recognizing him, led me to believe he was looking for a handout. The name—Mr. Howard

Hughes—rang the bell. When I told Perry I presumed Mr. Hughes was an old Canonsburg friend looking for some bread, the Como grin spread over his face as he reminded me: "A handout??? That guy could buy and sell me any day of the week!"

On the rectory bulletin board a note awaited me: "A Mrs. Eric Van Arlo called to say she will be here Sunday to attend Mass and visit with you." Who is Mrs. Eric Van Arlo? I never heard the name. Sunday morning arrived and I was informed a visitor waited for me in the office. Draped in immaculately white sable stood Caterina Valente and her little son, two years old, Eric, Jr. The girl is an absolute genius. "Esprit" would be the better choice of word, because she's not only clever but vivacious and witty as well.

Little Eric assumed all the features of his paternal lineage. His hair was blonder than blond, cut in a very close crop, and his complexion fairer than fair. He looked like a little Dutchman, ready to present arms. At one point in our conversation, Eric interrupted us to ask his mother a question. Caterina reprimanded him for such a lack of etiquette and for good measure said something that sounded like German. Much to my surprise, the youngster walked to the corner of the room, turned and faced the wall. Caterina gave me a big wink, waited a few seconds and spoke again in German to acquit him of all charges.

At the star table of the Nook Room at Danny's Hideaway sat Nick Conte and his party. It was the night after the *Godfather* premiere, a film in which he enjoys a fat role. To his friends he is Nick; professionally he is known as Richard Conte. I sat with Nick and his party for some time. He was overjoyed that particular day, he informed me, because his dad and a friend of his father visited him at his hotel. Papa, who lives in New Jersey and is eighty-three years young, brought along his mandolin and music. The two old men entertained the movie star with songs *italiano,* old and new.

Mr. Conte invariably portrays the role of a gangster, hoodlum, racketeer. In person he is quite the contrary: soft-spoken, kind and genteel. As I was about to leave his table, explaining I had already dined, we shook hands. At this point something happened that surprised and startled me. Only in southern Europe do I recall that people kiss the back of a priest's hand out of respect and reverence. There, right in the middle of the Hideaway Restaurant, the Movie Star kissed the back of my right hand, in deference not to me, but to my priesthood.

How much money do they want? How much money does one need? These are the recurring questions which hammer at my mind as I watch Arthur Godfrey, Henry Fonda, Edie Adams, Perry Como, Danny Thomas, Bing Crosby and their families doing TV commercials. These people are indisputably in the superstar genre; they've been on the big-money scene for a combined period of over a hundred years. There's a certain amount of vicarious pity I experience when I see an actor of the caliber of Robert (*Stalag 17*) Strauss screwing up his face and rolling his eyes for the sake of a dollar. However, the man is a professional actor and needs the money for food and rent. Equally, there's a certain amount of personal revulsion and contempt I experience when I see multimillionaires pushing aside the have-nots and adding thousands of dollars to their already padded bankbooks. To view these superstars peddling their wares would repel me to the same extent as to see a David Rockefeller peddling his Chase Manhattan Bank. After all, you have a friend there.

Commercials possess tremendous potential. What commercials have accomplished for Milt Moss and Jack ("Try it—you'll like it") Aaron they can achieve for other unknowns. When the former mayor of Cleveland, Carl Stokes, accepted the offer of NBC-TV to co-anchor the local New York news, newscaster John Chancellor took exception to the offer and acceptance. Mr. Stokes, claimed Chancellor, is a nonprofessional newscaster who takes advantage of his political prestige. When asked if he would consider advertising a commercial product on TV, Mr. Chancellor submitted the perfect answer: "Maybe if I was real broke I'd do it, but I doubt it."

Did you ever hear of plans being made for a christening at a supper-club table? Hardly the place, you say! Strange as it may sound, it was.

Actor Don DeLeo and I sat nursing a Scotch-and-water when Pat Henry made a surprise appearance. After the preliminary questions regarding our health, Pat inquired about Mr. DeLeo's wife and baby.

"My son is still waiting to be baptized, and you're never around to be his godfather," the actor told the comedian.

"How can I be around when I spend half of my life on the road?" the comedian reminded the actor. "How old is your son?"

"He's four!"

"My God," Pat exclaimed, "what in the hell are you waiting for? Do you expect that kid to bossa nova his way to church?"

Then and there Mr. Henry decided on the arrangements: "Father Bob, you have the booking. It will be in your church. Let's make it Thursday—around five-thirty so we'll have time for an early dinner. I'm the godfather and Patti, my wife, will be the godmother. Tell Roseann," he instructed Don, "to have the kid ready."

The plans were perfectly executed with one exception: Pat's new godson had to be removed from the dinner table—he was terribly loud and noisy.

In the wing of Lincoln Center's Philharmonic Hall sat Phil Silvers, David Frost, Liza Minnelli and Jerry Stiller and Anne Meara each awaiting their turn to entertain. It was a charity show, "Fight for Sight," to raise money for visual health. The mere sight of yours truly with a shining white Roman collar turned Miss Meara on. "Father Bob, have I got a nun for you!" To which I retorted, "The way things are in Rome, they'll be *none* for me and *none* for the rest of my associates."

Mr. Frost discovered some relevancy in our lives, informing me his father was a Protestant minister in England.

Phil Silvers was his own amiable self, soft-spoken, courteous and gentlemanly. Sergeant Bilko reminded me a dozen years had passed since we both flew from Toronto to New York and hadn't seen or heard from each other since. For the past six years he had lived in the anonymity of forgotten success: no bookings, no work, no friends, no anything. Since then Fortune has turned again, and the name PHIL SILVERS has once again blazed in Broadway lights as the star of *A Funny Thing Happened on the Way to the Forum.*

Phil told a story about a friend, also a man of the cloth, Monsignor William McCormack. It seems the Monsignor as a priest and a youngster was a staunch rooter for the New York Rangers hockey team, which invariably finished at the bottom of the league. On the day of Father Bill's first mass, as he blessed the members of his family and friends, he encountered Mr. Silvers. Plagued with nervousness and allied diseases on such an occasion, the neophyte stammered, "I'll pray for you, Phil." Sergeant Bilko hammered him with a classic Silverine line: "Don't pray for me, Padre—pray for the Rangers. They're in last place again."

To me Carlos J. Montalban is a friend. To millions of others he is El Exigente—The Demanding One—the Crowned Connoisseur of the coffee samplers. The entire nation of Colombia depends upon his nod of approval, without which that Land of the Coffee Bean would disintegrate and starve to death. But once he nods and smiles his approbation, the entire city goes delirious with joy, music, dancing and a striking display of colorful fireworks. Not only is he El Exigente; Carlos is a well-known Spanish-speaking actor, and when he is not performing, he plays the role of United States representative of Madrid's Suevia Films. It is not generally known that the Coffee Cognoscente is a brother to film actor Ricardo Montalban. Ricardo married one of the Young sisters. Unless my knowledge of genealogy is completely distorted, this union makes Carlos the brother-in-law of Miss Georganna Young and Ricardo the brother-in-law of Miss Loretta Young. Bravos to the two Montalbans—Los Exigentes.

Myriad are the number of sick calls I performed during my priestly life, but one in particular remains etched in my mind as the most memorable and unforgettable. A parishioner asked if I would visit his nephew at Memorial Hospital in New York. His name is Brian Piccolo but, he advised me, they call him "Pic" for short. Brian Piccolo . . . being an incurable aficionado of professional football, the name cascaded a number of faces, places and things. Gale Sayers; the Chicago Bears; "Pic," the running fullback and sometime running halfback.

Carmine Esposito, a cousin of "Pic," drove me to the hospital. The powerful athlete was resting in bed while his beautiful wife, Joy, sat beside him. Our meeting was cordial indeed; cousins kissing and friends handshaking. I asked to see a large photograph of Joy and her three daughters, then five, four and two, each of whom looked like a delicate Dresden doll.

To me Brian appeared enigmatic. He was so soft-spoken, genteel, courteous, considerate—yet place a football in his hands and he'll hit you with the kick of twenty mules. Brian realized the gravity of his illness and asked for prayers that God's will be done.

Brian's Song tells about "Pic" and his black roommate, Gale Sayers—the respect, love and admiration each had for the other. This TV film, starring James Caan and Billy Dee Williams, won an accolade of awards. Among the eleven honors bestowed on *Brian's Song* are the George Foster Peabody Award, the Mass Media Brotherhood Award, the Black Sports Magazine Award, the Directors Guild Award, the Writers Guild Award, and a special citation by the American Cancer Society. The film has also been cited in the *Congressional Record* and by the NAACP. Its future appears equally illustrious, as it has been nominated for a Golden Reel Award, a Golden Globe Award and the Eddie Award. But the greatest reward of all is to believe there is a celestial bowl and a heavenly gridiron and "Pic's" doing his thing.

I finally met the inimitable Vince Barnett as he and Jackie Coogan joined our table. It was on the eve of the Memorial Day holiday; consequently, Danny's Hideaway entertained very few customers. Mr. Barnett stretched his neck to look around, turned to Danny and wisecracked: "You have a nice place here, Danny. When do you open it?" In a more serious tone, Vince declared his pride in being affiliated with the acting profession: "You won't find them anymore like the great Gable, Jimmy Stewart, Spencer Tracy, Robert Young, Tyrone Power, Barbara Stanwyck, Loretta Young, etc. These were pros." To assert his point, he quoted Jerry Lewis' definition of a pro: "A pro is a pro is a pro."

Then Mr. Barnett inquired if it was true that I was in the process of writing a book. "If you are, you may add this piece of memorabilia. During World War II, my people contributed greatly to the country, not merely by entertaining troops but actually fighting and shedding blood. Jimmy Stewart commanded B-17 planes for the Air Force; Tyrone Power and Bob Young commanded PT boats for the Navy."

At this point Vince grew apologetic. "I'm hogging the table with all my talk, but I must tell the priest one more story." Jimmy Stewart and his unit of thirty-six B-17 planes were returning to England having just bombarded a section of Germany. One of the planes was badly damaged, so Stewart commanded all thirty-six planes to reduce their speed to a hundred and twenty miles per hour. This course of action drew the ire of every four-star general in the service. To jeopardize the safety of thirty-five planes and their crew for a solitary plane and only ten men was considered foolhardy. Generals Ira Eader, "Tooey" Spatz and Jimmy Doolittle were among the first to condemn him. Facing a possible court-martial, Steward defended his action: "I would do the same for one plane and ten men as I would for one plane and one man."

"Good afternoon. This is the Hotel Delmonico."

"Good afternoon. Barber shop, please. . . . It's Saturday afternoon, I have two weddings to attend today and I'm in desperate need of a haircut." My regular barber is off on Saturday, so I spoke to his partner. He informed me only three-quarters of an hour was unbooked and available. "So hop a taxi and come as you are." At the time I wore light beige trousers, a dark brown pullover sweater and a blue zippered jacket. Mike clipped and cleaned my head. As I'm about to leave the Delmonico lobby I spot Ed Sullivan. "Hi, Ed," I saluted him. "Hi, Padre, how are you?" "I feel much better now that I've gotten my hair clipped and my head cleaned." "Padre, I'm going across the street to Faith, Hope and Charity to attend Mass." Then, with a quick sweeping glance of my beige trousers, brown pullover and blue jacket . . . thinking I was headed for the greens . . . he grinned: "I'll say an extra prayer for your golf game."

I sat with Morey Amsterdam, who is a very delightful man of the Jewish faith. He loves to tell stories. Here's a sampling. In San Francisco's Saint Mary's Hospital, Morey rested on a hospital bed minus his appendix. Typical of most Catholic hospitals, a nun supervised his floor. The good sister had already enjoyed four scores of living and seemed to be eternal. Someone gifted Morey with a double-face medal: one side representing Saint Christopher; the other, the Star of David. One afternoon as he lay in bed he held the medal between his fingers, deeply studying one side of the medal and then the other. Meanwhile the little sister entered the room unnoticed, observed this entire scene and softly remarked, "Undecided, Mr. Amsterdam?"

For many years Morey lived directly across from Saint Joseph's Seminary in Yonkers, New York. His feelings about living at that particular location were ambivalent. Certainly he enjoyed the sylvan beauty of the seminary grounds, the tree-lined roads, the manicured lawns, the kaleidoscopic coloring of shrubs and flowers. However, he suffered from one unmitigated frustration: his dog. It seems the animal would invariably pay a hurried call across the street whenever nature beckoned. "I couldn't make that mutt understand that good Jewish dogs don't desecrate holy Catholic grounds."

Gene Fowler was a writer's writer. He belonged to the era of the Damon Runyons and the Paul Gallicos. Among his literary achievements, *Good Night, Sweet Prince* is considered by many to be his greatest. It concerned the life and derring-do of the talented and erratic John Barrymore. Later he added another biographical endeavor, *Schnozzola*, the life of Sir James Durante.

"Gene," I once asked, "whom do you consider to be the greatest comic of them all?" Without a moment's hesitation, he declared: "W. C. Fields." He wanted desperately to biograph the comic's life, but could not find W. C. sober enough . . . long enough . . . to do so. Many are the tales he told about the corpulent comic. This one I found terribly amusing: Mr. Fields considered himself an agnostic, or perhaps even an atheist. One day Gene found W. C. fingering through the pages of a Bible. Surprised beyond belief, Mr. Fowler inquired what the great atheist W. C. Fields was doing with a Bible in his hands. "Looking for loopholes, my boy, looking for loopholes!"

What is today the Johnny Carson *Tonight* show used to be the *Broadway Open House* show starring Jerry Lester and Dagmar. Dag personified to the letter that timeworn cliché, the dumb, busty blonde. Busty she is—but dumb, never. Dagmar married a would-be actor, Danny Dayton, who smartly renounced the stage for the hard sell. Today he's a very successful Madison Avenue personality in the land of commercials.

It was a cold December night when I visited Danny at his Central Park South apartment. As yet, I hadn't met Dagmar. A scarf swirled around my throat, my coat collar high on my neck, my hat brim covered my eyes, my Roman collar nowhere to be seen, I entered the three-storied building. Dag and I came face to face in the lobby. "May I help you, sir?" came the gentle offer. "I'm here to see Danny Dayton." She excused herself and left for her apartment with the suggestion that I wait a few minutes in the lobby. A short wait and Danny appeared. "Oh, my God—it's Father Bob!" he exclaimed. "My wife told me there's a character in the lobby completely dressed in black and looking for me. She described you as 'an Irish, baby-faced hood.'"

On a rainy July morning my phone rang. "Father, Sam Berger is dead. Services will take place this afternoon at one." To the layman, the name Sam Berger is unimportant. To showbiz, that name connotes the epitome of success in personal management. He and his longtime partner, friend and buddy, Harry Steinman, operated a "stable" of talent not to be believed. Jack Carter, Cyd Charisse, Tony Martin, Billy Daniels, Zsa Zsa Gabor, Fran Jeffries, Meredith MacRae, Barbara McNair, Carmen MacRae, Pat O'Brien, Fran Warren, Jimmy Roselli. These are some of the nearly fifty acts these two managerial Goliaths represented.

Services were held at the Park West Memorial. Its chapel, which holds five hundred people comfortably, proved to be much too small for Sammy's friends. Everyone was there; the stars and the unknowns, agents and managers, stagehands and receptionists, writers and song pluggers, and even a Catholic priest. Rabbi Mann, who conducted the services, arrived a little late. For a while, because of his age and ill health, it was feared the Rabbi wouldn't make an appearance at all. Justifiably worried, Harry Steinman mused as he passed me: "Stand in the wings, Father. You might have to do the act."

"Harry," I encountered, "it's been four decades since I studied Hebrew. All I can remember is Aleph, Beth, Gimmel, Daleth . . ."

Joey Adams delivered one of the eulogies and reminded the audience not to cry for Sam. Right now, he told us, he's seated ringside, watching the greatest show the world could ever see.

It is the opinion of many experts that pound for pound, Sugar Ray Robinson was the greatest fighter in the world. If I could enjoy a second spot, I would nominate Willie Pep as the second-greatest fighter of the world. This youngster was a delight to watch. In fact, many were the times I became convinced I was witnessing a ballet rather than a fist fight. He moved with the finesse of a ballerina. We met, Willie and I, in Boston and became steadfast friends. It delighted me to watch him in training—punching the bag, jumping rope, sparring. His wife, Mary, came to Boston and begged me to return with her to Hartford in an attempt to save their marriage. My efforts proved futile.

Willie had signed to fight the challenger, Sandy Saddler. On the night of the event it seemed all Hartford had been transported to Madison Square Garden. Pandemonium broke out inside and outside his dressing room. Lou Viscusi and Bill, Pep's manager and trainer respectively, tried to restore order. The fight was rough and bruising. At the end of the fifteen rounds, Willie lost the fight and the featherweight championship title. He returned to his dressing room, his face crimsoned with cuts and blood. No fans returned to the room to extend a word of sympathy. Only his trainer, manager and myself. All the world loves a winner!

This bit of information might interest the F.B.I. or perhaps even the C.I.A., and I'm sure New York's Finest: There's a smuggling ring operating between New York and Las Vegas consisting of a Catholic priest, an airline stewardness and a public relations man. And what is the contraband? Gold, silver, narcotics, unstamped cigarettes? Hell, no!—beautiful clusters of tasty cream-filled Italian pastries. Tony Zoppi, public relations man of the Vegas Riviera, is the recipient, Jill Bugler of United Air Lines is the courier and Father Bob is the pusher. Evidently Las Vegas, San Francisco and Los Angeles cannot compare with the incomparable aroma-packed goodies from Ferrara—La Bella Ferrara and Roma of Mulberry Street in Little Italy. Anyone tapping my phone would hear this conversation: In her sweet "milk, coffee or tea" voice, Jill informs me: "Tony asked me to call you. Is the stuff ready?"

"It's packed and ready to go," I assure her.

"Good. I'll pick it up later today and have it there tomorrow evening."

"Is it worth all this bother?" Tony Zoppi was questioned. "You're damn right it's worth all that trouble. How do you think we keep our president, Dino, happy and content?"

Frank Morales is a bartender at the famous Manhattan steak house, the Pen & Pencil. In the art of dispensing the golden liquid Frank has no peers. His surname is misleading; it sounds Spanish. However, it's pure Sicilian—in fact, Palermitano ("native of Palermo") to be exact. There's neither rhyme nor reason for the name Frank Morales to be mentioned in this book. He is as far removed from showbusiness as I from the Ku Klux Klan, except for one incident which occurred in his life. His daughter, Carol, developed a very strong friendship with another Brooklynese lass, Concetta Ingolia. This camaraderie continued to flourish throughout grammar and high school days. Finally, Concetta left Brooklyn for the cerulean-blue skies of California in search of a life as a movie-recording star. While struggling for stardom, she met and fell in love with a young actor. As was to be expected, Carol was nominated to be the bride's maid of honor. Today both Carol and Concetta are Californians; Carol often baby-sits while Concetta continues to pursue her career. Frank's adopted niece, Concetta Ingolia, is today's Connie Stevens.

I met Lea Rae and Sonny Werblin through a mutual friend, Miss Jane Wyman. As I prepared to write this anecdote, I realized my total ignorance regarding Mr. Werblin's real name. It necessitated a telephone call to learn his nomenclature is David. However, he is affectionately called "Sonny" by everyone, friend and foe. It seems Lea Rae and "Sonny," Jane Wyman and Ronald Reagan all started in showbiz about the same time: Wyman and Reagan as actors, Lea Rae as a singer and "Sonny" as an agent. If ever a man has been gifted with a charismatic Midas touch, he is David "Sonny" Werblin. Accruing incredible affluence, he transferred his allegiance from showbiz to the gridiron. As owner of the New York Jets, Werblin made sport history by paying Joe Namath an unheard-of fortune to sign with his organization. When I ran into "Sonny" some time ago, he hurled at me one succinct question: "How would you like to be chaplain of the Jets?" "Chaplain????" I practically shouted, "I've enough problems with my temperamental make-believers, but at least I can argue with them. How the hell do I argue with your six-foot-ten three-hundred-pounders?" Finally "Sonny" abandoned the human horses of the gridiron and is presently dedicated to the art of breeding real horses.

Although Anthony Quinn's movie is titled *Across 110th Street*, a special segment of the actual filming took place on Mulberry Street. Quinn was its star and executive producer. An extra, Bob Balantine, spotted me and introduced himself, reminding me we had previously met during the filming of *The Godfather* in our neighborhood. He further enlightened me that there were some dear friends of mine on the set. Out of the famous clam house "Umberto's" appeared Ralph Serpi, producer, and Barry Shear, director. Kiddingly, I asked Barry if he could use me in a priest role. To the contrary, he advised me; he's looking for a killer type. You came to Umberto's "two months too late" was the response. Among the extras I met a towering, massive, young black gentleman, standing six-four and weighing about three hundred pounds. He told me many people mistake him for Rosey Grier. "With a frame like that, have you ever considered playing professional football?" I inquired. "I played football for ten years, but not professionally." "Where did you play?" "I played where they use striped uniforms."

Amid the scores of federal and Congressional committees, the intelligentsia of our nation's capital created still another: the House Crime Committee. The purpose of this select body is to probe criminal influence in sports. One of the witnesses was Sammy Davis; another will be Frank Sinatra. It is quite evident that the Crime Committee is more interested in names than it is in crimes. As Sammy departed from the hearing room, a reporter asked to what extent crime had infiltrated show business. His response was superb. "Ask Marlon Brando—he's the Godfather." Corbett Monica, music publisher Al Gallico and others discussed this Davis episode. Someone inquired if the diminutive star was in trouble for mentioning names and places. I had no answer to that question. However, I did present a strong suggestion: "I've got enough problems of my own. Let his rabbi worry about him."

There was a unique quality about the Conference of Personal Managers East Salute and dinner honoring Jean Stapleton from the award-winning television show *All in the Family*, Ed McMahon from NBC's Johnny Carson Show and Harold J. Gibbons, vice-president of the International Brotherhood of Teamsters. No master of ceremonies. However, there was a mistress of ceremonies: Miss Virginia Graham. The Women's Lib! It's the first time in the many yesteryears of my life that I witnessed a woman operate in that capacity. Virginia loves to talk, and talk she did. In a tone quite surreptitious, she revealed she had indeed been a mistress for thirty-two years—to her dearest Harry, her husband. In introducing the dais, I became the first of her many victims. "And now . . . dear, dear Father Bob. I personally think he's from Central Casting," her rapid-fire voice fusilladed the microphones. "We want him on our side so badly, we made Father Bob a proposition. If he will convert to Judaism and become a rabbi, we've offered him a stunningly beautiful house in Beverly Hills, with a gargantuan swimming pool. And a seventy-five-thousand-dollar yearly salary. For fringe benefits we'll throw in a chauffeured limousine and a young, vivacious wife. But," she giggled, "he'd rather live on seventy-five dollars a month without a wife."

Actor John Marley's sudden success came with *Love Story* and *The Godfather*. Now, he tells me, he will star in his next release with Otto Preminger as producer and has signed as leading character for two more pictures. In *The Godfather* he portrayed the role of the pompous Hollywood tycoon who vehemently refuses to contract Al Martino as the vocalist in his much-publicized film. His avocation as a horseman, his prize possession being a six-hundred-thousand-dollar stallion, is common knowledge among the Hollywood hierarchy. Now the singer has the blessings and assurance of the Godfather that he will definitely play the role. In one of the gruesomest scenes I've ever witnessed, Mr. Marley awakes in his king-sized bed to find the head of his prized stallion at his feet, blood liberally covering the bed sheets. I asked Mr. Marley how the technicians were able to fabricate that head and make it appear so convincingly realistic. Much to my consternation, he informed me there was no deception: it was really a horse's head; only the blood is unreal. What about the A.S.P.C.A.? The animal had enjoyed a long life, was about to be converted into dog food, so Paramount had it decapitated.

My first view of the new Madison Square Garden was indeed gratifying. The Italian-American Civil Rights League held its second annual show with a magnificent cast including Sammy Davis, Don Rickles, Jimmy Durante, Sonny King, Buddy Greco, Paul Anka, Enzo Stuarti, Pat Henry and many more.

I couldn't understand the most exuberant welcome I received until I learned of the anonymous telephone call. It promised to shoot and kill one of the performers while onstage. Presto, last rites. Amusing yet tragic was the sight of Johnny Anka, Paul's uncle. Gripping a satchel of his nephew's music, obviously pained by nervousness, he was begging an usher to investigate the area beneath the stage in search of bombs.

Pat told the vast audience he and Father Bob rode a subway (Pat in a subway???) when opposite us a drunken Irishman kept shouting, "There's no heaven . . . there's no heaven." Pat grew tired of the tirade and shouted back, "If there's no heaven, then go to hell, but be quiet about it."

We were advised Don Rickles couldn't make the trip by helicopter from Westbury, Long Island, because of bad weather conditions. When Don did arrive, shocking everyone, we questioned him. "To hell with weather conditions," he told the pilot. "With these Italians it's either the Madison Square Garden or a funeral parlor. Have your choice."

Sammy Davis simply asked me, "How do you keep so damn thin?" "I do a hell of a lot more praying than you, Sammy. My Boss takes good care of me."

Enzo Stuarti stole the show. It's no surprise to me. I've seen it happen time and again. In his tenor-baritone voice he sang arias from *Man of La Mancha,* the "Battle Hymn of the Republic" and *Pagliacci.* As he sang the "Battle Hymn," every spectator either struck their hands in unison or lit matches in the darkened arena. The spirit of patriotism that pervaded the cavernous Garden held each of us spellbound. With the last note of *Pagliacci* spent, everyone stood up and cheered. As Enzo returned to the dressing room, his eyes were moist with the success he had just witnessed. I whispered into his ear: "Thank God you're not a cantor in some synagogue. I'd be out of a job." "I sang my heart out. Never have I worked so well in my whole life." Their response, he confessed, was so tumultuous, so spontaneous, he felt he was driving three Ferraris all at the same time.

Occasionally I drag my wearied body and aging bones to the office of a dear friend, Dr. John Barone. Doc, after many years in the world of advertising, spent an equal amount of time studying the human body and its functions. Today he is one of the finest chiropractors in the City of New York.

On one of my visits, the Doctor asks me to linger awhile. Conscious of my devotion to professional football, he wanted me to meet one of his clients, the coach and player of the New York Giants, Alex Webster. Ten minutes passed when this massive, leonine figure walked—or rather, hobbled and wobbled—into the office. "Meet Alex Webster," the Doc introduced.

Never did I realize the amount of physical abuse and punishment a professional football player endures until I laid eyes on that pitiful man. He appeared completely exhausted, practically crippled and very dejected because the previous day the Giants had lost their game. Dr. Barone told me the only nonmedical description of Mr. Webster's condition after a game is "Lumps and Bumps." Now when I sit before a TV set and watch the boys bang one another as Howard Cosell and Frank Gifford word-paint the intricate plays, I'm less critical, less censorious and much more compassionate. Personally, I'd rather hit a golf ball. It's more my cup of tea.

It was a strange, peculiar sensation. In the presence of two hundred delegates of the American Guild of Variety Artists, with Joey Adams, their president, Mr. Karl Wallenda knelt before me to ask for my blessing. The Wallendas, as any circus aficionado knows, are the noted high priests of all high-wire families. This occurred some years ago, in Manhattan Center; after the occupational deaths of both his adopted son and his nephew, Wallenda sought God's blessings for his and his family's physical safety. Not quite a year later, another relative fell from the ropes to her doom.

What singular and unique motivation drives these people to continue in the face of death I cannot explain. A single mistake, the slightest slip, spells death. "Why do you continue, Karl?" was my simple question. "The high wire is our life" was his simple answer.

Again the radio news divulged another tragedy in the life of Karl Wallenda and his family: Richard Guzman, the twenty-nine-year-old son-in-law of Wallenda, died from a sixty-foot fall.

Occupational hazards do exist in many professions. Policemen and firemen face the ultimate every day of their lives. However, they stand a chance—perhaps even can afford a mistake; but not so with the high-wire act. It's complete paralysis, if they're lucky, or death, if they're not. Might the answer be: The Show Must Go On?

Knowing a vast multitude of people may be fun, but it isn't easy. In my younger days, recalling names was difficult but possible; today I find it equally difficult and impossible. I attempt to avoid any confrontation with my memory by greeting people with a wide-dentured "Hi"—or "Hi, dear" if my words are directed to the female species. My efforts to categorize people into their particular branch of work—comic, writer, actor, columnist, dancer, musician, etc.—succeeded for a while, until my latest tragic experience. Comedian Bob Melvin, who works frequently with Tom Jones, unexpectedly joined our party. My mind went blank! "Hello, Mr. Comedian," I blurted out. "You've forgotten my name!

You've forgotten my name!" clamored Bob loud and strong enough for everyone in the room to hear. However, the pièce de résistance occurred a good many years ago. Having finished dinner with a nephew, we passed a table when someone greeted me. I turned my head from whence the voice emanated, stared a few moments and introduced the couple to the relative. "I want you to meet Mr. and Mrs. Earl Wilson." A few seconds of frigid silence. Then the bomb: "Sorry, Father. You have the correct profession but the wrong party. We are Mr. and Mrs. Hy Gardner."

I have always been a firm believer in the old showbiz cliché "The bigger they are, the nicer they are." We sat in Danny's Nook Room when a party of four walked in to occupy the star table. I faced the wall and consequently did not notice the foursome. Soon someone tapped my shoulder, greeted me and invited me to meet his son and daughter-in-law. Bert Bacharach, Sr., politely walked me to his table. He stopped momentarily and hesitantly asked if I hadn't met his son at the March of Dimes dinner, in which his son was honored. I reminded him the invitation had been extended but an out-of-town commitment prevented my acceptance. "Burt," said Dad, "this is Father Bob." "Father," said Son, "this is my wife, Miss Angie Dickinson." I told young Burt I was a great fan of his and pointing to the vivacious and angelic Angie, I volunteered to be a greater fan of hers. "I like your taste" was his comment. The young composer who made the covers of *Life, Time* and *Newsweek* placed his arm around my shoulder and whispered, "Dad and Mom have told me so many wonderful things about you." Like I said, "The bigger they are, the nicer they are."

In the Monticello Supper Club, Framingham, Massachusetts, the robust baritone voice of Sergio Franchi filled every inch of space. Like the white-peak swells or the thundering waves of the majestic oceans, his voice rose to magnificent heights or softened to a mere whisper. Sergio is a real showman. The show concluded, I met him in the corridor as he returned to the room to sit with some friends. "How is Donna Valery's brother?" I greeted him. Incidentally, whenever I meet Donna Valery I always ask, "How is Sergio Franchi's sister?"

After an exchange of some friendly platitudes, he placed his arm around my shoulder and we began to walk. "Che bella fabrica!" (What gorgeous material!) he observed as he touched the fabric of my mohair suit. "How does a Franciscan with the vow of poverty manage to dress this well?" he wondered. "It's easy. This Franciscan happens to be a charity case. My clients dress me, sometimes from head to foot. Jack E. Leonard, in a reciprocal mood for some favors I performed, bought me this mohair suit, a cashmere coat and a pair of Bostonian shoes. Maybe, Sergio, someday you'll like to join my club and be a client?" To that question the only thing Donna Valery's brother *flashed* was a large mouth of white pearly teeth.

I first met Merv Griffin when he arrived in New York, having left the Freddie Martin orchestra as the band vocalist. His penthouse pad was located in the sophisticated area of Manhattan's East Fifties, in the same building where Miss LuAnn Simms, of the Arthur Godfrey era, made her residence. In fact, that's where I met him. He dated quite frequently with a bevy of beauties— models, stewardesses and showgals—but these shenanigans stopped the first time he met Julann, the daughter of a New Jersey judge. Many were the times our group—Julann and Merv, Dorothy McGuire and Julie La Rosa, LuAnn Simms and Loring Buzzel, Tommy Leonetti and Jaye P. Morgan and (today's top director) Alan Rafkin—bowled at the Madison Square Garden lanes and ate pizza at Frank's Pizzeria on Second Avenue at the foot of the Queensboro Bridge. I candidly felt hurt when Merv and Julann decided to marry and didn't ask me to officiate. He had an Irish clergyman do the job.

At this particular period Griffin was unemployed. At a Catholic Actors Guild dinner, its president, actor Horace McMahon, turned to me and commented, "This kid will make it big someday." He pointed to Merv. Soon the word was out: Merv Griffin had signed for a TV coast-to-coast network talk show, in the same format as the Johnny Carson, Joey Bishop shows. Westinghouse would syndicate the show on one hundred and sixty stations.

Since this happy occasion, I haven't seen or heard from Merv except for one encounter. It was at Sophie Tucker's funeral services. He spotted me among a group of mutual friends. "And how is Father Robert Perrella?" he greeted me. "Merv," I replied, "I knew you WHEN you called me 'Father Bob.'"

I sat in the barber chair of the St. Regis Hotel while barber Paul Montera clipped whatever locks still penetrate my scalp. How many years have you known my dad? the young tonsorialist wanted to know. "Many years, perhaps from 1945." Rudy Montera, considered one of the best barbers in the trade, was well known in theatrical circles. Rudy would take second spot to no one—in his estimation, he was the best.

We met on a Como appointment at the Trans-Lux Barber Shop at Forty-ninth Street and Broadway. Perry kiddingly lambasted Rudy's technique, claiming his own far superior. A chair became available for Como to prove his tonsorial prowess, and he asked me to be seated. In the meantime, Tommy Dorsey was Rudy's next appointee. Both barber and ex-barber began cutting away. The first few strokes of the scissors produced a nervous spasm throughout my system. I've heard Perry sing and appreciated his voice; I'd never seen him cut hair, so I could hardly be appreciative of his barbering savoir-faire. His long absence from the barber's chair didn't help encourage me, either. I suddenly jumped from the chair, removed the large white cloth from under my chin and reminded the ex-barber, "If you're looking for guinea pigs, why don't you try the Bowery?"

Throughout these many years, Rudy's Barber Shop never charged me the price of a haircut. A small tip was accepted and appreciated. But the Montera tradition, father and son, will not take my money. I reassured young Paul that his dad, now deceased, was the greatest barber ever to touch my head and scalp. Far greater than Como, the ex-barber.

I love the game of golf but cannot play it well. I cannot play it well because, bereft of an automobile, I cannot get to a golf course. Ask any professional golfer and he'll tell you, without practice you cannot play golf well. Since this syllogism makes a lot of sense, let me get to my story.

Bob Strauss invited me to a golf tournament, as a spectator and not a participant. As his golf partner Mr. Strauss drew Danny Thomas, his buddy. The time to tee off arrived. Mr. Thomas grew more nervous as each minute clicked away, because Bob Strauss was nowhere in sight. A man characterized by a keen sense of punctuality, *Stalag 17*'s "Animal" did not even telephone to explain his tardiness. "Where the hell is the 'Animal'?" Danny definitely wanted to know. No one could help him or even suggest a possibility.

Then the shrill cries of a siren. Was it a police car? Moments later we learned it was a local hospital ambulance. Perhaps a golfer or a spectator collapsed from the summer heat. Perhaps someone became ill. As our eyes searched for a sick, prostrated victim, all we could see were perfectly healthy people anxiously awaiting the tournament to start.

The ambulance came to a sudden halt. The driver and his assistant leaped out of their seats and opened the back doors of the vehicle. They pulled out the stretcher with something sprawled across it and covered with a bed sheet. The stretcher-bearers began walking in our direction, as Danny Thomas collapsed in a convulsion of laughter. Danny removed the bed sheet, and there lay the "Animal"—Bob Strauss—and his golf bag.

The ambiance of my neighborhood isn't exactly a landscape for a scenic-view postcard. It's New York's "Little Italy." The area comprises a conglomerate of nondescript tenements interspersed with a variety of factories. The local businesses are strictly *italiano:* Italian cigar store, Italian-record shops, Italian pastry places, Italian newspapers, magazines and souvenir shops, Italian-bread stores, Italian restaurants, pizza parlors, scungilli and calamari dispensaries, Italian-cheese outlets specializing in mozzarella and provolone, Italian-clothing boutiques.

Many thousand of tourists walk our streets; thousands more eat our food. It's no surprise to see Frank Sinatra, Jackie Gleason, Sophia and Gina, Robert Strauss, Peter Falk and John Cassavetes and many more celebrities dropping into our local restaurants for linguine with marinara sauce, or dipping into a platter of scungilli with hot or medium sauce, or some other Italian delicacy. This occurs more than frequently.

Writers often referred to the thickly populated district as slum property and its people living in squalor and wretched living conditions. It's not the Waldorf or the Pierre or the Plaza. But it is far from squalid or wretched. I've visited many of these homes, and each visit provided me with greater surprises. Each apartment, though modest in size, is furnished with good or moderately priced furniture. Each apartment is immaculately clean and spotless. More roaches have been seen in condominiums in Sutton Place than Mulberry Street. I've witnessed more charity, compassion and camaraderie among my people than I would hope to see in the Silk Stocking District, where neighbors know you by sight rather than by name. Ad rem: a case in point.

A lethargic and comatose young man, apparently on narcotics, appeared early one morning on Mulberry Street. He was seen approaching The Block from Canal Street, completely stark naked. Adam himself could not have been more au naturel. What would be the normal reaction of a community in such circumstances? The odds are one hundred or one thousand to one: call the cops.

Not my neighborhood, thank Almighty God. First, someone threw a blanket out of their window to wrap around the sick man, who was then taken out of the cold into a warm hallway. Heads and hands sticking out of windows like a completed crossword puzzle; cries of anxiety rushed down the street. Evidently some people do give a damn. "What size pants does he wear?" "What size shoes?" "Angie's husband is about his size; call her."

"How about Funzi, Levio and Johnny the Butcher?" Then a cascade of clothes came flying through many windows. It looked like New Year's Eve without the confetti but men's apparel hitting the street. Shorts, jerseys, socks, shoes, trousers, jackets. Still dazed and comatose, the young man was completely fitted from head to toe within ten minutes. He left The Block with an extra pair of pants and a jacket under his arm and a prayer of thanksgiving in his heart.

To complete this opus without a mention of Mr. Irving Chezar would constitute a grave and mortal sin of omission. If, in the argot of mobdom's citizens, you need a godfather or a rabbi, Irv was both my spiritual father and my rabbi. Unlike many theatrical agents, Mr. Chezar achieved superior educational training, passing the New York bar exam with the appellation Mr. Counselor. However, he preferred the role of agent to the art of jurisprudence.

On one of his multiple assignments, Irving found himself in London when Roselle and Perry Como and family arrived in the City of the Falling Bridge. General Artists Corporation, Mr. Chezar's employer, ordered him to remain in London, assist the Comos in every possible way and await further orders from the main office. To his knowledge, his next destination was to return to New York and home. A telegram arrived and Mr. Chezar was busily arranging another trip to Rome: The powers that be commanded my friend to visit the Eternal City as soon as possible. Contact Mario Lanza. Inform him of a prospective weekly TV musical series, alla the Como show. Next came the monotonous procedure of packing and rearranging tickets and hotel reservations, etc. On the morning of his departure, still another telegram arrived with this message: CANCEL ROME TRIP. RETURN HOME. MARIO LANZA DEAD!

I read where Harvey Schmidt, who composed the score for *The Fantasticks,* has been signed by Paramount to do his first film score for *Bad Company. The Fantasticks* is the longest-running play in the history of the New York theater. It is housed in a little brownstone building in the Sullivan Street section of Greenwich Village, a stone's throw from Washington Square Park. Hence the name, Sullivan Street Playhouse.

What vivid and delightful memories that edifice brings to my mind! Long before the transformation, it housed Jimmy Kelly's Night Club. To describe Jimmy is to describe a saint. Kelly came from Italian stock. In those days only Irishmen were fighters, so when Jimmy decided to enter a prizefighting career, DeSalvio became Kelly. A local politician, his deeds of charity, including tons of food for the poor at Christmastime, read like a litany of love. When I was sick, he would order his chef to cook up hot, delicious soup. On sizzling summer nights he would sneak me into his kitchen, which faced the street, and serve cool, delightful drinks. Many were the times in my younger years I stood, dazed and amazed, in front of Kelly's to watch Jack Dempsey, Gene Tunney, Mayor Jimmy Walker and Irving Berlin visit his bistro. In fact, it was Jimmy Kelly who introduced Irving Berlin to lovely Ellin Mackay. This introduction made history when the little Jewish songwriter married the daughter of the New York Telephone and Telegraph magnate.

Having been a participant, Jimmy loved to watch prizefights. His many invitations for me to accompany him were rarely denied. I shall never forget one particular evening in the lobby of the old Garden when Jimmy placed a bet with a bookmaker. A detective spotted the transaction and arrested Jimmy and the book. As the three were leaving the lobby, Jimmy winked. "Aren't you coming, Padre?" "Not this time, Jimmy boy!"

Why are obese people invariably so good-natured, considerate and altruistic—in short, good Samaritans? I don't buy the old gag that fat people can't run so they have to be nice. One of the nicest obese gals I've ever met is singer Julie De John. In the past I had heard of the De John Sisters, but failed to meet either of the two girls. George Scheck, her manager, did the honor in introducing us. "So you are the famous Irish priest," laughing Julie chortled.

"You've just made two mistakes: I'm not famous and I'm not Irish."

Big Julie expressed her nervousness as she sat in the wings of Philharmonic Hall. The presence of some of the biggest names in the business, mostly singers, caused Julie to ask, "I wonder how I'll do tonight?" "You sing and I'll pray," I admonished her. Julie gave a great performance, returned to her chair and tried to relax. "You know," the sweet fat girl confessed, "my kid sister did the best thing. She quit and raised a family. Me, I'll never quit this damn business."

One of the funniest lines I heard that night came from Julie. As she stood, stage center, facing the audience, she timidly observed, "I hope this microphone isn't hiding me."

"White Christmas" has always been associated with Crosby, "Prisoner of Love" with Como, "I Left My Heart in San Francisco" with Bennett and "The Donkey Serenade" with the veteran Allan Jones. Reflect on Allan and there pops into your mind the magnificent portrait of his onetime wife, graceful Irene Hervey. Reflect on the Joneses and you have Jack Jones. Recently TV News showed Jack tenderly embracing his soon-to-be Mrs., as Mother commented he's already had three unsuccessful marriages.

Young Jack never impressed me as a vocalist. He seems to lack that distinctive quality, that vocal trademark that would set him apart from all other vocalists. Turn on the radio and after the first four bars you'll know if it's Crosby, Sinatra or Bennett. Not so with Jack Jones; he strikes me as just another singer. Be this as it may, some time ago I attended a benefit at which Jack was to appear. He arrived with his mother, as lovely and attractive as ever. Backstage, she and I crossed paths and she introduced herself. "Hello, Father. I'm Jack Jones's mother." "To me," I bouqueted, "you're still the lovely Irene Hervey."

What was once glamorous and sophisticated can in time become boring and tedious. This about explains my feelings towards cocktail parties. First, there's never enough chairs to accommodate the guests. Secondly, it's always the same people being invited. Thirdly, what is there to talk about after you've answered the question "How do you feel?"

Most of my friends know when I order a drink it's one piece of ice or no ice at all. This obvious eccentricity developed as a result of cocktail parties. I'm repulsed with the feeling of my hand sticking to the glass because of the ice and cold. And in the majority of cases, you'll never find space available to rest your glass.

I recall one such party, many yesterdays ago, on Central Park South. Rosemary Clooney was the hostess. She invited a dozen people on that Thanksgiving Day afternoon. Some—like Betty, her sister, José Ferrer and his brother—I recognized. Among the unacquainted I met was a darling, attractive young lady, a budding actress, Miss Ruth Cosgrove. Many years passed and I often wondered, What ever happened to the actress Ruth Cosgrove? The revelation finally reached me. She is no longer a budding actress but a Beverly Hills housewife. Her new name is Mrs. Ruth Berle. She's Milton's wife.

Songwriting is an art. Song plugging is a way of life. Regardless of the quality of a song—good, bad, or indifferent—its fate remains dubious. The plugger will devise every trick in the book to get it spun by disk jockies. Take the unforgettable hit "I Left My Heart in San Francisco." Tony Bennett and I were returning from the Singer Bowl at New York's World Fair. Incidentally, he had been presented on that occasion with an award as the outstanding entertainer of the year. On our way to Englewood, New Jersey, where Tony's home is located, I asked him how such a hit was created. It surprised me to learn when "San Francisco" was first released, it flopped with the velocity of the Frisco earthquake, except in the city whose name it bore. The publishers smartly decided to recall the song and let it die a sudden death. This coup de grâce was not to be its destiny. After an interim of time, the publisher pontificated its second release. Mind you, it was the same, identical recording. It exploded into a coast-to-coast hit, on the *Hit Parade* for months, making all the music charts in the country. When I attend a wedding and hear the espouseds' favorite song, "San Francisco," a knowledgeable smile spills over my face, because The City by the Sea almost didn't make it.

I feel a deep poignancy concerning the amount of divorces occurring among showpeople. Husbands and wives are exchanged with the same shameless frequency that one would change a shirt or dress. There's a great gag around town about the Hollywood boutique that sells drip-and-dry wedding gowns. The irony exists, however, not in Hollywood or showbiz but in America and every profession known to man. Statistically, three and one half out of every five marriages are assassinated by the weapon of divorce in America. This means seven out of every ten clergymen's "I pronounce you Man and Wife" are nullified with the judge's "I declare you divorced and free." These are frightening figures not only for showbiz but for the world. One group of entertainers ostensibly unaffected by this craze to separate from their spouses are the comedians. George Burns, Jack Benny, Fred Allen, Eddie Cantor, Jimmy Durante, Danny Thomas, Joey Bishop, Buddy Hackett, Corbett Monica, Jack E. Leonard, Shecky Green, Don Rickles and many, many more. Why? I do not know the elements of this miraculous panacea. Perhaps, as someone suggested, it's one hell of a laugh living with a comedian. As Kay Leonard, Jack E.'s deceased wife, once told me: "I got to laugh or I don't eat." NBC's Midnight Johnny must be doing something wrong!

I dislike the use of words like "prolific" or "ingenious." They are employed with such monotonous frequency as to lose their meaning and significance. However, when I enumerate some of the songs for which Mitchell Parrish has written the lyrics, only two words surface to my mind: Prolific! Ingenious! "Stardust," "Deep Purple," "Moonlight Serenade," "Stars Fell on Alabama," "Stairway to the Stars," "Take Me In Your Arms," "Sophisticated Lady," "Sweet Lorraine," "Does Your Heart Beat For Me?," "Sleigh Ride," "Ruby," "Volare."

Recently Mitch and some friends visited me and we made the "Italian route" with pasta *al dente* at a local restaurant, cappuccino at a coffee shop and Italian ice at a confectionery store. When it was time to return to their homes, I suggested we wait for a cab on the corner of Canal and Mulberry Streets. Cars went streaking by for five or six minutes when we finally spotted a cab. As we raised our hands to stop the vehicle, the driver just continued to drive past us. We all did a double take. No, there was nothing unusual about the chauffeur; he was behind the wheel, where chauffeurs are supposed to be. In the passenger area, there sat a dog, all by his lonesome. I turned to Mitch and suggested, "Can you write a love song about a dog being chauffeured alone around the streets of New York?" The proposed title: "Now I've Seen It All."

The Showbiz Priest does not necessarily administer exclusively to the needs of showbiz folks. Whatever borders on the periphery of the entertainment world is oftentimes included. He may baptize the grandchild of an NBC special policeman; marry the daughter of a stagehand; bury the mother of a CBS page. Will you do us the honor to officiate at my daughter's wedding? requested Mrs. Julia Moore a few years ago, and Mrs. Frances Pallazzola only a few weeks ago. Julie and Fran are hatcheck girls at Danny's Hideaway.

Julie's wedding went flawlessly, strictly according to the script. Fran's was something else. Preparing for my barbering chores, I learned too late and much to my regret the injector was defective. The blade stuck halfway in and halfway out of the case. The moment the blade touched my face, I dropped the razor and it slashed across the index finger of my left hand. I applied a Band-Aid to the incision, which ordinarily would have required a couple of stitches. Then into a chauffeur-driven limousine to transport me to church.

We hadn't driven five minutes when my Italian chauffeur passed slowly through a green (naturally) light and a Chinese tried to hurriedly jump a red (naturally) light. He missed us by the length of an egg roll.

During the services I felt something warm and sticky beneath my left hand. It was my blood from the incision. The assisting priest offered me the purificator—a cloth used to purify the chalice—and I applied it to my hand. It's the first time in thirty years I celebrated the Holy Mass minus one hand. My soliloquy? Greater love than this no one hath that a priest bleeds while officiating at a friend's daughter's wedding.

Miss Pat Moore is one of the lovelier of New York citizens—Bronx-bred, a Fordham University beauty queen and one of the highest-priced Madison Avenue models. It is customary for Pat to throw a yearly Christmas party for her friends—who, understandably, include some tiptoe-prancing hairdressers. On one such occasion, fortunately, I met two interesting guests, both children of showbiz: actor Ralph Meeker and vocalist Morgana King. I was enlightened and thrilled when I learned Miss King originated from the same neighborhood and, in fact, the very same street (Thompson) where I was born and raised. It is Little Italy. Likewise, it surprised me to learn Morgana is of Italian extraction.

Today Miss King has attained incredible success in the world of the cinema. It is she who portrays the role of the Godfather's wife, Mrs. Corleone ("Lion-hearted"). To obtain the role, Morgana was forced to stuff herself with plenty of pasta and pizza. Producer Al Ruddy and director Francis Ford Coppola demanded she add to her frame twenty-five pounds of extra adipose tissues; this supposedly would represent the typical Italian wife and mother. Miss King had read Mario Puzo's book and was convinced the role was hand-tailored for her. She pleaded for the part, and her pleas were not in vain. How could a vocalist turned actress be so terrific in her first acting role? someone asked. Considering Morgana and my neighborhood background, how could she lose?

Paul Blye is a dear friend. He owns and runs a very exclusive men's shop on Fifth Avenue. The remaining part of the organization, Blye International, is managed by his brother. Believe it or not, Paul initiated this million-dollar business years ago by going to Orchard Street, on Manhattan's Lower East Side; buying a dozen pairs of socks and selling them to friends. From socks to riches. Paul, like myself, is a great fight fan. Friday nights became our temple nights out, when we would dine at Frankie and Johnnie's and arrive at the Garden just in time for the main bout.

On one of these occasions, Paul, I and some friends sat third row ringside. As we relaxed, waiting for the announcer, Johnny Addy, to introduce the gladiators, someone walking the aisle stopped suddenly at our row, quickly removed his jacket, threw it on the ground and was in fighting position. Another man, a powerful Negro, seated next to Paul, jumped to his feet and he too was ready for action. It seems that the aisle-walker and jacket-thrower was none other than Mr. Cassius Clay—pardon: Muhammad Ali—and the other gentleman, the next contender Clay would meet in the near future. What an act! Such élan, such enthusiasm, with the perfect setting: the Madison Square Garden and twenty thousand spectators.

Comics Jack Carter and Morey Amsterdam are good friends and golf partners. But camaraderie ends once Carter places a golf club in his hands. Jack would hope to play with the finesse of a Jack Nicklaus or a Lee Trevino. Morey plays for the hell of it. Since Jack seeks near perfection with every stroke of his game, he'll go into a rage at the littlest imperfection. In the meantime, Mr. Amsterdam slices it here or hooks it there, overshoots the green or drops it into the pond, and all this time overworking his vocal cords.

Morey loves to tell a golf story about his partner. It's his way to infuriate Carter even more. It seems one day Jack could do nothing right. From the very first tee-off, Carter began bungling, and with each stroke his performance became worse and worse. Suddenly, the nonpolluted air filled with obscenities and broken golf clubs and golf balls. Came the final hole, Jack asked his caddie for the seven-iron. "I'm sorry, sir," the youngster muttered. "What the hell are you feeling sorry for?" Mr. Jack Carter retaliated.

"Because the only club you have left in your bag is the putter. You've broken all the others."

"Guess what?" Morey will ask anyone willing to listen. "Jack threw the putter, the golf bag and the *caddie*—in that order—into the drink." It's a very funny story—but, sad to say, apocryphal.

It's common knowledge that that great bit of Runyoniana, *Guys and Dolls,* enjoyed a long and splendid Broadway run. Among the starry names that blazoned the marquee were Robert Alda and Vivian Blaine. Both are Broadway favorites whose names relate to many Great White Way musical hits. Bob, the cinematic George Gershwin, is a native New Yorker, but is more at home on the streets and boulevards of Rome; born in Gotham, he spent most of his time in the land of his ancestors, Italy. Now that he wants to live where it's all at—New York—he is forced to live elsewhere, preferably the Eternal City: his wife suffers a respiratory ailment, and doctors have eliminated both New York and Los Angeles as a residential locale. Presently he's fattening the purses of Trans World Airlines and Alitalia commuting at least a half-dozen times a year from Where He'd Rather Not Live to Where It's All At. His greatest claim to fame: he's the father of Alan Alda. Vivian is a lovely thespian with a number of matrimonial adventures, one of which briefly involved an old friend of mine, Milton Rackmil of Universal Films and Decca Records. She is proud, terribly so, of one noncareer event in her family life: she reminds me, loud and clear, as often as she sees me, "My aunt who lives in New Jersey is a Catholic nun." How often I've been tempted to ask her, "Does the Reverend Sister know how many nephews-in-law she's had?" Ouch!

If the words "dangerous," "perilous," risky," "hazardous," "precarious" demand a complementary noun, the dictum would be "personal management." There is no business in showbusiness as dangerous, as perilous, as risky, as hazardous and as precarious as a personal manager. The success and danger of the manager's role depends upon the amount of energy expended in "pushing" his clients and the vacillating and prima-donna temperaments of his stars. One day he's the greatest; the next he's a creepy bastard. To the bourgeois, a contract is a contract, a written agreement that can be enforced by law. Not so in showbiz. There are ways to break the contractual agreement, and one of the easiest is to buy out that valuable piece of paper.

History proves there have been many happy marriages between star and manager; however, many other similar marriages terminated in divorce courts. The ten-percenter invariably is responsible for failure, but never for success. How terribly false! Without Tom Rockwell, Como would still be barbering in his home town in Pennsylvania. Many years ago, Bullets Durgom lost Jackie Gleason. Ken Greengrass lost not only a client; he lost a family—Eydie Gormé and Steve Lawrence. Al Bruno lost the *Tonight* show when he lost Johnny Carson.

Look what managerial know-how accomplished for the career of Nina Van Pallandt. Hers was just a dirty name in a dirty story. Enter Mr. John Marshall, her manager and agent. She's booked into the St. Regis Hotel Maisonette room at six figures, her nightclub tour booked solid, and is contracted to make a movie.

I stood in the lobby of the Americana Hotel with a house phone glued to my ear and the most hurt expression across my face. Someone had just informed me Rosemary Clooney was too preoccupied to accept any visitors. Even Father Bob. My pride crushed, I began to curse showbiz and some ungrateful bastards that comprise it. How could she treat me so? I've known her and her kid sister as young teen-agers. They were practically part and parcel of my life as a young priest. I didn't marry Rosie and José because I could not: José confirmed the fact that he and Uta Hagen had been married in a Catholic church and divorced; otherwise, I would have had the job.

What ever possessed Rosie to act in that fashion, I didn't know then. Ironically, the answer appeared some years later. Down in Miami Beach for a short stay, I visited the home of Mr. and Mrs. Pupi Campo and found no one home. I left a brief note. The following day I was intercomed at the pool, and Betty Clooney Campo kept apologizing for her absence. Within an hour, she and two of her strikingly beautiful daughters sat poolside with me.

"Have you seen my big sister lately?" the dark-haired beauty inquired. I told her what occurred at the Americana. Betty shook her head in disbelief. "The next time," she practically commanded me, "don't call; just crash her pad." "What's happened to our Rosie?" I simply asked. With the expertise of a psychiatrist, she clearly explained her sister's problem: It seems, in her opinion, that Rosie refused to meet any close, personal friends, because she had become too obese. She will work before an audience, but will not face a friend. Women's prerogative.

I don't want to appear hard and impenetrable. Certainly I have met many people in all walks and fashions of life. Admittedly, yours truly fell prey like so many others to star-gazing and hero-worshiping. But that was many, many moons ago. It brings to mind the story of a nephew-in-law. He originated from a speck-on-the-map town in northern New York State. Graduated from a Utica, New York, college, he came to the city and married my niece. He knew as much about showbiz as I do about moon shots. Through my intercession, he was employed at RCA Records headquarters. At this locale all RCA artists record their songs. It didn't take him long before he assumed using the typical show-biz spiel and jargon. "Hey, Unc," he'd crow, "Per and Dinah were in today." The put-down: "Who the hell are you talking about—Per and Dinah Schwartz?"

My greatest put-on came in the form of a postcard from Teheran:

Dear Father Bob:
  I hope you get this—
The Shah and Empress send you their best.
Also love & XXXX from
Cindy and I
  Pal Joey
  Adams

Hereeeeeeeeeeeeeeeeeeeeeeeere's your Per and Dinah!

Of all the human frailties humanity is asked to endure and sustain, blindness is the most depriving. The reason I feel so related to the visionless is my sister was numbered among them. I'm terribly saddened whenever I find myself on East Fifty-ninth Street and watch a coterie of the blind tapping their way to the Lighthouse. One such girl, pretty Mary Jo Lovascio, lived in our parish and attended school at the Lighthouse. She and a classmate, a Puerto Rican boy, José, matriculated at that school until they graduated. Again they both attended the Bernard Baruch High School for the Blind and graduated four years later.

At a very early age, José started strumming a guitar, and as each year passed he became more proficient with the melodious strings. In fact, he played well enough to entertain at Mary Jo's Sweet Sixteen birthday party. Often he would visit Mary Jo's uncle, Tony the Florist on Hester Street, and after a dish of spaghetti alla marinara and a couple of appetizing meatballs, José would cuddle his guitar as though it were a newborn baby, string and sing for hours.

Today Mary Jo is a happily married Mrs. Pascal and the mother of a darling baby. Sadly, she informed me she doesn't see or hear too much from José. He's busily traveling the country, playing his guitar and singing his songs and making lots of money. You see, the little blind boy, her classmate at the Lighthouse, her inseparable friend at the Bernard Baruch High School is today the international showbiz star José Feliciano.

Nick Brady, salesman, introduced me to Scott Brady, actor. The introductions were negotiated over glasses of Scotch that rested on a table of Joe & Rose's Restaurant. "I understand you're friendly with my brother," Scott surmised. "Not really friendly," I reminded him, "although we did meet several times right here in Joe & Rose's." His brother is also an actor, with the nomenclature Lawrence Tierney. Most friends refer to him as "Dillinger," because it was Mr. Tierney who enacted the lead role in the life of that most notorious gangster. Perfect casting. Unless mistaken, I believe this was the one and only lead role Larry Tierney enjoyed. It's said of him that he fought his way into and fought his way out of the movies.

Both brothers long were fighting fools. And they drank as well as they fought. They didn't look for trouble; they weren't particularly keen on brawls. However, I never heard of them turning their backs on either. More often than not, a well-known actor is a target of envy—especially those who customarily enact the roles of the cinematic tough guys. A wise guy will try to impress his girl friend by embarrassing the thespian with a filthy epithet or a sly remark, or a drunk will take a swing at him. If the actor happened to be "Dillinger" or his kid brother, God bless the wise guy; God help the drunk.

Mr. Nick Brady now tells me his friend Scott Brady has reformed—totally renounced drinking and is on his best behavior. In all probability, he is correct. On frequent occasions I've seen the name of Scott Brady on movie credit lists, and this doesn't happen if you're a cantankerous, fighting drunk. Larry evidently has vanished from Screenland. It's been years since I've seen his face on celluloid or his name in print.

My acquaintances are legion; my friends, manifold. There is a man who is neither an acquaintance nor a friend. He rises far above the plateau of acquaintanceship or friendship; he is something "very special" because he's a very special man: Mr. Victor Riesel. To categorize Mr. Riesel's facets of endeavor is impossible. His mental attributes are not to be believed. He's a writer, reporter, columnist, commentator, political analyst, a crusading crime combatant. He and Harry Hershfield are probably the two most sought-after dinner speakers in America.

I run into Vic and his lovely wife at least a half-dozen times a year, invariably at some testimonial dinner or political banquet. If possible, I ask to be seated next to the Riesels. It's an honor and privilege. The world knows of Vic Riesel's total blindness.

The world knows why and how he was attacked and blinded by the slimy snakes and stinking scorpions of the underbrush. His total blindness metamorphosed into a shining golden badge of honor, courage and tenacity. Fear will not deter a man of Mr. Victor Riesel's courageous caliber. He continues to write, continues to comment on television, continues to fight the crime commissioners of the world. Had they instead amputated his hands and feet, he would continue to write and walk. That's the kind of a man Victor Riesel is. A very special man!

I was lost. Hopelessly lost. In the meandering corridors of the Sahara Hotel in Las Vegas I didn't know which end was up. Logically, I was there for a reason. Mike Douglas, the Kennedyesque TV talk star, invited me to attend his opening at the hotel. After the show an invitation to a party for "invited guests only" had also been extended to me. It would be held in a special room, of whose name and location I was completely ignorant. I made several inquiries, but no one seemed to know what I was talking about. Finally a young lady, sensing my problem, approached me. "Are you looking for the Mike Douglas postshow party?" she inquired. "Just follow me," she encouraged the lost soul.

We walked through the lobby, corridors, the casino, corridors, the dining room, corridors, finally into an elevator. We exited the lift only to find myself on one of the hotel floors. "Honey," I said in passing, "are we going to the Mike Douglas party or a party of your own?" "Have no fear," she girlishly admonished me, "I'll get you there." By this time she pressing a doorbell. The door swung open. A lovely and attractive woman greeted me. "Larry," she calls out, "look who's here." I found myself in the penthouse suite of Norma and Larry Storch. Larry, a funny, funny, funny man, made up the first half of the Mike Douglas Sahara show. With Norma and Larry and the young lady, I finally got to the party.

Christmas germinated a very special significance a few years ago. It verily represented the spirit of giving. Mr. Joseph "Sonny"

Ventola, proprietor of the Gun Hill Manor, Bronx, New York, set aside an annual pre-Christmas date for a very illustrious affair. He sponsored a dinner dance in behalf of the Dominican Sisters of the Sick and the Poor. Sonny's strategy for this once-a-year labor of love worked in categorical maneuvers. It was his job to approach his grocery suppliers, butcher, liquor man, baker to donate toward the party. It behooved Sister Rose Terese and her cohort of angels to distribute the tickets to the many friends of their convent.

Sonny demanded of me a very specialized contribution: deliver a showbiz name, preferably female, to entertain the party. On my very first venture, lovely Janice Harper sang her heart out for exactly one hour. On the second expedition, red-haired (natural) and beautiful Miss Louise O'Brien, of Mitch Miller fame, sang to her kinfolk, ninety-five-percent Erin. And on the third try, we really hit the jackpot. Stage, film and television star gorgeous Gloria De Haven sang and danced as though she were working the Cocoanut Grove.

Then one day Sonny telephoned me and at the mere sound of his voice I knew the news to be distressing. "What's wrong, Sonny?" He proceeded to tell me that Sister Rose Terese and the other nuns sold their convent to the State of New York. They'll be moving to Roxbury, Massachusetts, to attend to the needs of the black sick and poor. "May I ask you a question?" Mr. Ventola practically whined. "Don't we have any more *white* sick and poor in New York?"

Julie Budd and her dad were backstage at Lincoln Center's Philharmonic Hall. She was ready and set to open her golden, Streisand-like pipes to entertain a jam-packed house of anxious listeners. Julie is one of the luckier nightingales in the business. She made it big while still a teen-ager. We chatted awhile, during which time I casually congratulated her. "I understand you headlined a show in Vegas. That's quite a feat for a young lady still in her teens." Julie took exception to the remark. "Others go to Vegas to enjoy themselves and be entertained. I have to do two miserable shows every night of the week for two and three weeks," she complained.

The folly of life. O tempora! O mores! I have known legions of entertainers, working, struggling, sweating in dilapidated roadhouses and clubs, with one goal in sight: to work Las Vegas. I have been approached by countless showfolk who offered to work for no money provided it was on a Vegas stage. As one young thespian put it: "I'll pay my own traveling expenses, work for nothing, just food and board. Just get my name on a neon sign—provided the sign is embedded in Las Vegas soil." And Julie complains. . . . O tempora! O mores!

The name "Bobby Darin" first came into earshot when a song made its appearance on the music charts across the country. Bobby wrote "Splish, Splash." Later the songwriter was transformed into a singer. My initial meeting with Mr. Darin was in Mr. Frank Barone's office. Bobby desired to employ Mr. Barone managerially, but Frank was too busy with "humble-pie" Julie La Rosa. I liked Mr. Darin instantly. His voice might not be categorized as great. However, as often is the case, a singer's voice need not be great to be successful. It's the "whole" artist that really counts. Once on stage, Mr. Darin is all pro; he moves with such savoir-faire; he handles his audience as though he were distributing lollypops to kindergartners.

Bobby comes on strong, but he's gifted enough so that coming on strong is easily and simply overlooked. He's brash, arrogant and completely uninhibited. However, his manner is not really offensive. Ordinarily guest stars will thank their host after a show. To watch Bobby expressing his gratitude to Como, you didn't know who was host and who was guest. Even one of the NBC pages reacted, "Who the hell does Darin think he is?" The absolute absence of an awestricken neophyte facing his idol pervaded the scene. I honestly believe Bobby has no idol. Ironically, after so many years of experience and success, Mr. Bobby Darin performed no differently on his very first Como show. A pro from way back. He is, much to my surprise, part Jewish and part Italian. What a combination! Perhaps this explains the overwhelming success of his alltime best-selling record "Mack the Knife." Bobby is not a fair entertainer; he's a very good entertainer. And he knows it.

It was a sultry August Sunday morn. Hot and humid. My phone rang. Mr. and Mrs. Morty Morton were on the other end of the line. "My wife just spoke to the Bob Strausses, and we suggested a walk through Battery Park. Are you interested?" Certainly. On such a hot day, where can a poor man find a better and more refreshing patio than Battery Park?

We wound our way through the maples and elms of the Battery, stopped for a hot dog and a cool drink and arrived at the Staten Island Ferry terminal. How can you go wrong at the price of admission: a twenty-minute ocean voyage at five cents a head? We boarded the ship and within minutes were invited by the captain to be his guests on the captain's bridge. I've sailed the ferry since I was five years of age, knee-high to a grasshopper and half a century ago, and never came close to seeing, let alone relaxing, in the captain's bridge compartment. The entire nautical procedure fascinated me, especially when the pilots docked the ship into the narrow-mouthed gap of the pier without touching a single pile. It was an inexpensive adventure, since we remained aboard ship and saved twenty-five cents in toto on our return to Manhattan.

After our navigational experiment, we returned to Bob Strauss's apartment and prepared for our journey to the Bronx—Sonny Ventola's Gun Hill Manor. Actually, it was the Mortons' and the Strausses' first encounter with Mr. Ventola, one of the most generous and gracious hosts in the restaurant business. He'll feed and liquor you until you're ready to burst. All that hits the tabletop is food and liquor—never a check.

When we arrived, a wedding party had just begun celebrating. Unbeknownst to me, the groom's father was my Bronx taxi driver. Unsolicited and unpaid, Mr. Bob Strauss became a part of the entertainment committee. He told jokes, rolled his eyes and made funny faces, to the delight and glee of the newlyweds. It's a nice way to start a married life: to be entertained by a Hollywood Heavy without signing a check. This was a typical day in the life of a real nice guy, Robert Strauss.

"Paul, I'm terribly sorry about your mother's passing away. Kindly extend my sympathy to Dad and the family." "Will do, Father." The bereaved and saddened figure walked alone on East Forty-fifth Street toward Lexington Avenue, the uplifted collar of his mohair jacket hugging his neck as he struggled with a cold, wintry blast, in search of a taxi. Paul's surname is Anka. My introduction to Paul occurred shortly after he farewelled his beloved Canada to invade New York with his multifaceted talent. Within a few years of his arrival, the teen-ager reached the pinnacle of success in nightclubs, television and recordings. His records spiraled in sales, leaving the likes of Laine, Como and Bennett gasping for breath. Ironically, some of his record hits were written, music and lyrics, by Paul himself. Although he still entertains, he is considered today primarily as one of the most knowledgeable songwriters in the business. Among his many hits, he's written "My Way" for Frank Sinatra and "She's a Lady" for Tom Jones.

Several years ago, Tony Ford, a General Artists Corporation agent representing Anka, called me. "How about christening my firstborn?" I assured him it would be a pleasure indeed. "Paul Anka will be the godfather," he advised me. To my knowledge, Paul was Catholic; hence, he presented no problem. A later conversation with Tony Ford and he enlightened me that Paul was Catholic but not Catholic like you and I. "What the hell are you trying to tell me, Tony?" "He's an Orthodox Catholic."

According to the effete and antiquated laws of the Church, only Roman Catholics may act as sponsors at a baptism. I took matters into my own hands. Since the godmother was Catholic, I designated Paul as the "honorary godfather" of the child. Why should I deprive a child of this intimate spiritual relationship with a man of Paul Anka's caliber—especially, when the word "godfather" means so much today? So "I did it my way."

I intensely dislike Tiny Tim the singer. I very much like Tiny Tim the man. I have the utmost respect and regard for the man, but cannot accept him as an entertainer by any stretch of the imagination. My feeling of ambivalence toward Mr. Tim isn't difficult to explain. We met at a Joey and Cindy Adams party. His ubiquitous shopping bag and ukulele also made an appearance. Tiny graciously entertained the audience, singing a number of his popular songs. The shrill sounds of his mousy voice nauseated and offended me. I instinctively resented him. I've encountered so many fine talents, struggling for a break to make the big scene, working at Macy's and Gimbels to scratch out a living, and here is a vocalist who is voiceless earning thousands of dollars yearly, playing top-named clubs, shrilling "Tiptoe Through the Tulips."

I speak of Tiny Tim the singer. Meeting him personally at the Adams' party, completely transformed my emotions toward him. He is terribly taciturn, refined and modest—incredibly so. He sincerely believes in his craft; he's an honest-to-God entertainer. Friends tell me in his Greenwich Village days, long before he rubbed elbows with success, Tiny was known for his kindness and charity toward the unfortunates and have-nots. Literally, he would give the proverbial shirt off his back.

Tiny's obviously a very religious man. His deep-rooted convictions have been beautifully expressed on various occasions. He and his Vicki, unfortunately, are in the throes of some serious marital problems. Invariably, when interviewed on this topic, he always refers to the Almighty and prayer as the only true panacea for marital happiness. Recently, when asked if his marital problems can be solved, he answered: "Certainly. Everything is always resolved through prayer." I speak now of Tiny Tim the man.

I know nil about the great power plays, the long, sweeping end runs, the double reverses, the long bomb pass which emanated out of the prodigious mind of Mr. Vince Lombardi. I do know his alltime favorite New York Italian restaurant and his favorite New York host, the Amalfi and Mr. Jimmy Toriello. Whenever the

Green Bay Packers found themselves in the City of Gotham, the odds were one to five Mr. Lombardi would find himself sitting in the Amalfi. Like most Italians, Vince loved to eat and eat Italian. A disciplinarian of remarkable psychological insight, Mr. Coach knew his men well—and believe me, the men knew their coach equally well. To Vince football was not a business—not even a game; it was a dedication—a devotion—a shrine (Would anyone dare cut up or play around in a church or a shrine?)—a quasireligion. In the Lombardi estimation, the gridiron demanded the same respect. At one of the Amalfi meetings, he told us religion plays an integral part in the making of a genuine football player. "As long as they profess to be Catholics or Protestants, then I think it's their duty to attend services on Sundays and my duty to see that they do. It never hurts to have God on your side."

Some describe Vince as a stern despot of some sort, a martinet in the uniform of a football coach, a tyrant among men. I have often thought what a great and outstanding United States President this leader of men would have made with his no-nonsense way of life. I'd pay a scalper's price for a ticket to see beatnik protestors marching in front of the White House while President Vincent Lombardi and his forty-strong platoon were scrimmaging, preparing for the onslaught. Is there a doctor in the house???

In the prose of Gertrude Stein, a restaurant is a restaurant is a restaurant is a restaurant. You may describe most eating places in such terms. Most places lack that certain indefinable something that makes it shine among the others. Some possess that certain something. Luau of Rome is such a restaurant. Located in the very heart of Rome, it is a stone's throw from the Via Veneto and the Excelsior Hotel. The decor is far from smashing, as the British would say; its accouterments are proper to any of the Pacific South Sea Island settings.

Luau spells home to many showbiz personalities. Its proprietor, Mr. Jerry Chierchio, is a former Brooklynite who staked a small fortune in a basement on the Via Sardegna and came out a winner. Jerry shakes hands and kisses knuckles with royalty, potentates, film superstars, financiers with the same cordiality and warmness as he would handshake an old buddy from Flatbush Avenue. Big John Wayne sits at a sidewalk cafe on the Via Veneto and shouts in his booming voice, "I'm going to the Luau Restaurant for dinner." A procession of hysterical fans follow him into the eatery. The exiled ex-King Farouk converted the Luau into his temporary throne and newly found kingdom. Rita Hayworth assumed possession of the bar stool at the very end of the bar. During my stay in the Eternal City, the Luau became a meeting place for Harry Guardino, Richard Basehart and myself. Neophyte actors Brett Halsey and Wayde Preston gathered there in the hope of meeting a producer, director or writer and thus achieve stardom as a rootin', shootin' Italian cowboy. In name, Luau is Polynesian; in soul, it is *italiano*.

The labels sex goddess and sex symbol are oftentimes deceiving and misleading. Neither should connote the erogenous, but unfortunately do. A perfectly chiseled face crowned with long shimmering hair, a transcendent figure, a voluptuous bosom, panther-like legs and gait equates a sex goddess, a sex symbol. Press agents romanticize their lives to greater extent than the typical Hollywood actress. Some girls accept this dubious title in a laissez-faire attitude.

One such young lady is Miss Joey Heatherton. Joey presents the perfect enigma in showbiz. To cast eyes on her beauty, you almost want to forget "thou shalt not"; to know her personally makes one proud to call her friend. A most unique girl, thoroughly steeped in showbusiness, she's been singing and dancing since she was a child. A native daughter of Long Island, the teen-aged entertainer was always accompanied to rehearsals and shows by her dad, Ray Heatherton, also a glowing name in showbiz. She worked the Como show for an entire season and I can't recall the presence of the lovely daughter without her handsome father. In fact, Ray could almost plead guilty to the transgression of overprotectiveness where his teen-age daughter was concerned. He was the proverbial hen, and she the colorful chick. In showbiz perhaps, Father knows best. I subscribe wholeheartedly to the axiom: Believe in one-third of what you hear and two-thirds of what you see. In Miss Heatherton's case, believe in one-third of what you hear and absolutely nothing in what you see.

In her film effort *Bluebeard,* with Richard Burton, Virna Lisi and Raquel Welch, Miss Heatherton disrobes au naturel. Interviewed by Miss Rona Barrett, she was asked, "What will your parents say when they see you on film in the state of nudity?" "Oh, my goodness"—she blinked surprise—"I don't know what my father will do. . . ."

Bob Hope is a plagiarist. An inadvertent one; nevertheless, a plagiarist. Let me bring my case to the people. My intimate association with comedians over the span of many years has rubbed off on me. Some of their routines I can tell you backward. I personally have been responsible for two stories. I created them; they are my personal property.

No. 1: At a church bazaar, a monsignor orders his curate to do a little gambling, thus stimulating the parishioners to do likewise. The curate returns to the rectory with a small parcel. "Monsignor," he giggles, "I've just won a set of towels, HIS and HERS. Should I return them?" "Hang on to them," the stern monsignor pontificated. "The way things are going in Rome you'll never know."

No. 2: I'm in favor of priests marrying, but not for the obvious reasons. There are a couple of monsignors and bishops I want to see married and stuck with a mother-in-law.

I related both these stories to Mr. George Burden, assistant to Mr. Earl Wilson, syndicated columnist for the *New York Post.* In his latest literary opus, *The Show Business Nobody Knows,* Mr. Wilson credits both stories to Bob Hope under the category "Religious Jokes Bob Hope Tells." Perhaps Hope is the innocent victim of this inadvertent act of plagiarism. Certainly, I am the offended and aggrieved party. A much better and astute suggestion: let people (clergy) like myself stick to the Gospels and leave the jokes to the comedians.

To the juvenile mentality, the job of a movie critic is super. You see movies for free and get paid for it. Likewise, sportswriters rank very high too. When our Franciscan magazine, *Padre*, came into being, the editors assigned me to the movie department. Incidentally, a reward was promised to any friar who might propose an accepted name for the new monthly periodical. "Padre" was my baby, but went unrewarded. To my knowledge, this is the first time this fact has ever been printed. Nevertheless, I finally shared the fulfillment of a lifetime dream. Now I belonged to the ranks of Judith Crist, Wanda Hale, Louella Parsons.

I felt the title of the column, "Views and Previews," appropriate enough. To fill the column with word fodder indeed involved backbreaking work. Paramount, Metro, Universal and 20th Century-Fox would advise me of the upcoming previews, shown privately. To do the job well necessitated my previewing at least six pictures a week, on some occasions two a day. To aggravate matters, oftentimes the showings were held late in the evening. Regardless of the merits of any particular film, regardless of the superstars enacting the heroes, my reactions constantly remained the same: monotony, boredom and ennui *usque ad nauseam*.

Feeling perhaps a personal touch with known names might enhance the column, I interviewed Jimmy Durante, Rosemary Clooney, Danny Thomas, Perry Como, among others, and little sob sister Margaret O'Brien. At that time Miss O'Brien, eleven years of age, was the houseguest of José Iturbi. When *Padre*'s circulation started to falter, the editors decided some departments of the magazine should be eliminated. Thank God, "Views and Previews" was the first to the guillotine.

A great amount of admiration must be showered upon anyone working under a severe handicap. Especially when the handicap is part and parcel of one's work. A prime example of a man with a bellyful of guts—a dancer without a foot—is Peg Leg Bates. Peg has been stage center for at least thirty years that I can recall. And as evidenced only a few weeks ago on television, he's still around and working. The pianistic wizardry of the blind trinity,

Art Tatum, Alec Templeton and Ray Charles, makes you wonder. Did the Almighty place two tiny eyes in each of their fingers? More fortunate is Peter Gennaro. His hearing impaired many years ago, Peter controls music and sounds by way of hearing-aid devices. For many years Peter choreographed the Como show and appeared personally on many occasions. Since then, he's directed and staged dance numbers of several Broadway musical hits. Today, Mr. Gennaro is employed in that same capacity in the mammoth Radio City Music Hall.

I'm proud of my friendship with Pete Gennaro. Despite his diminutive size and impaired hearing, he reigns as the greatest jazz dancer in the country. To meet him is indeed an unforgettable pleasure: quiet, shy and unassuming, genteel, soft-spoken. Even at rehearsals, when mistakes occur frequently and routines must be repeated over and over, you'll hardly hear him speak above a whisper. On one occasion I requested a favor of him for a friend. A young Boston ballerina asked me to intercede. She wanted Mr. Gennaro to appraise her dancing ability and, if he would, create a short routine for her act. She offered him a sizable amount of money. This Paramus, New Jersey, gentleman who refused to create routines for some Hollywood superstar dancers quietly accepted the offer, but refused the money. He accepted the offer, he told me, because the ballerina was my friend.

A factotum, according to *Webster's New Collegiate Dictionary*, is a person employed to do all kinds of work. We have a factotum in the Rectory and Church of the Most Precious Blood. He is Mr. Joseph Guadagno, a lay member of our Franciscan family for a quarter of a century. "Joey," as we affectionately call him, was afflicted since birth with a slight case of retardation—God's gifted people. To see him operate, you begin to question your own sanity. "Joey" acts in the capacity of our sacristan, our one and only altar boy, our usher and collection-taker. In the rectory he answers doorbells, phone calls and runs every errand for the cook, including food shopping and picking up our clothes at the tailor's. Besides, he operates a side business on his own. Unable to read and write, he delivers flowers for a local florist—traveling to all parts of the five boroughs of New York City, and oftentimes he crosses the Hudson into Jersey. All of the local gentry employ "Joey" to do their errands. He delivers—and you had better deliver when it comes to tips. His anathemas are more powerful than the Pope's. When Ed Sullivan and his Sylvia made their annual pilgrimage to the San Gennaro feast on Mulberry Street, I made it my business to introduce "Joey." The ever-gracious Mr. Sullivan shook "Joey's" hand warmly. "Joey" in turn immediately recognized the very famous Sullivan profile. Smiling, "Joey" observed, pointing a finger at Ed: "I know you. Sunday. Eight o'clock. Number two."

I have often enjoyed the sweet smell of success and just as often had to endure the wretched stink of defeat. Although all the world loves a winner, there are too many losers to make it exclusive. Actor Harry Guardino, having perused the smash, best-selling *Godfather,* telephoned me. He was inordinately enthused by the story of the Mafia and the characters that compose its membership. Especially the role of Sonny, the elder son of Mr. Corleone.

"Father Bob, the role of Sonny fits me like a glove. Sonny is me," Harry assured me. "Would you know anyone connected with the book; the author, the publisher—anybody?"

"I've never met the author, Mr. Mario Puzo, personally, although he's in the neighborhood during the summer at least two or three times a week."

"What the hell is he doing down there so often?" came the legitimate query.

"Believe it or not, he comes down to La Bella Ferrara, across from the rectory, to buy Italian ice. Ordinarily, he consumes four and five extra-large cups. A glance at his rotund figure will prove me true."

I managed to obtain the telephone number of Mr. Puzo's brother, who in turn supplied the author's phone number.

"How did you make out, Harry?" I asked.

The sound of his voice had already answered my question. "Not so hot. Puzo tells me Paramount is casting exclusively, and most of the guys are unknowns." The role of Sonny ultimately went to Jimmy Caan. "The guy is not even Italian," complained Harry.

Most successful men love to bask in the sunless days of their poverty-stricken youth. There's a certain aura of charm about the "rags to riches" stories. Most successful entertainers aren't too keen talking about their indigenous backgrounds. This awareness of the past cuts too deeply into the flesh of opulence and affluence that they enjoy today. Their cry "Don't remind me" rings almost universally among the make-believers of the stage and screen. They refuse in any form or fashion to be identified with the somber reminiscences of the pastrami days. Psychologically, this negative philosophy acts as a defense mechanism on the part of the entertainer and as an offense mechanism on the part of the talent buyers.

The little Mexican boy from Dallas supported his brothers and sisters with the paltry pieces of change he earned nightly playing his guitar and singing in Dallas dives. He'd beg local columnists and newspaper reporters to write his name in their columns and news reports. This same Mexican youngster would jump at an opportunity to act as a substitute or a replacement any night of the week and work in any Dallas club at a salary of ten dollars a night. Now when the Mexican vocalist sits to sign a contract and is forewarned he worked in Dallas for only ten dollars a night, Trini Lopez drools in his finest Mexican olé, "Don't remind me, amigo! Don't remind me, señor!"

The name Shecky Green was just a name that kept popping up in *Variety* and newspaper columns. The showbiz insiders repeatedly reminded me Shecky rated as the best in the field of comedy. He's highly proficient in every form of the art. His lines are fast and furious, he'll devastate any and every name in the business, his pratfalls are dangerously genuine, his mastery of different languages is very believable.

Shecky virtually destroyed himself with Las Vegas success. He refused to leave his desert habitat. Rarely did he appear on any variety show and adamantly refused to make any appearance on talk shows, be it the Johnny Carson, Merv Griffin or the Mike Douglas shows. He was a tremendous success, a big showbiz name only in Las Vegas.

When he speaks of Dean Martin, he openly exhibits his disdain for the man. "Dean became a big shot," Shecky tells the audience; "he only wants to do one show a night. So Mr. Martin pulls out of the Riviera as its president to the tune of two million three hundred thousand dollars. I break my back every night doing two shows for the past eight years filling this room for Mr. Martin and he winds up with two million three hundred thousand dollars. And I wind up with craps."

Contrary to most of showbiz parlance about this star being a very dear friend and that star the godfather of my son, Shecky calls it as it is. Joey Bishop? "I don't like Joey Bishop," Green startles the audience. "Maybe Joey doesn't like me. To tell the truth, I hardly know him. But he's too serious, and I don't like serious guys."

Shecky's favorite religious joke: A lumberyard manager steals much lumber from his place of work. He goes to confession and reveals to the priest the theft of lumber. The good padre suggests that the manager make a retreat. "If you can get the blueprints, Padre, I've got the lumber," the manager suggested.

His name is Shecky Green, but I guarantee you he'll turn you purple with convulsive laughter and tears happily streaming down your face. I too confess, he's the greatest.

What is a Hollywood pretty boy? He's a Hollywood actor, one hundred percent man, with a pretty face—in fact, a little too beautiful to be a man's face. Years ago, Mr. Robert Taylor filled the role. Intermittently, John Derek filled the role. Today the role seems to be held by Jimmy Darren.

What is a Broadway pretty boy? He too is an actor, possesses the same liabilities or assets—whichever you prefer—but works on a Broadway stage. Whom would I suggest as a candidate? Mr. Jack Cassidy. His finely chiseled features crowned with silver-golden hair would set any female heart aflutter.

Although he possesses all the physiognomical qualifications, he's also endowed with a strong, booming voice. In the lexicon of showbusiness, anyone who enjoys a half-dozen lead roles in Broadway hits is a Broadway star. Jack's glorious voice rather than his pretty looks brought him that honor. Jack's beautiful wife, Shirley Jones, is equally well known among theatergoers and cinema addicts.

I was ignorant of the fact that Jack and Shirley parented a family of three. I was even more ignorant of the fact that a son born from Jack's previous marriage is named David. "FATHER BOB, you mean to tell me you never heard of DAVID CASSIDY?" a pre-teen-ager blasphemed. "That's correct. I never heard of him," I confessed. Trying to restore her faith in me, I added, "The only Cassidys I know in showbiz are Hopalong Cassidy and Jack Cassidy." With a look of utter disgust and contempt she stammered excitedly: "Jack Cassidy is David's father. But David is much prettier than his daddy."

Backstage at the Mayflower Hotel in Washington, D.C., I found my roly-poly friend the Big Bridgeport Belle, Totie Fields, in tears. And they were not tears of joy. She had just read a review of her act by a local theater critic and he described it as disgustingly vulgar. Totie's routine is basically a sight act, as she depends rigorously on her height and obesity for gags and laughs. She possesses the body of a full-grown, mature woman with the legs of a midget. "You have a choice," she tells her husband: "where do you want me to be my greatest—in the kitchen or in the bedroom?"

How did two people so diametrically different ever meet? Totie an absolute extrovert, obesely funny; George totters on the brink of introversion—quiet, unassuming, tall and on the thin side. In those days, Totie Fields entertained as a vocalist, while George Thompson's routine was comedy. They met frequently in the usual places where entertainers gather. At one affair in which both were to appear, Totie, instead of singing, did all of George's material, which she knew by heart. Since George couldn't sing, he returned home without appearing. Dates followed dates, and eventually marriage. Two daughters were born of this wedlock, and because Totie's Jewish and George is Catholic, the spiritual heritage was left to the girls when they could decide. They chose their mother's faith. Consequently, George converted to Judaism and underwent the ritual of circumcision. Now the Big Bridgeport Belle has an all-Jewish family.

His A's are uncommonly broad, as a proper Bostonian's A's should be. But what he does to the English language is something else. Were I to designate anyone as assassin of the King's English, the title no doubt would be conferred on Mr. Norm Crosby. Such is his mastery over words and phrases, Norm enjoys the easy facility to mispronounce and misconstrue the language. The result is a hilariously funny routine. Mr. Crosby is another victim plagued with a physical handicap. He is stone-deaf, and without the help of a hearing aid, sound is completely alien to his ears. It's ironic that a man so physically impeded should make his livelihood on sounds and words. "Count your blessings" has always been Norm's credo. Indeed, there are times when he considers his deafness a blessing in disguise. Norm and Jeannie, his wife, have been blessed with a baby boy, little Daniel. Since nightclubs and late hours constitute the greater part of his life, sleep becomes a very precious commodity. "What happens," I once asked Norm, "when you're rolling into bed at five in the morning and little Danny is just about ready to jump out of his crib to begin his day's activities?" "It's easy," Mr. Crosby winked. "I just take the 'bug' out of my ears and I don't hear a sound. The only other precaution: I must make sure my bedroom door is locked. I could never hear him walking around in my bedroom. A couple of times, the Little Tempest tried swinging his bat at a baseball.

The only trouble is, my head sticking out of the bed sheets was the ball."

Very English, very proper, very beautiful, young Miss Jill Haworth is an eighteen-carat British charmer. Her name has been romantically linked with my old Westchester buddy, Sal Mineo, for the past ten years. In fact, my last meeting with Sal he reminded me that I had finally met up with his old flame. Miss Haworth has been involved in a few films, none of earth-shattering importance. However, she is much too talented and much too beautiful to be deserted among the Hollywood relics.

Jill and I met at a testimonial honoring the film magnate Mr. Spyros Skouras. The tedious formality of the evening finally got to most of the dais guests. A number of us, including Jill and myself, wound up sitting on the rug-covered dais floor, stretching our limbs to our hearts' content.

During the feast of San Gennaro I was visited by two lovely young ladies. One was my little English elfin Jill. Her companion struck me as rather strange: A babushka completely covered her head; she wore sunglasses and it was nightfall. She appeared much more elfinish than Jill. At the time her name was unheard of—but things have definitely changed. "I want you to meet," Jill introduced, "a dear friend of mine—Miss Mia Farrow."

I know not how doctors, lawyers, bankers, engineers interact. How do doctors act among themselves? And lawyers, bankers and engineers? Is there a certain format they pursue? Are they forever discussing business, their last operative experience or the possibility of steel-spanning the oceans? Showbiz, I know, walks certain avenues of peculiar behavior. Male entertainers rarely handshake. The Frank Sinatras, Sammy Davises, the Dean Martins will invariably greet you with a large bear hug. And if you're a dear friend, a kiss on each cheek is bound to follow. Female artists like their counterpart will plant wet lips on your cheekbone, if you're a friend. Otherwise, a slight rub of her cheek against yours will do. Comics respond very physically, almost violently, to a real funny story. No career indicator need be exhibited to realize five comics are seated two tables away from yours. If the joke is sensational, you'll hear foot-stomping, handclapping and table-banging, with roars of guffaws splitting the air. There are some exceptions. The charm-school proponents, Don Rickles, Shecky Green and Jack E. Leonard, rarely laugh. They make peculiar guttural sounds.

If it is opening night and, among the many congratulatory or best-wishes telegrams received, one might contain the expletive BREAK A LEG or the French-oriented equivalent MERDE, no offense is intended. Much to the contrary, both idioms are felicitous well-wishers. "Merde" literally translates into "Shit." They say the French use the expression as endearingly well-wishing. "Break a leg" in no way refers to any anatomical fractures. It merely implies "Wish you luck."

If ever a sainted restaurateur walked this earth, I would say his name is Max Asnas of the famed Stage Delicatessen. An immigrant boy from Russia, Mr. Asnas harbored a love for America second to no man, not even the President of these United States. Only in America, Max would preach loud and hard, can a poor boy like myself grow up to become a multimillionaire. He credited his phenomenal success and the tremendous sums of money he accumulated not to himself but to the beloved country he adopted. A very docile man, Mr. Asnas hated passionately two things in American life: Communism and the Communist. They were traitors to a sacred cause. He would spend hours explaining with the expertise of a political-science professor the inherent fallacies of the Marxist and Leninist doctrines. A man who once tasted the bitter morsels of poverty and hunger, his heart was ever opened to the poor and the unfortunates. At Thanksgiving time, he'd rebuke me if I didn't collect some turkeys for the poor families of the parish. Max dispensed the turkeys. At every benefit in and around New York City, it was always Max Asnas who provided the goodies backstage for the entertainers.

The "Stage" became the mecca of showpeople, the gathering place of most comedians in fair or inclement weather. It became a meeting place for actors and agents where routines were worked out and prices discussed. Little Max assumed the image of "Father Confessor" and "Mother Superior" to every showbiz guy and doll that walked The Street. On any given night you'd find the likes of Fred Allen and his Portland, Milton Berle, Jan Murray and many, many more. Swapping jokes or stealing them from one another.

Max spoke with a heavy Yiddish accent and possessed a very keen Yiddish sense of humor. On one occasion a matronly woman wanted to know if the pastrami was hot or just warm. "My good lady," Max asked her, "did you come into my place to eat, or are you looking for a weather report?"

Some friends live in Verona, New Jersey. This statement preludes one of the most embarrassing faux pas of my life. I sat backstage entranced by the artistry of two young black entertainers. The boy and girl sang medleys from the Broadway hit *Two Gentlemen of Verona*. It was a new show and I hadn't seen it. As the two youngsters went through their histrionics, I stood mesmerized, oblivious to anyone or anything around me. Suddenly I felt a soft touch at my back. My half turn became a quick full turn. Liza Minnelli was asking me a question, and I couldn't for the life of me understand her. Then I realized she wanted to know what show that beautiful music came from. I stammered, stuttered and spluttered, "Two guys from Jersey!"

Another gem to add to my diadem of faux pas occurred only recently. An agent advised me Liza Minnelli had been booked by a Vegas hotel for a six-week appearance. "Who'll work with her?" I wanted to know. "She'll work with a comic for the first three weeks and with Joel Grey for the remaining part of the engagement," he said. Joel Grey: I looked askance. What the hell is she doing with Joel Grey? came my callous, opinionated opinion. A "Listen to me, idiot" stare stopped me in my know-it-all-tracks: "Did you ever hear of *Cabaret*???"

The Good Book strongly recommends, "Be all things to all men." The recommendation is most noteworthy—but how do you help newly married belated honeymooners in distress? Cathy of *No, No, Nanette* and Russ, a trucking-firm executive, expressed their desire to be married. Danny Stradella went into immediate action. His first phone call came to me: "Get me a judge." Next, he decided to utilize the second and third floors of his restaurant as the wedding locale. All went well. The judge made his appearance, loquaciously inspired, as most judges are. The beautiful bride and handsome groom were united in the name and authority of the State of New York. Obviously, everything ran smoothly. Where was the problem?

Cathy harbored a lifelong desire to spend her honeymoon at the Beverly Hills Hotel in California. From childhood she read about this famous hostelry, its celebrated cabanas festooning the pool and the movie moguls and stars living there. She contacted the hotel and was disappointingly informed all rooms were occupied. Reservations were impossible. Cathy related the bad news to Mr. Stradella. A quick telephone call, little white lie spelled success. The manager of his restaurant, Danny told the manager of the Beverly Hills Hotel, was about to be married, and the young man was interested in a suite facing the pool. To add an air of sophistication and intrigue, Danny further informed the management that the newly married couple would be escorted by a bodyguard, in the person of Jerry Joseph, of the Colony Record Shop on Broadway. Regretfully, the hotel could not provide the suite facing the pool; however, there would be a suite available for the new Romeo and Juliet. At the Beverly's poolside, they're still talking about the newlyweds—unknown, unheard of, uncelebrated—and their six-foot-two handsome bodyguard hovering in the honeymooners' shadow.

Mine is not a showbiz family. Perish the thought! My parents migrated from Italy to the teeming slums of lower Manhattan. Dad worked as a carpenter; mother, a housewife. After my father's death in 1933, mother was employed in a rag shop sorting out different kinds of material. Later still, she worked at home, bouqueting artificial flowers. I don't believe my dad and mother ever strayed into a movie house in their lifetime. The only remote affiliation we enjoyed with the world of entertainment occurred through the marriage of my sister Connie. She married a buck-and-wing man who quit the business on the day of wedlock. My mother was always "my girl" and "my sweetheart." Death, the ubiquitous stranger, called upon her on May 18, 1956. An unexpected phone call at three in the morning conveyed the sad and disheartening news. I recall standing on the corner of Forty-second Street and Tenth Avenue, tears streaming my face, as I hailed a cab. "What's wrong, Father?" the perplexed cabbie asked. "I've just been informed my mother passed away." Without inquiring my destination, he began to drive north. After a few minutes' wait, he resumed the conversation. "If you feel a little better, Father, can you tell me where we're going." I did.

I have seen life and death throughout my priestly life. Discounting any precise numerical figures, I probably baptized as many babies as I have buried adults. You would expect a priest by reason of his profession and faith to be able to accept death. Normally we do. However, in the case of his mother, acceptance is improbable, especially for a priest. Perhaps in the language of the psychologist, a mother fulfills the human demand of nature necessitating the presence of a woman in the life of every man. As a woman, the mother of the priest, she fulfills the human exigencies of a sweetheart, a wife, a companion, a confessor, a consultant, an adviser. Maybe the old song says it better: "You're my everything underneath the sun. You're my everything all wrapped up in one."

Mother was waked on Sullivan Street in the heart of the Village, one hundred yards from Saint Anthony's Church, where she spent countless hours attending Mass, in prayer and meditation. She always expressed the desire to be buried from "her" church. Flowers began to arrive at an incredible pace from every part of the country. Mr. Como arrived on the first midafternoon of the wake, so as to spare us any disturbance. The funeral director seemed slightly annoyed as each floral piece appeared. At the last count, there were one hundred and seventy-five pieces, with little or no room for the mourners. Suddenly I sensed an element of the macabre, a sense of eeriness: there were complete and total strangers in the funeral parlor who were present just to see what celebrities would show up.

Durante, Jackson and Jack Roth appeared on the last night, in between shows at the Copa, minutes after the arrival of Durante's floral offering, a six-foot orchid-clad cross. Jimmy respectfully knelt before the bier and recited his prayers. He stood up and studiously viewed the body for a few minutes, turned to me and asked, "How old was Mama?" "Seventy-eight," I replied. Jimmy appeared stunned at the numeral. "Seventy-eight!" he exclaimed, "you're putting me on; you're kidding me. She looks like she's in her middle fifties." My sisters, Jo and Connie, verified my answer. Once again Jimmy studied my mother and remarked: "If she left any pills, give them to me. I sure can use them."

If it is humanly possible to derive any pleasure on such an occasion, the sight of fifteen hundred people attending her farewell Mass filled my heart with indescribable joy. More than half of that attending number were affiliated with showbiz, from usher to stagehand. Como offered to pay the entire funeral bill. I gratefully and appreciatively declined. Unbeknownst to me, some friends did leave monetary gifts. With that money I managed to arrange her memorial as a part and parcel of the church. Today in Saint Anthony's Church—"her" church—a huge stained-glass window sun-brightly proclaims: IN MEMORY OF ROSINA PERRELLA.

I love young Nancy Sinatra. I love her with the same affection and esteem any adopted father can lavish on his adopted daughter. She was my ward whenever as a single young lady she would visit New York. Ordinarily her companion was one of Jack Entratter's daughters, Carol or Michelle. I vividly recall taking Nancy and Carol to Frankie and Johnnie's Restaurant in Gotham's theatrical area after a Broadway matinee. Johnnie Phillips, the proprietor, recommended the onion soup, but Nancy remained skeptical. With my personal endorsement, she decided on the soup with the contingency if she didn't relish it, the soup would be returned to the kitchen. And if she did, she promised the proprietor a big kiss on his Irish cheek. She ate the soup, he got the kiss and—thank God—I got no check.

Nancy fell in love with an up-and-coming vocalist, Tommy Sands. They planned to be married in the Church of the Good Shepherd in Beverly Hills. She had always promised herself, when I get married, I want Father Bob to perform the ceremony. Evidently, the good monsignor at Goor Shepherd thought differently; he strenuously objected to anyone performing the marriage rites except himself and his curates. Nancy's tears were evidenced on the transcontinental call as she explained the befuddled situation. I assured her to play it by ear and everything would eventually be straightened out. Mama Nancy, distraught by the tide of events and fearing the pompous ire of the good monsignor, weakly suggested that I and her daughter forget our plans.

I've read much about the famous trait of Irish stubbornness, the good monsignor's nationality. However, as a member of the MAFIA (Mothers' And Fathers' Italian Association), I fear no man. So my next move was to contact the prelate himself. I explained to him my background with the Sinatra family, our friendship in good times and bad. My bonds with them go back many, many years. I knew Marty and Natalie when they lived in Hoboken and not Beverly Hills. I emphasized this request was not a frivolous act on my part; I honestly and sincerely felt entitled to perform the ceremony. The most reverend monsignor succumbed with the admonition it will be my first and last time insofar as The Good Shepherd Church is concerned.

My superior's permission to make the trip granted, reservations completed, my American Airlines return ticket in hand, I awaited the happy event. Then one morning, as I poured some coffee into a mug and a fellow priest scanned the *Daily News,* the young Levite floored me with an impious ejaculation: "Holy Cow! your girl got herself married." My reactions were complete disbelief.

"Seeing is believing," the cleric ventured. There on page three of the *Daily News* lay a photograph of glowing marital happiness. Nancy, Tommy, Papa Frank, Jack Entratter, Carol, Michelle, all smiling after the civil ceremony at the Sands Hotel in Las Vegas. The only missing one: me. That's showbiz!

Years passed. The voice on the phone sounded vaguely familiar. "It's Nan . . . Nancy . . . Nancy Sinatra." "Hi, Nan," I greeted her; "long time no hear, longer time no see." "Father Bob, I want you to be the first to know: I'm getting married again." "Who's the lucky guy?" I queried. "Hugh Lambert." The name rang a bell, but I couldn't quite catch the tone. "Hugh Lambert?" I repeated questioningly. "You know him, because he knows you," the bride-to-be assured me. Suddenly I realized he was the choreographer who worked the Como show on several occasions.

"Nan, it is humanly impossible for me to make the trip. However, do me one big favor—please, pretty please: get married in church."

"And you do me a pretty favor: don't tell anyone about my plans. No one knows, not even Daddy."

A week elapsed. Again a west-to-east call. Again it's my little Nan. She tells me tomorrow is the date of her forthcoming marriage. It will take place in a tiny Catholic church, more resembling an army hut, just outside Cathedral City. Her final words, tremendously uplifting to the morale of an adopted father: "I'm doing it this way because this is the way you wanted it."

"Do you know a funny story, something that happened in this casino?" I asked a Riviera change girl. "Yes, Father," she replied, "something almost tragically funny. A man was playing at the poker table. The only reason I noticed him was he collapsed and slumped underneath the table." He remained there practically unnoticed for a minute or two; then the place broke out into pandemonium. Call the house doctor, call an ambulance, get the emergency squad. . . . "The man has suffered a heart attack," a man yelled. Someone untied his necktie and belt and began revival procedures by mouth-to-mouth resuscitation. The heart-attack victim, practically dead, opened his eyes slightly. A strong blow against his chest, his eyes now completely opened, he began to breathe normally. This entire episode occurred within the space of a few minutes. He was offered a glass of water and gulped it down unceremoniously. "Now, what do you think happened?" giggled the change girl. The man got to his feet, shaking slightly, retied his necktie and belt, drank a little more water and, lo and behold, he returned to the poker table and started to gamble again. "You're kidding," I ventured as though in a state of shock. "Kidding, hell," she replied; "he took the house for over ten big ones."

He's a nice Italian boy. So nice, he bought his parents a beautiful home in Westchester County. The nice Italian boy has been in showbusiness so long I can't recall when he wasn't in showbusiness. He's Sal Mineo. Sal is a showbiz enigma. Still a young man, it appears to me and many others he's been in films for the past fifty years. With his dark, boyish face, wavy hair, toothy smile and black Sicilian eyes, Sal has the audacity to refer to me as "the perennial youth." He lives a bachelor's life in the Hollywood Hills of Los Angeles. However, judging by his gestures, carriage, postures and dialect he's never left the confines of his favorite borough, the Bronx. We met frequently at the Como show, and when Perry left the scene, my only contact with Mr. Mineo was a lonely little Christmas card. *L'affaire* Jill Haworth–Sal Mineo is questionable. When I first met Jill and saw her youthful face, I suggested she must have started dating Sal when she was six years old. If Sal finally decides to renounce his bachelorhood, the "perennial youth" will be the first to congratulate him, or possibly perform the wedding ceremony.

Rocky Graziano, born and raised on Manhattan's Lower East Side, now resides with his Mrs. on Manhattan's gold coast, the Upper East Side. The view is the same: the East River. The only difference is the price of the rent: from twenty-five dollars to three hundred and fifty dollars monthly. Ironically, the Rock lives in the same highriser on East Sixty-fourth Street as Danny Stradella. The last time I visited Danny and ran into Rocky, he introduced me to the building doorman. "I want you to meet Father Bob," the Rock mumbled; "he's Danny's priest and mine."

I remember meeting the ex-pug many years ago on Broadway. "I gotta buy you a drink," he offered. "It's a very special day in my life." He then steered me into Jack Dempsey's restaurant. "What's the celebration all about, Rock?" I asked. "I just sold my life story to the movie people. I'm gonna get a fortune for it. So let's drink to my good luck."

Today, Mr. *Somebody Up There Likes Me* is richer than ever. He's probably the most popular TV-commercial-maker in the business. At our last encounter he was heading for a midtown advertising agency. "I'm gonna make another TV commercial. Twenty-five hundred bucks for the day. Not bad, hey?" "How do you like the advertising business?" I asked him. "It's better than getting your nose punched in and your brains plastered and shattered," he mused. Rough and tough, a shoulder-swinging gait, yet a lovable and ingratiating character, the Rock's heart is like his pockets: filled with gold.

Although I live in the heart of Little Italy, it is an area rapidly developing into Big Chinatown. Unfortunately, I'm acquainted with very few Chinese. Fortunately, however, there is one I can count among my many friends: a nonresident of Chinatown, Mr. Dong Kingman. He is a noted, outstanding, world-recognized watercolor painter. I would venture to say Dong is the most popular and most accepted Chinese painter in America today. Like myself, Mr. Kingham is a board-of-trustees member of the Actors Youth Fund. On many occasions he has raffled much of his artistic works for the cause of the American youth.

Dong is a very slightly framed man, five foot three inches tall, about one hundred and twenty pounds, give or take a few. If you're ever in the lobby of the Plaza, the Americana, the Waldorf, or Drake hotels and you see a slightly framed, five-foot, tuxedoed Chinese man walk in with a Manhattan telephone

Yellow Pages directory tucked under his arm, don't be dismayed. It's Mr. Dong Kingman, noted Chinese painter. The Yellow Pages directory? Mr. Kingman invariably sits on the obese volume so as to keep his nose out of the soup and see eye to eye with the other dais celebrities.

On one of his infrequent visits to Chinatown, Dong stopped by to say hello. He showed me a brochure of his more recent paintings, and I in turn showed the brochure to one of our parishioners, a mother of three sons, affectionately called "Chicken." "How much is this painting? I'd like it for my home," Chicken asked Dong. "Five thousand dollars" came the astonishing response. Stunned by the awesome figure, the brochure unceremoniously fell out of her hands to the pavement.

Marty Burden literally covers Broadway. He is living, breathing proof that walking is a great panacea for good health. Mr. Burden is columnist Earl Wilson's assistant. Odds are better than even money you'll find Marty during the course of the night at the Royal Box, the Copa, the Empire Room, Danny's Hideaway, the Casino Russe, the Maisonette Room, etc. Earl writes the day's story; Marty supplies the celebrity-studded one-liners. Who is seen with whom. When. Where. A man of Mr. Burden's professional status is welcomed anywhere, anytime; every line he writes is a free plug for a hotel, a club, a room. He helps the cause by informing his readers what an outstanding act young Liza Minnelli performed at the Empire Room. That Charlton Heston and his wife dined at Danny's last night. Occasionally he comes up with stories which touch the perimeter of showbiz and crash into the bullet-riddled mobster land. Marty and I cross paths frequently—so much so, he had this remark to pass on to friends: "Father Bob attends so many dinners, testimonial and otherwise, that he is now confined to giving confession and absolution only to captains, headwaiters and checkroom girls."

Mr. Lou Perry, onetime manager of young Dean Martin, sold Dino's contract to agent Abby Greshler for three thousand dollars

—cash. At that time Mr. Greshler held Jerry Lewis' contract, and once the two Pagliaccis joined forces, it remained a question of time as to who would buy out whom.

Despite his disastrous decision and consequent loss of potential wealth and prestige, Lou Perry still retains a staunch and fervent faith in humanity. Once a year at the Biltmore Hotel in New York, Lou stages a benefit show for the Holy Name Center for the Homeless Men of the Bowery. Through his many personal contacts with showbiz personalities of every sort and variety, Mr. Perry's benefits read like an astronomical chart. At one of his affairs, Joey Heatherton walked in sporting a beautiful black eye—accidentally kicked in the face by another dancer during an intricate routine.

At a more recent occasion, Anthony Quinn, who played the Pope in the film *Shoes of the Fisherman,* reminded the audience that Terence Cardinal Cooke was in Rome, explaining Quinn's presence that evening for the Homeless Men of the Bowery. "That's why I'm here. You see, I'm Cardinal Cooke's boss—I'm the Pope!"

Later, comic Pat Henry appeared. Impressed by the number of Roman collars and nun's garbs at the benefit, he decided to tell one of his religious jokes. Publicly professing his faith, Pat informed the audience of a theological dilemma he could not resolve. As a youngster he was taught if anyone ate meat on a Friday and died thereafter, he went to hell. What happened to those people now that they've changed the law? Did they keep them on ice for all these many years and finally ship them north?

At this same affair I met Mr. Milt Moss and his wife. Milt reminded me that we were introduced on several occasions, but always in the midst of much confusion and commotion, usually backstage. He philosophized on the perplexities of fate . . . the many years on stage as a comic without an iota of success or recognition. Then one lousy commercial on TV and the miracle occurred. The master of ceremonies introduced him to the audience and the name "Milt Moss" conveyed no message to the onlookers. He appeared before the audience and very few recognized him. His first line was the commercial "I can't believe I ate the WHOLE thing!" Suddenly he's the star of the show. Alka-Seltzer, anyone????

Most Catholic organizations—the Holy Name of Jesus, the Knights of Columbus, the Children of Mary, etc.—living in communities within striking distance of New York City, involving a two- or three-hour bus ride, visit this town at least once a year. Such is the parochial tradition of the Church of Mount Carmel in Watervliet, New York, an upstate city west of Troy and directly north of Albany. The men's Holy Name Society will hire a bus, come down to the city to catch the New York Giants football team or the Yankees baseball team, have dinner and return home. As for the Mothers' Club, the plans are usually more elegant and sophisticated.

I made arrangements with the Short Line Bus Company to transport fifty of the parish women to New York and through a rabbi was able to obtain the same amount of tickets for a leading Broadway show, *Man of La Mancha*. Dinner plans were set with the proprietors of Delsomma's Restaurant.

Through a very fortunate coincidence I ran into a dear friend and a brilliant stage star, Miss Bernice Massi, who at the time was the leading lady of *Man of La Mancha*. It was she who provided me with the tickets. Bernice graciously accepted my offer to join us for dinner after her matinee performance. The parish women enjoyed a delightful day, the show was great and the dinner sumptuous. The presence of Miss Massi, whom we had just seen perform so brilliantly, constituted the dessert. And the proverbial cherry on the cream came in the person of Sidney Poitier, the man who came to Delsomma's for dinner. Sidney spotted me and my contingent, walked to our table, sat and chatted with us and, gentleman that he is, shook the hand of each and every lady in the party. It was a day, they told me, they'll never forget!

I'm wanted on the phone. A curt "hello" and my tone immediately changed. It's my big boss, the Superior, Father Charles

Tallarico. "Robert," he greeted me, "I've got a newly married couple, honeymooners, visiting with me. The guy is a boxing bug, knows about every boxer who ever stepped into a ring. How about arrangements for dinner at Jack Dempsey's Restaurant?" No problem, I politely informed him. But there was a problem. As a guest of Jimmy Durante, I had spent a week in Las Vegas without official permission from my superior. (Can you imagine him granting me permission to spend even a day in the Devil's Playground?) During my stay at the Desert Inn, most of my time was spent with Mr. Dempsey and his two lovely young daughters, Ted Lewis and his Ada and writer Gene Fowler, who resided at the same hotel.

I made it my business to get to Jack's restaurant a couple of days before our dinner date with my boss and the honeymooners. "Jack," I explained, "my big boss and I plus a newly married couple will have dinner here in a few nights. Please, under no circumstance mention the fact that I was with you in Vegas this past summer. It could get me into a mess of trouble." He assured and reassured me he would never mention it. When that blessed evening arrived, as we crossed the threshold of Jack Dempsey's Restaurant—my boss; the honeymooners, holding hands, and I— the great Manassa Mauler greeted me with a huge bear hug and exclaimed to a friend with whom he was conversing: "Here's my Las Vegas buddy. Boy, what a ball we had there with Durante this summer!" My boss merely grinned, and I haven't heard a word about it since—twenty-five years ago.

Very often it is physically and morally impossible to keep in constant touch with friends. Letter-writing becomes boresome; telephoning, expensive. Thank God, friendship isn't measured by physical meetings, correspondence or telephone calls. Freddie Fields and wife, Polly Bergen, are friends. I haven't seen or heard from them or they from me in years. My recollection of our last meeting involved a hospital room where I visited a sickly Polly. Freddie is a bigwig Hollywood manager-agent. In the realms of personal management, he is considered a superstar.

We are all familiar with Polly's film career. She never achieved the fame and prestige of an Ingrid Bergman; nevertheless, she did accomplish a more-than-average amount of cinematic success. Now she's enjoying a double dose of success. Diverting her efforts from the cinema to cosmetics, Miss Bergen is about to become a tycoon millionairess. It's inconceivable how a woman is able to rechannel her efforts into a new and totally strange endeavor and be so miraculously successful. The Pulchritudinous Polly manufactures chemicals and powders for those women not as pulchritudinous. Now that the Movie Queen has been transformed into a Cosmetic Queen, let's hope she'll transform the women of America into beautiful and pulchritudinous Polly Bergen look-alikes.

A surprise birthday party isn't exactly newsworthy. However, a surprise birthday party replete with the cast of the dancing girls of *No, No, Nanette* and Victor Jory, Bob Strauss, Benny Baker and *Nanette*'s superstar, Montana-born Miss Margie Yvonne Reed—known to the theatrical world as Miss Martha Raye; known to her many friends as just plain Maggie—that's newsworthy. "Have you met Maggie?" dancer Cathy Rinaldi asked me. "On many occasions, but a century ago." "Come with me," Cathy suggested; "I'll do the honors." I became skeptical about the encounter. My pride faltered. Would it embarrass me if I turned out to be a complete stranger? I underestimated this beautiful woman. Maggie immediately informed one and all that she and Father Bob had met on many occasions, most of them in the company of Mr. C.

Like many Catholics, she entertained several gripes about our changing religion. "Would you believe it," she wryly observed, "I can't find a medal of the patron saint of actors, Saint Genesius, in all of New York City. If automobiles fear leaving their garage since they removed Saint Christopher from the heavenly list, what's going to happen to us actors?"

Her many years' association with Rocky Graziano converted the Irish lass into an Italian volcano. Everyone is "Gombà." She greeted an unrestrained sneeze by a gentleman at the party with "*Figli maschi*" (May all your children be males)—apologizing to the priest that her words were certainly not directed to the clergyman. Her parting words to the first person to leave the party for home—me: "*Salute per cent'anni*" (May you be healthy for a hundred years).

I endeavored to soothe her ruffled feelings about the demise of Saints Christopher and Genesius by presenting her with a gold crucifix ring. "Now, Maggie," I assured her, "you belong to The Family." Cognizant of her herculean efforts to entertain the servicemen in Vietnam for so many years, I thanked her for myself and every true, red-blooded American. "Did you ever consider," her misty blue eyes inquired, "what the boys have done for you and me?" Martha's dignified sign-off, "Good night, Sisters," were words of affection and thanks to the Franciscan Sisters of Saint Francis Hospital in Miami Beach. "The good Sisters pulled me out of a tight one and I shall never forget them," she signed off appreciatively.

If the name Johnny Mathis creates an aura of sophistication and elegance, forget it. Johhny happens to be a levelheaded, down-to-earth nice guy. For all the success he has enjoyed throughout his fabulous career and the incredible sums of money he has earned, he still remains a quiet, dignified and unassuming young man. Johnny has been in showbusiness about sixteen years, and ironically, his voice is now more cultured and disciplined than when I first heard him at the Copa. Where some stars demand an entourage of dupes at their beck and call, Johnny is completely different. He is by nature a loner. I've seen him on many occasions dining solo at the Amalfi Restaurant. It's not that he is antisocial; he merely enjoys the privilege of his privacy.

I shall never forget seeing Mr. Mathis and a matronly-looking woman proudly hanging on to his arm in front of Radio City Music Hall. When I got close enough to the couple, the matronly-looking woman suddenly became stunningly beautiful. Johnny introduced his mother. "With a mother as beautiful as yours,

Johnny, I'd have her on the bill, if only to wipe the sweat from your face or offer you a glass of water." She thanked me profusely; Johnny beamed even more so.

Mr. Mathis has suffered some crippling financial setbacks and reversals throughout his career. This happens to the biggest of names and in the nicest of families, especially when the family members want to drink the well dry. Thank God, Johnny's back again where he belongs, stage center, singing his love songs to love-hungry human beings, from age eight to eighty. In Johnny's own lyrical exhortation: "Wonderful, Wonderful."

Everyone has heard of Tallulah Bankhead, Jack Carson, Milton Berle, Jimmy Durante, Sid Caesar, Groucho Marx, Garry Moore and Perry Como. But have you ever heard of Miss Selma Diamond? She's the femme fatale—the laugh machine—the gal who writes the funny lines with which the celebrities I've just mentioned and many more make people laugh. Selma belongs to that uncredited battalion of geniuses whose name you rarely hear, whose face you never see. Yet without her talent, many comics are comicless. Selma is a female rarity. Vocally, she speaks in a basso profundo. Professionally, she competes with the male-chauvinist world. On the fingers of one hand you can count the number of female gag writers. A highly successful, top-notch, high-priced female gag writer, such as Miss Diamond, is considered phantasmagoric in showbiz. This miracle of success was compounded when the gag writer turned actress. Now she appears regularly in such commercials as Wash 'n Dry, Uncle Ben's Rice and Hertz (Number One) cars. She has also appeared in films and stage plays.

Once, after an absence of many weeks on a preaching tour, I reappeared at a rehearsal. "Where have you been?" Selma asked. "We haven't seen you in months." "I've been on the road, Sel," came my reply. That statement, in Selma's opinion, made history, because "on the road" belongs exclusively to the argot of the troupers and certainly not a preacher. "You better stop praying," I kid her. "What's wrong with me praying?" she wanted to know.

"I heard from the grapevines that your gravel voice is irritating the good Lord."

Nick Vanoff is just a name. In TVbiz, it's a name that belongs to a man who can practically walk the waters. Nick Vanoff left the smoke-smogged city of Pittsburgh, P.A., to come to the filth-festooned city of New York, N.Y. Like Gene Kelly, who hailed from the same P.A. location, Nick was a dancer. He joined the Como ranks of high-kicking boys and girls and was considered about the best in the group. Affable and ingratiating, Nick showed a solicitousness about everyone around him. He would not hesitate to do an errand for the errand boy. Would anyone like some coffee? How about a Coke? He could make a stewardess feel self-effacing.

We met frequently at the rehearsal hall. Otherwise, we would congregate at Jimmy Toriello's Amalfi Restaurant. Watching little Nick plow through those big Italian dishes explained the significance of "the sparrow who ate the lion." A quiet, unassuming, practically introverted young man, he seemed ill at ease on stage or in showbiz, in my judgment. Alas! How often appearances deceive.

Cognizant that a dancing career, much like a sport career, cannot last a lifetime, resourceful Mr. Vanoff began to pry into the technical aspects of television and communications. Aping so many New Yorkers, Nick and his bride left the City of Merry Muggers and settled in Los Angeles. In those days, the East dominated the world of television, but opportunities were opening out West. He must have learned his craft well, because Nick owned and directed the seemingly endless variety series of the *Hollywood Palace*. Just how good a TV director is Nick Vanoff? One way to determine the talent of any man is to learn the identities of those who seek that talent. This year, Nick directs the *Julie Andrews Hour*. That, my friends, is Big Time.

We are all familiar with AA, whose bête noire is alcoholism. But have you ever heard of the Tennessee Squires? I hadn't until

I met a representative of Jack Daniels, the bourbon people. The Tennessee Squires is quite unusual in scope. Where AA discourages and denounces the curse of drinking, the Tennessee Squires encourage and promote the art of imbibing. However, a very fine distinction permeates the entire picture. The liquid in the glass must of necessity be Jack Daniels. Among those selected for membership to the Squires are Frank Sinatra, Elizabeth Taylor, Paul Newman and J. Edgar Hoover. As a promotional gimmick, each member receives one square foot of land, their names clearly printed thereupon, in Lynchburg, Tennessee, where the Jack Daniels distillery is located. In the case of Mr. Sinatra, a newspaper in describing the event mistakenly allotted the singer an acre instead of a square foot of property. The officials of the bourbon company, realizing that Sinatra is their greatest and most vociferous promulgator, acknowledged the printed mistake and presented him with the acre of land. I can understand in the event Mr. Sinatra desired to utilize the acre for burial purposes, he would have more than enough space. What I fail to understand is what are the others going to do with only one square foot of real estate? Maybe a burial ground for squirrels and their nuts!

In a mahogany-paneled suite of the Hotel Fourteen, adjacent to the Copacabana, sat Frankie Avalon, screenwriter Bob O'Brien and myself. It was an in-between-shows friendly confab. The slightly built, boyish-looking Frankie is the good-humored target of many showbiz wisecracks. At an early age, he's already fathered seven children. "Do you expect any more, Frankie?" I suggested. "I would like maybe one or two more, but I'm ashamed. You know"—he stammered—"population explosion." "What the hell do you care about population explosion?" I thundered. "If you can support them, have them." It seems Frankie participated in a TV talk show on the West Coast to which actress Evelyn Keyes was also invited. She verbally excoriated the singer for fathering seven babies and being so humanly selfish as to completely ignore *l'affaire* population explosion. The actress is married, she reminded him, childless by choice, and all this sacrifice in the name of that cause célèbre.

Personally, these do-gooders and bleeding hearts, who espouse every cause from galloping gerbils to stray cats and dogs, give me an acute pain—you know where. They view life as though it were a cul-de-sac; there's only one way to rationalize: their way. They arbitrarily forget that the world would have been deprived of countless great and celebrated names who were a fourth, fifth, sixth or even a seventh child. Unless I'm mistaken, didn't Someone command us to increase and multiply and fill the earth? "Frankie," I exhorted him, "the next time you see the winsome Miss Keyes, ask her how she spells her middle name. Could it possibly be G-O-D?"

If years ago someone suggested I write a paper on cuff links, I would have strongly recommended the straitjacket treatment for the spokesman. Undoubtedly, many people have hangups with photography, stamps, coins, rare books, etc. We all suffer some crazy quirks; why shouldn't I? I enjoy collecting cuff links, primarily with a religious motif. My present collection includes the Face of Christ, the Immaculate Conception, the Cross, the meeting of Pope Paul VI and the Patriarch Athenagoras and two more pairs about which I shall now expound.

Years ago, Miss June Valli presented me with my very first pair of gold cuff links. They bore the facial likeness of St. Genesius with the inscription ACTOR-MARTYR. According to the *Catholic Encyclopedia:* "Genesius, the leader of a theatrical troupe in Rome, performing one day before the Emperor Diocletian and wishing to expose Christian rites to the ridicule of his audience, pretended to receive the Sacrament of Baptism. When the water had been poured upon him he proclaimed himself a Christian. Diocletian at first enjoyed the realistic play, but, finding Genesius to be in earnest, ordered him to be tortured and then beheaded. This occurred in the year 286 or 303." Hence today he is revered as the Patron Saint of Actors. These links are worn whenever I'm involved in a very important personal enterprise—just as I wore them the night I met Mr. Len Forman, an executive from Trident Press, to discuss the possibility of publishing this book.

Another pair of links I profoundly cherish depicts the portrait of the Praying Hands. They were a gift of Tony Bennett. These I wear on two very distinct and polarized occasions: at wakes and opening nights. Now I know I'm ready for the straitjacket.

Visiting the sick constitutes a corporal act of mercy and a sizable part of my job. The patient need not be a superglamorized star; a stagehand or an usher will do. It's amazing how sickness and disease tend to deglamorize most people, including showfolk. The locale of my visit was Polyclinic Hospital on Manhattan's West Side. Peter Gennaro, whom I affectionately refer to as the Dancing Fool, was about to undergo another ear operation in the prayerful hope of recovering his auditory faculties. Peter certainly possesses one faculty about which very few dancers can boast: I have never seen any human being move his dancing feet as fast and rapidly as Peter.

When I arrived at Poly, Peter greeted me with a guessing game, which I personally detest. "Guess who's occupying the room directly above me?" Attempting to systematize my conjectures, I successfully gathered that the above occupant was a female, rather young, a leading lady in films and married. There are just too many married young leading ladies in films for me to guess. So I gave up the attempt. "Why don't you kill two birds with one stone?" he advised me. "Take the elevator to the next floor and say hello to Marilyn Monroe."

I stood breathlessly at the threshold of the door and peeked in. Her eyes were closed in sleep, and I asked the nurse not to awaken or disturb her in any way. Till my dying day I shall never forget the natural beauty of her face with her shimmering golden locks caressing the pillow. I still contend she was one of the most beautiful women on or off the screen. What a pity such beauty had to be destroyed long before its allotted time. What a pity that she who gave so much of herself received so little in return. Much more can be told about the sad, unfortunate, grief-stricken life of this beautiful girl, but we'll close the chapter here.

It was a dreary autumnal Friday night. I grew tired of writing, rewriting, editing and trying to recall my past personal history. Physically and mentally I was fatigued. I decided to leave my typewriter for a couple of hours and go to my *refugium,* Danny's Hideaway. Perhaps a little Dewar's with water and a conversation with my *gombà,* little Danny Stradella, might provide the perfect panacea. I sat alone at a corner cocktail table while Danny, all five feet of him, stood tall and erect beside me. Bob Strauss and his lovely Ginny walked in, formally dressed to attend a United Nations dinner, and sat at my table. They enjoyed a fast drink and left. Moments later, a party of four arrived. I could not recognize anyone in the party. Suddenly I hear a familiar voice greeting me.

"Johnny Carson," I responded, "what are you doing in New York? I thought you blew this town months ago." Johnny's party consisted of his latest wife, his son and his latest mother-in-law. The striking resemblance of the present Joanna to the previous Joanne is startling. I recalled the first time I met the NBC midnight Giant at a party and mistakenly kept referring to him as "Jack Carson"—until he politely notified me: "I know people nickname John 'Jack,' but my name is officially 'Johnny.'" His parting words were to tell me he'll be back in New York next month for three weeks to perform at the Westbury, Long Island, Music Fair. "I'll contact you then," he promised. "Good enough, Jack," I farewelled.

I found Liberace to be a perfect gentleman. We met in Boston a week before he was to appear for a concert in the Boston Garden. In fact, on that very evening of our meeting he was scheduled to appear in Providence, Rhode Island. Then the outré-appareled pianist received an SOS from the Garden authorities. The ticket sale for his concert had virtually stopped. They asked he return to Boston for a few hours for some publicity shots to stimulate the sale of ducats. I distinctly recalled one photograph of the pianist in a kneeling position kissing the ring of Richard Cardinal Cushing.

It seemed I was directly responsible for this crisis. Our show, the Festival of Stars, was scheduled to go on two weeks after the Liberace concert. The moment our tickets went on sale at Filene's, Jordan Marsh and the Garden, there was an abrupt stop in Lee's ticket sale. Certainly this is no reflection on "Mr. Showmanship's" artistic ability. It was one solitary Star fighting a foursome of heavyweights: Como, Nat Cole, Eddie Fisher and Patti Page.

In a friendly gesture of hitting me, Seymour Heller, Lee's manager, growled: "Here's the villain giving us the headaches." "Don't feel badly," Lee volunteered; "business is business." He assured me, "There's enough pie in Boston for all of us to eat." Then, gentleman that he is, he reassured me: "With a lineup like Como, Fisher, Cole and Page, you could run a dozen shows in Kalamazoo and make money." I attended Liberace's concert trembling at the thought that I was responsible for this catastrophe. Once I arrived in the cavernous hall, my heart and soul lit up like a Roman candle. There wasn't one empty seat in the house. In fact, S.R.O.

Some in showbiz consider him a square or some kind of a freak. However, I noticed, for example, the billing at the Westbury Music Fair: JERRY VALE—LOUIS PRIMA. JERRY LEWIS—BOBBY VINTON. SADDLER AND YOUNG—PAT COOPER. ENZO STUARTI—STILLER AND MEARA. JOHNNY CARSON—DOC SEVERINSEN—PHYLLIS MCGUIRE. But when the Square appears, there's only one name on the billboard: Mr. Showmanship. LIBERACE.

Radio City Music Hall is as much a part of Manhattan's landscape as the Statue of Liberty and the Empire State Building. It is a must on any tourist guide's agenda. When RCMH first opened its doors forty years ago, a bit of piracy was perpetrated: they managed to entice most of the personnel from the Roxy Theater, including a dear friend, Anthony Policano. Similar to his previous position, Tony was in charge of all head- and footgears. Mr. Policano's assignment demanded he fashion new headpieces and shoe wear for each and every new presentation. It wasn't an easy task. Each show presents two permanent acts: precision numbers by the toe-kicking Rockettes and a mini ballet, gracing a stage big enough to play a football game. Obviously, Tony needed help in such a mammoth project. He received this assistance in the person of his much younger brother, Albert.

If the wheels of fortune play havoc with the destiny of men, such was not the fate in the life of young Al. He spent weeks and months gazing upon the pulchritude and loveliness of Forty-six Rockettes whose en masse anatomy would open the eyes of a blind man. Albert left the Music Hall to go elsewhere. After many long years of study and sacrifice, Albert was renamed Rosario. "Mister" became "Father." He was ordained a Franciscan priest on June 8, 1944. Christ took him unto Himself to the City of Heaven and the Halls of Peace on June 22, 1966. *Requiescat in pace.*

Relaxed and refreshed, I sat in the barber chair of the St. Regis Hotel while my barber, Paul Montera, clipped away. "Look who's sitting next to you," whispered the bushy-haired Mr. Barber. All I could see was a completely hairless, very bald head. My own "crown of glory" is rapidly vanishing. However, I still suffer the necessity of visiting a barbershop at least once a month. My tonsorial neighbor, Mr. Otto Preminger, does not really suffer the same necessity, unless it is to clip some invisible particles of hair from the back of his neck. Later I find myself with Larry Gengo, an agent with Creative Management Associates, sitting in the Empire Room of the Waldorf. The room is ablaze with excitement because Judy Garland's daughter, Liza Minnelli, was about to make her first public appearance. "Look who's sitting behind you," whispered Larry. Again all I could see was a completely hairless, very bald head. Again Otto Preminger. On this occasion, however, he sat beside a strikingly beautiful woman. Although we have never formally been introduced, I profess a great admiration for this professional genius. A gifted and astute producer-director, he stands by his convictions be the opposition the United States Government, the entire Catholic Church or one of her princes. Preminger's *The Moon Is Blue* made cinematic history. Opposed by Francis Cardinal Spellman, the Legion of Decency and the Church, he emerged victorious. Ironically, by today's standards, *The Moon Is Blue* may be viewed by kindergarten children.

Is it possible to be an integral part of a famous international act and still remain in anonymity? It is in the case of Mr. Jack Roth. Jack who? Except for people in the trade, the name Jack Roth signifies absolutely no showbiz recognition. Yet for fifty-two years Jack has been beating drums for Clayton, Jackson and Durante and more recently Durante and Sonny King. Mr. Roth is a tall, quiet, subdued gentleman who resides in *Hello, Dolly!*'s city of Yonkers with his wife, Marge, and family. For most of his earthly existence he identified the Bronx Borough as his homestead.

Jack plays the part of the clown who persistently interrupts Durante with loud invectives, and pounds the drums while Schnozz performs his skits. And in more recent years, unbeknownst to the general audience, Jack supplies the Nose with lines that Jimmy may have forgotten. In the act, Mr. Durante always appears annoyed and disturbed by Jack's conduct. Jimmy's forever shouting, "Stop the drums, stop the music." Jack's children, grown and married, still refer to Sir James as "Uncle Jim."

Fifty-two years is a lifetime in anyone's estimation. Nevertheless, for Durante, Jackson and Roth, who started out as young men and now face the sunset of life, fifty-two years created one long, uninterrupted act which carried them to all parts of the world to entertain royalty and masses alike. Jack has always maintained a very mundane, pragmatic philosophy: "I'm not complaining being a nobody. I've worked steady and supported my family for fifty-two long, beautiful years. That's good enough by me."

It sweetens the heart to see struggling unknown youngsters heading for the big time. One is lovely, red-haired Kaye Hart of The Bronx. She's a protégée of Jack Benny, who invited her many times to work with him on his personal-appearance tours, including his international treks. Another is an Italian import from Bari via Rome, Tony Galante. A young man of twenty-five years of age, Tony's name is a household fixture throughout his native land. He's acted in Italian films, enjoyed his own TV series and made hundreds of personal appearances in the land of sunshine. Today in America Tony is just another unknown reaching out for the golden rainbow. The locales of his singing engagements are typical of most youngsters: local bistros, the mountains and occasionally a concert at Carnegie Hall or at some other location.

He told me how one night he arrived at Jenny Grossinger's hotel too late for rehearsal and was forced to face his audience "cold." When he finished his last tenor note, the entire assemblage rose to their feet to give him a standing ovation. "I wanted to cry," he confessed, "not because of the ovation but because I was completely disgusted with myself. I could have sung so much better."

Mr. Galante is aware of a tragic mistake he's committed in his professional life. At the very first sight of money and the potential he could possibly earn, he forfeited many long years of formal operatic training. There are three instruments with which a person sings, he informed me: the brain, the heart and the voice. The brain interprets the song, the heart searches for the meaning and feeling of the song and the voice, naturally, does the actual vocalizing. Lacking any one of the three, you're not a singer; you're a fake. Whom do you consider the prime possessor of all three prerequisites? I inquired. "Sinatra, without the slightest iota of doubt; maybe Tony Bennett, and possibly Steve Lawrence. But," he pontificated, "no one comes close to the King."

I knew Buddy Hackett when ninety-nine point nine percent of the American population wouldn't have recognized his name or his face. Buddy owes his present popularity to one man, Perry

Como. Of his own admission, in my presence, he talked about his automobile trips to Miami for club dates where very few people recognized him on the road. After he guested on the Como show several times, he himself became amazed at his growing popularity among all types of people. Mr. Fat Boy is a funny man. There's something funny about his face, his speech and his stature. You laugh when you see his oval-shaped, distorted face; you laugh when you listen to him speak; you laugh when you just look at Mr. Bubble.

The mischievous, roly-poly comic once enrolled in a Duke University–affiliated, medically supervised diet clinic in Durham, North Carolina. He did not receive a diploma; he did not even finish the weight-losing course. The clinic officials expelled him for leaving the premises, sneaking down to the city and buying food for himself and the other inmates.

I have not seen or heard from Buddy or Sherry, his pretty, petite ex-dancer wife, since the grand entertainer's invasion to the West. Unlike *The New York Times*, the Hackett brand of comedy isn't fit to be printed or even heard by virginal ears. He uses the four-letter word onstage with the same frequency a clergyman uses the "amen."

Paul Lynde is certainly flying high. Not on junk or junkets, but achievement. He's reached the pinnacle of success. Movies and now his own television weekly comedy show for ABC. Paul is a graduate of the Como College; in fact, he's probably the most successful alumnus of the Perry's Kraft show. His brand of comedy remains unchanged. Facially frenetic, spastic. Over the years he perfected his technique to such a degree he's now a national and international movie and television personality.

Mr. Lynde is a sweetheart of a guy. Blessedly devoid of any "make room, folks, here comes a star" pomposity, he'll chat with anyone willing to listen and autograph a dollar bill or even a giraffe to make someone happy. Often a performer resents direction. He feels, This is my bag, I know what I'm doing and this is the way I want it. Not Paul. He would pay heed to the least suggestion and tiniest proposal the director offered. And always with a gentlemanly "Thank you." Always friendly, quiet and subdued, you hardly knew he was in the studio.

Many years ago I visited the NBC Burbank, California, studios. What a treat for my sore eyes to see the tall, slim figure of Paul Lynde heading in my direction. It was another Kraft rehearsal day, with zany jokes, stories and reminiscences of the good old days. When I first met Paul, he was a struggling actor trying to make the big time. Today he's big-time and, like his brand of comedy, he remains unchanged and unaffected by fame and prestige. Some people change with success; many more, thank God, don't.

Where Sammy Davis is concerned, you always expect the unexpected. He'll appear at a Harlem street-corner benefit and might refuse to attend a black-tie affair. He's black and a convert to the Jewish faith. Some people consider this double jeopardy. Now if some idiotic racist doesn't hate him for his color, some Nazi-oriented facist might hate him for his creed.

Wittingly or not, Mr. Davis represents his race in showbiz. When you speak of an outstanding, all-around great entertainer, his name is the first to echo through the canyons of Broadway. Hence his presence was sorely missed at the funeral services of Louis "Satchmo" Armstrong. Many well-known black stars within hearing distance of Louis' famous trumpet came to pay their final respects—except the Candy Man. Some blacks were quite vociferous in their condemnation of their soul brother. Others alluded to the fact he was seen just two days previous on the TV news visiting an alleged racketeer in a New York City hospital and could not find the time to attend the final services of one of the world's greatest black artists.

I'm sure Louis and Sammy were dear friends. It could not be otherwise, since Satchmo never knew an enemy in his lifetime. Whatever the reason for his absence, I felt a tinge of sympathy for Mr. Wonderful. There must have been other black entertainers who should have been there and weren't. Somehow they weren't missed. It doesn't always pay to be a Winner. Sometimes you're better off in the Place or Show slot.

Amid the glittering and garish trappings of Caesar's Palace in Las Vegas there lies a very sad and pathetic story. How does a world heavyweight boxing champion from 1937 to 1949 wind up a pauper? How does a man whose hands were raised in victory over ninety-five percent of his opponents now extend his hand to tourists as a hotel greeter? It's the sad story of the great black champion of champions, affectionately called "The Brown Bomber": Joe Louis. It's almost sacrilegious, to say the least, to see this humble, calm, benign man quietly walking the different rooms of the Palace greeting people. To have seen him within the confines of the ring—doing what he did best, fighting and winning—and to meet him personally as a greeter nauseated me. He earned as much money as the punches he's thrown at his opponents and punching bags. Yet today he is penniless. The hotel provides him with board and a minimal salary. Sadly, Joe doesn't fit the role of greeter very well. As a world champion, he had very little to say. As a greeter, he is even more taciturn. The Champ merely extends his hand with an unsolicited "Hi." Nevertheless, the Brown Bomber is still Champion in the eyes of many people, including myself. Truthfully, I experienced an indescribable thrill to meet personally the man who has done more for his people and his race than all the Black Panthers of America.

Sixty-five stories above the sprawling borough of Manhattan; electric bulbs flickering as far as the human eye can see; countless tons of lifeless concrete backing in the warm glow of moonlight. The vast panoramic candelabrum creating a certain breathlessness as people—notables and unknowns—marched into the Rainbow Grill of Rockefeller Center. Roy Cohn, Ed Sullivan, Jack Dempsey, Harold Gibbons, Jacqueline Susann, Irving Mansfield, Earl Wilson, Bert Bacharach, Jim Farley, Jr., Attorney General of New York State Louis Lefkowitz and the proprietor of this gold-lined real estate, Governor Nelson Rockefeller were present to honor Joey Adams on his opening night. Tiny Tim also played the same bill.

At first Joey addressed the Governor and the General in terms respectful and submissive, which are comme il faut on an occasion such as this. However, the Governor and his Happy, the General and his Mrs., sat ringside, a little too close to Joey to go unscathed. Mr. Adams reminded the audience Rockefeller worked so hard that at the age of three he was already a millionaire.

Joey continued his let's-have-fun tirade about the Rockefeller fortunes. "President Nixon," he told us, "sent me these gold cuff links to wear tonight. [He really did give him the cuff links.] You, Governor Rockefeller, haven't ever given me a thing. Nixon is not a millionaire; he's worth about seven hundred and fifty thousand dollars—a quarter of a million short. You, Governor, make seven hundred and fifty thousand a year from your candy concession at Radio City Music Hall."

He further informed us Rocky's son, Nelson, Jr., who is about eight years old, still plays with blocks: Forty-ninth Street . . . Fiftieth Street . . . Fifty-first Street, etc.

Tiny sang (?) an uninterrupted fusillade of twenty-five songs including "K-K-Katy," "Over There," and "God Bless America," causing the onlookers to jump to their feet in an outburst of patriotic fervor and cheers. Introducing the falsetto-voiced singer, Joey described him as an incredible square. "He thinks," Mr. Adams wisecracked, "Rockefeller Center is the Governor's navel."

My turn came to take my bow. Joey told his fans: "I asked Father Bob when does he think the Pope will change the rule on celibacy? Father answered, 'With my luck, the Pope will change the law when I'm seventy-five.'" It was a night long to be remembered.

On the second phone ring, I placed the receiver to my ear and was greeted by a tiny, British-accented voice. "This is Anne, Maggie's secretary," she purred into my ear. "You are invited to a cocktail party prior to her departure at four P.M. for the Caribbean on board the *Sea Venture*." I arrived at Pier 84 and inquired about the location of Miss Martha Raye's suite. A young lady standing directly behind me overheard the request. "Excuse me, Reverend," she hedgingly interrupted, "did you say Miss Martha Raye?" I nodded. "The movie actress?" Again, I nodded. "Will she entertain us during the voyage?" "I can't really say. But I can assure you of one thing: after this trip with Martha Raye, the *Sea Venture* will never be the same."

I arrived at Maggie's suite, christened the Owner's Cabin, the most deluxe on board. The room was filled with men and women, mostly young and twenty-ish. After the proper introductions and some light banter, I began to realize these were not just ordinary young men. They were all Maggie's Boys. All amputees from Vietnam. One of them, Bill Clark, from Clark, New Jersey, related a fantastic story to Maggie and the group. On one occasion when he first had begun using his artificial limbs, he hurriedly secured them to his body. Later, in a restaurant, as he tried to maneuver some difficult moves, he realized the price of his hastiness: the wooden leg had slithered right through his trousers onto the restaurant floor. Undaunted, the ex-Marine politely turned to his bewildered waiter and asked, "Will you please pick up my leg?"

It is not my intention to philosophize on the morality of the Vietnam War. Today, thank God, that war is ended and peace prevails. However, I have never witnessed such camaraderie and such empathy as I have seen in this group of veterans. Each of them spoke of Maggie's selfless sacrifices and glowing exploits on the battlefields of Vietnam and Europe; they extolled her total commitment to every boy and girl in uniform. She wears on her pinkie finger a ring emblematic of the Marines and the Navy presented to her by "her boys." They literally idolize her. A mother showed me a colored photograph of her son and Maggie together on a Viet battlefield. "He's been killed in action," her mournful eyes told me, "but I'm as proud of Miss Raye as I am of my son for what they both have done for their country." In the eyes of every serviceman and woman who ever saluted the American flag, Miss Maggie Raye is their Goddess Athena—the Goddess in War and Peace.

With such a scene of tenderness and compassion, a fadeout is certainly in order: Miss Maggie cautiously pushing one of her wheelchair boys down the gangplank.

I've spent two and a half years writing about The Showbiz Priest. Many of my friends knew of this particular endeavor. Many were interested enough to ask on many occasions, "How's your book coming along?" Toward the finale of my writings, I had to change "just fine," in answer to the many questions, to "I expect to submit the book to a publisher." Through the instrumentality of a dear friend, I found the courage to bring the manuscript to Trident Press. They promised to let me know in two or three weeks. Instead, the twelve-week wait became excruciatingly unbearable day by day. For once in my life I could relate with the agonizing anxiety of parenthood, waiting for the baby to be born.

The good news eventually arrived in the voice of Mr. Leonard Forman who floored me with "You better blow a kiss into the phone. Trident accepted your manuscript." I couldn't believe my ears. I wanted assurance—total, absolute assurance. "You mean I'm in!" said I, reverting to my old New Yorkese days. Soon another of my compatriots, Saint Vitus, rushed into the scene. My phone-holding arm began to twitch spasmodically and uncontrollably. The conversation over, I sat in an armchair in the reading room stunned beyond belief. Filled with untapped enthusiasm, I told some friends in my neighborhood of my good fortune. Aside from some congratulatory words, most people were not too impressed. To some, Trident sounded like a new chewing gum. It seems in certain areas of New York you're more a hero making book than writing book!